SEXLESS IN THE CITY

D0169446

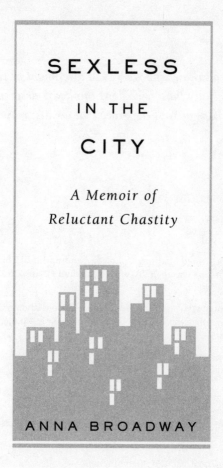

SEXLESS

IN THE

CITY

A Memoir of
Reluctant Chastity

ANNA BROADWAY

GALILEE

DOUBLEDAY

NEW YORK LONDON TORONTO SYDNEY AUCKLAND

For all those who wish such love might be true,
especially those who don't think you deserve it.
You are perhaps nearest the grace that awaits; may it find you.

———————

A GALILEE BOOK
PUBLISHED BY DOUBLEDAY

Copyright © 2008 by Christi Foist

Published in the United States by Doubleday, an imprint of The Doubleday
Broadway Publishing Group, a division of Random House, Inc., New York.
www.doubleday.com

GALILEE and DOUBLEDAY are registered trademarks of Random House, Inc.,
and the portrayal of a ship with a cross above a book is a trademark of
Random House, Inc.

Credits for song lyrics and poetry appear on page 304.

Book design by Gretchen Achilles

Library of Congress Cataloging-in-Publication Data
Broadway, Anna.
   Sexless in the city : a memoir of reluctant chastity / by Anna Broadway.
— 1st ed.
      p. cm.
   1. Broadway, Anna. 2. Christian biography—United States. I. Title.
   BR1725.B6855A3 2008
277.3'083092—dc22
[B]   2007026495

ISBN 978-0-385-51839-0

PRINTED IN THE UNITED STATES OF AMERICA

10 9 8 7 6 5 4 3 2 1

First Edition

CONTENTS

CONTENTS

ACT III
THE PILGRIM

ACKNOWLEDGMENTS

Years after reading Anne Bradstreet's poem "The Author to Her Book," I finally understand the metaphor, though *this* gestation lasted far more than nine months and took a village of friends and family just to "bear" the babe. I won't attempt to name all those whose lifeprints helped shape the manuscript, but heartfelt thanks go out to you all, especially those who believed in my writing years before I actually took it seriously.

To Grandpa D., though I'm not sure if I'm brave enough to actually let you read this, thanks for all those birthday poems and your ever-helpful tips about titles and pseudonyms. *Marching Single File* almost happened, but I'll leave that title to Sis if she wants it. To Dad and all the rest of the clan whose tales have kept my lungs limber, thanks for modeling good storytelling. Mom, thanks for nudging me into that first journalism class— without it I never would have put my preteen *Tardy Tribune* together with efforts to dictate early stories to you and thought *I should try writing.*

To all the teachers, editors, and bosses who came later, thanks for nurturing and helping hone my instincts. Thanks especially to Mrs. G. for encouraging my prose style, and to Peter for that interview question on five-year goals. This isn't the book I hoped to write then, but it's far more than I ever dreamed of accomplishing on that December day in Chelsea. Finally, thanks to Rick for concluding a less-than-stellar performance review with an admonition to write because you'd heard I had a gift for it. You're part of the reason I'll always say this book happened mostly in spite of me.

Jane, Beth, and Trace: you're another big part of that. Thanks for taking a risk on such an unknown and cowardly writer, and for giving me time for that final pass through the book. Annie, you were indispensable on so many different judgment calls and narrative snags, and the redemption of *tNP* for me. Your friendship will always be one of my sweetest memories of New York. And Garnette, I am eternally grateful for all your help and encouragement with permissions, "the sound track," and everything else music-related. Rich is the woman who counts people like you all among her friends.

Finally, profound thanks go to those long-suffering, stalwart souls who gave feedback on the entire manuscript and never flinched from speaking your minds. You have been perhaps my fiercest critics, and thus everything I asked you to be. Thanks for being friends who loved enough to wound when needed; this book owes quite a debt to your feedback. I look forward to the time when we can all rejoice, side by side, in whatever God's redemptive purpose was for this.

And lastly to all those who prayed for this book—whether often or sometimes, with me or based on an e-mail or just a sudden thought that you should—my deepest thanks. I'm no Moses, but you were certainly Aaron and Hur to me and this book. I thank you, my parents thank you, and undoubtedly my editors thank you as well.

PROLOGUE

No one can serve two masters. Either he will hate the one and love the other, or he will be devoted to the one and despise the other.

—MATTHEW 6:24

My reckoning started not long before high school, with the recurring dream of facing my deathbed a virgin. That was the choice, anyway. Each time I had the dream, it was the night before the world was ending and I was marooned on a spit of mud with a young man I somewhat liked. The death's eve dilemma was always whether to pass up this final chance to partake of life's best—enduring a last, supreme Missing Out for my obedience—or to cave in favor of dying with just a little taste of true "heaven." Although I quit having the dream long before adulthood, the longer I lived as a single person, the more God seemed to be shorting me in my share of a normal life's pleasures—and, worse, denying me a fully realized humanity. I worshipped a God whose son said he came to earth that we might "have life and have it to the full," but I feared being a Christian meant living only a half life at most.

Fear anything more than God, and it will take you places you never dreamed you would enter so boldly or blithely.

NEW YORK, FALL 2003

The sex shop was quite neat and tidy inside—so much so, you could almost begin to forget you were walking past not the banal wares of the grocer or drugstore but things far too obscene for even Urban Outfitters. I'd expected lurid displays and dim-lit shelves—a kind of horror house of sex that gloried in all its trappings and varied sundries of sin. Instead the place could have served neat red-velvet cupcakes like those gobbled up at the famous Magnolia Bakery nearby. Amazing how bright lights diminish guilt, as if what's seen is clean and wholesome. Perhaps it wasn't all bad, this place—wasn't that the card deck one of my Christian girlfriends received at a bridal shower?

Only we weren't after cards, Best Friend and I; we were on a mission to find specific sweets for teeth lascivious. After scanning the shop unsuccessfully, I marched up to the short-haired, nose-ringed female clerk and asked her where the chocolates might be. She pointed us to a small case we had to access by squatting down and sorted through boxes of "Naughty Nibbles." Prurience being what it is, we didn't lack for options—just goodwill and funds. No sense being too lavish. This was, after all, intended to taunt an erstwhile date with what he'd never get from me.

There had never been much "logic" maintaining a friendship with a guy who constantly hassled me for sex, but I felt Ad Weasel had few genuine friends—and when I first met him a year before, I had no friends here at all. He probably had the most repugnant character of any guy I've gone out with, but when I found him on Craigslist, barely two weeks into my New York relocation, all that mattered was that he talked back, and rather well.

Sure, I liked his attention—had compromised to get it, in fact—but beneath the curiosity that muted my "no's" when Ad Weasel got too frisky on our one date, and behind the loneliness out of which I had first gone out with him, was a deep longing for community. I desperately wanted to re-create what I'd left behind on the West Coast, to rediscover what I'd been born into—a world of talk and interaction that preceded my existence, thus didn't depend on my life to survive.

As the oldest of four children all taught at home and born into an equally close-knit maternal clan who regularly gathered together en masse, I was nursed on espresso-strength community in my formative years. All that I required—love, laughter, intellectual stimulation, and an indispensable role as helper with washing the dishes, making a bonfire, or other chores—was given to me independent of any efforts to seek it. Such freedom, correction, and welcome were like a mother's milk I never consented to be weaned from, and I sensed early on that re-creating this cycle as I grew older depended on getting married myself.

Over time this ambition became an obsession, from which a fixation with sex emerged. How could I find an intimacy as deep as that which a husband and wife exchange? And yet I feared such exposure just as deeply as I longed for it. *Get too close to me, and you'll find out how unwell I am, smell the stench of all this rotting flesh.* Surely no love was really good enough to actually deal with *that*—not even I had the courage to face it!

Consequently, I went through much of life giving others—and God—the parts of me I thought presentable (therefore surely too good to alter), albeit packaged with such candor you weren't meant to guess how much I was hiding. With Ad Weasel, I offered sexual banter in trade for attention and company, concealing for the most part just how orthodox was the credo I assented to . . . in theory if more than practice.

But God talk was only fine with him if it was bartered not for conversation but the activity that was my second-most-frequent topic in those days, sex. That point was cruelly driven home when I called up about seeing the last pre–World Series game between New York and Boston, one year into our unfortunate acquaintance. Who wants to watch such a game alone, with only the sounds of shouts from others' parties for company? Though we hadn't talked in a while, I figured my "friend" was the kind of guy one could call for casual baseball watching.

But he was only up for the sort of polite, pragmatic, businesslike affair I wouldn't give him. Ad Weasel wasn't impressed by this new pitch to play it platonic; only women with whom he'd relieved all sexual tension got such access. Unless I wanted to join their ranks, he had no interest in nonmetaphorical baseball or my calls.

"But I—"

He repeated the terms of contact—sex or nothing—and hung up.

Best Friend always said I should've called back to say I changed my mind—just to get him back—but I could never do that . . . Or could I? I'd never been quite as desperate for attention as when I first met him, then a lonely and jobless transplant to his city, so perhaps I'd never led with my sexuality quite as aggressively as with him. In any case, I'd never been as vulnerable to the crass rejection and disrespect delivered during that phone call.

My compromises had so far seemed so innocent I barely noticed them until these sudden wounds hardened into a state that bred an unprecedented openness to revenge. As Ad Weasel's greedy, ungrateful dismissal sank in—this from a man who'd already gotten far more from me than he should have—I decided to use his desire for me against him in a loaded and symbolic parting gesture.

I didn't stop to think if I should have some ethical problem dropping my money at the sex shop—or pursuing revenge in the first place—though the assistant's "unfeminine" hair and jewelry might have epitomized scandal to some Christians. When I asked her how her day had been, she visibly relaxed. Then I did too.

Asking not "How are you?" but "How's your day been?" was a subtle shift in greeting I'd started post-Berkeley, as part of acknowledging the humanity of those in jobs like hers no matter what reason she might have been an outsider in some minds. She wasn't just a clerk, but a woman with hungers and hurts and a heart; why treat her like a wax figure or robot? I looked her in the eye and paused a beat to let the woman be more than her job, feeling strangely more righteous than Best Friend beside me, though she'd been more reluctant than me to actually come here.

Reinhabiting this other self made me feel better—as if my kindness, the passing moment of human exchange, could somehow redeem this farcical perfidy . . . if not fully justify it. *Didn't Jesus party with prostitutes and sinners? Surely someone had to love the sex-shop workers.*

As that early autumn evening gave way to tawdry deliveries cloaked in dusk and fraught with adrenaline, I only grasped faint outlines of the truth. The issue was not just letting the woman be more than her job, but learning to be more than one or a sum of parts. I prided myself on holding to a virginity that was somewhere between technical and Amish, but that was the problem: that I prided myself on sexual terms at all. Define yourself as anything but the whole being God meant you to be, and it warps you into someone who says and does things you never thought you would do, much less so boldly and blithely.

I thought I was living for God, but serving my loneliness and sexual "needs" had led me into the arms of a man I trusted only for the constancy of his desire—and when he spurned me, the aisles of a West Village sex shop. But the ache that led me to this showed no signs of yet abating. Would I find the courage to leave this master, come love or spinsterhood, or would it finally snatch from me what I thought was my true treasure?

ACT I

THE INNOCENT

A million changes amass like storm clouds speeding at me from the horizon. I'm terrified—scared almost to tears, yet at the same time strangely excited (I think). Worlds are opening up to me—still vague and hazy, but still distinguishable as alternatives I hadn't considered before.

The beat and rhythm of the music that has been college life begins to change subtly—and I recognize that it is due to a movement on my part. I now stand between college and a life beyond—whose music and rhythm begin to mingle with the familiar cacophony, yet in a voice I begin to distinguish. And I stand transfixed—slightly terrified of this strange new sound, yet oddly attracted as well. I know not how to dance to this tune yet something in it excites me. The pace is at once faster and yet a slower bass part plays beneath, like the slow, sensuous rhythm I imagine in lovemaking. Trepidation. Excitement. Uncertainty.

I feel like a reluctant hatchling, unhappily inspecting the unused (or weak) wings which will shortly become her only protection against a broken neck, in her plummet from the nest. And yet . . . the world within the nest was dominated by images of home, with only scant glimpses of sky and tree without. On this scary edge of the nest, I suddenly discover a world completely unknown before, the sight of which is so startling and fascinating that it helps somewhat to calm the fear of flight and falling.

—JOURNAL ENTRY, NOVEMBER 23, 1999

CHAPTER I

A YOUTHFUL ROMANTIHOLIC

Portence hung in the air like a thick fog. She felt a shiver as she eyed him from across the bar. He worked the room as if he was running for office, calling everyone by name and seeming genuinely interested in their idle babble. When he touched her shoulder, she sat erect . . . "I don't believe we've met," he said with an all-American smile that revealed compelling dimples. "Oh, my God," filled her head so loud that she feared she may have actually uttered the phrase.

—E-MAIL FROM A FORMER BOSS, APING TYPICAL HARLEQUIN PROSE

Not long after Girlfriend #3 began her Peace Corps service in Africa, she reported: "There's a lot of 1950s Harlequins floating around over there. I'd never read one before, but I picked a couple up. And when I read it, I thought, 'Now I understand Anna.' "

The gist of such prose is aptly evoked in an e-mail response to my first interview in publishing. Shortly after moving to New York in 2002, I set off to find my dream job. I'd moved here days after earning my M.A., intending to take a break from the classroom, ponder a Ph.D. . . . and better my chances of someday being published myself by getting an editorial job. At one time my dream "literary coup" was to be the virgin who wrote convincing sex scenes—the Meg Ryan of the romance novel. Who better to hire me for such work than the top purveyor of all that pulp? Remarkably, Harlequin needed another assistant. Given my extensive reading of their catalog back in the day, and the entry-level nature of the position, no first job in publishing could have been better suited to my talents.

When I arrived for the appointed interview, there was little hint these offices churned out such salacious lines as not just Harlequin Desire (formerly their "sexiest" series) but now also Harlequin Blaze (just this side of pulp erotica, as I'd learned from preinterview research). No lustrous red walls worthy of any Vegas bordello; no life-size posters of Fabio, ravishing something other than butter. Rather, the front office conjured the environs that prompt many a wistful reader to *turn* to Harlequin in the first place, which demographic was also evoked by the middle-aged, portly receptionist. She told me I looked like the Brat Pack redhead, but had to call a friend to supply the name: Molly Ringwald. Ignorant of '80s movies, thanks to my homeschool education, I shrugged and returned to vain attempts at recalling business-reference phone numbers. When finished, I had time to inspect the various paperbacks installed in two glass cases flanking her desk. Apparently they didn't want guests flipping to the "good parts" and reading them impertinently aloud. *Pages must be certified FREE of reader palm sweat!*

The interview (with a mousy man of indeterminate sexual tastes and a sense of humor about his job in an otherwise all-female office) went well enough, but in the middle of crafting a follow-up letter, I hesitated. Maybe $26k per annum wasn't quite enough money for reading crap femme porn by day and by evening fending off horrified e-mails from the half of my family that rarely drinks. I settled for merely regaling friends— and alarming family—with an e-mail about the interview. As would be the case with many of my New York adventures, just getting a good story was enough.

The Harlequin habit meshed nicely with a life plotline I'd been developing since childhood. Some girls plan their wedding; I planned my courtship—right down to the anticipated engagement sometime near the end of college. But all that my leading man would share with the cads and smokers and rebels who tended to populate Harlequin romances was a commitment to pursuing me. Other than that, he'd be a man whose chief virtues were not swagger or bravado but integrity and kindness.

Initially this fantasy was just the best escape I could conjure up to fight insomnia; in a sheltered childhood defined by home and a close-knit extended family, I had little concept of growing up to do more than re-create that loving community with children of my own. I figured ten would do. As long as Hoped-for Husband married me soon enough, we'd have plenty of time to space them out, every two years or so.

He would be three years older than me, I decided, and the oldest of a family whose other children would probably give my younger siblings spouses as well. We would meet during college, I a freshman, he the dashing senior man about our California campus (since I imagined attending a SoCali Christian school known for its choir and music program). After college, he'd go off to the other coast to start his med school training, but we'd maintain contact through the mail . . . and eventually phone calls, probably one each week. We'd alternate the bill like good friends would, of course. Besides, he'd need time to recover from the betrayal of the girlfriend he had when I met him (in one version of the soap opera—er, story—she proved to have mothered twins with a much older man, during a hush-hush Parisian affair she had on a modeling break from high school).

During the course of our three years apart, Hoped-for Husband would not only get over his girlfriend but, unbeknownst to me, his clueless friend, fall deeply, madly in love with me—no doubt helped along by the power of my oh-so-delightful letters (during Gulf War I, I'd written a soldier from our church and knitted him slippers; when he got back he brought me a colorful, wood-bead necklace from Africa. Proof my method worked? I think so. I'd even baked him *cookies*).

In the early days it seemed God might let life conform to these dreams, including my carefully worked-out timeline. Sophomore year of high school, I fell for a boy in *The Music Man*—the show our school produced that spring. We were even cast as characters who *dated*. Musical Man was blond and had the requisite blue eyes, but his real feat was the ability to lift me.

Sometime during junior high, a well-intentioned parent had hinted a bookworm like me might need to watch my weight so it didn't spiral out of control. Well, I could be suggestible. Sure enough: as puberty kicked in, I watched the scales climb from a slight 110 pounds around sixth grade to a not unhealthy 136 by freshman year. A curvy five foot eight or not, I deemed this "spike" a sure sign that my parents' concern was prophetic (no one thought to tell me a womanly figure weighs more than a girl's does). As soon as I started giving my weight the brain time boys would later merit, it complied nicely by moving upward. By sophomore year I considered myself overweight, a perspective reinforced by regular fatherly admonitions regarding how I could be more self controlled in my eating.

Dad termed his role that of "coach." Since he'd also been my guitar teacher, it wasn't such a stretch for him. For me, though, our lessons had always been less about whatever I was learning and more about a chance for precious time alone with him. Probably half the reason I never took to guitar was that my studies were so often sidelined by Dad's work on his master's in engineering—well, his coursework and the fact my only female-guitarist role model in those years was Leona Boyd, whom I promptly deemed a "tramp" because her album covers showed cleavage, mind you, *cleavage*. She was like the Dolly Parton of the guitar world. Younger siblings got more focused, consistent lessons later, once Dad's diploma came, but I'd already moved on to an instrument I could learn on my own and with regular instruction—not to mention one whose role models were more decorous men like Horowitz and Van Cliburn.

Ironically, I probably would have had more father–daughter time had I not quit the guitar when I began public school in grade nine. But by sophomore year I was so engrossed in novel pastimes like journalism and theater I didn't realize how much I still longed for the conversation only Dad could provide, but rarely did.

If he sought me out to ask about my homework assignments or interesting topics in class, I don't remember it. Instead I found that the subjects that most inclined Dad to pay attention to me were music, God, and the changes in my body. The latter he was reluctant to praise, as if his acknowledgement I was becoming a woman would allow men to lust after me. Mostly Dad addressed the topic with warnings on how such "drooling dogs" would look at my blossoming figure . . . especially if I could lose the extra weight his coaching was meant to help me fight.

A book I once read on discipline in the classroom said that when tackling misbehavior in students who do it for attention, you have to be sure to balance your feedback on both the good things and the bad things they do, giving much more to the former, or you'll just reinforce the unhealthy behaviors they've learned. In large part, Dad's "nurture" was probably just a healthy parental response to alarming and baffling trends in his

oldest child's conduct—like a tendency to foreground a burgeoning sexual self. But somehow the way he handled these tentative feints at forming identity inadvertently reinforced such
bents in my "nature." I learned that even with Dad it was my
body that got his attention.

Ironically, in contrast to such "worldly" values as physical
beauty, Dad placed a constant verbal emphasis on the character
a good man should admire. Which was well and good for Mom,
whom he'd clearly admired *and* desired enough to actually
marry. But I was not so sure I wanted a man who merely "admired" me—and that for a few odd, fairly generic traits. Nor
was I convinced that Dad pursued Mom with such disregard for
her evident beauty! Their chemistry belied his condemnation of
desire.

He was by his frequent and candid admission a man who'd
been an adolescent bad boy—like the sort against which he
warned me—until God began reforming him into the kind of
man who went for righteousness in women. In my mind this
meant I needed both the virtue Dad liked to praise, and the
beauty I evidently lacked, to really get a man's attention. I
wanted to be loved for an inherent worth, but pragmatically
prepared to work hard to earn it, just in case. That seemed by
both Dad's reckoning and mine to depend on controlling my
weight. After all, such discipline would reveal not just the
beauty beneath the pounds, but also his much-celebrated character.

It proved far easier *being* a character. "Plump" or not, I was
undeterred from trying out for *The Music Man* early spring
1994. After being homeschooled through eighth grade, school
plays were something I'd never had the chance to join before.
But hadn't I long entertained my family by striking the models'
poses from Sears catalogs we got? What girl gets drafted at six

to play the voice of Satan (Mom and Dad were preparing a skit to dramatize Genesis 3 for the church youth, but their Adam and Eve required a third) without becoming a dramatic sensation? Clearly I was destined for a career before the stage lights.

Sure enough, I made it through to the coed dance auditions, in which men and women were taught an individual part then paired up to dance a brief duet. But when we were told that at one point the guys would perform a brief lift of the girls, I mentally wrote this out of my tryout. Sure, maybe my hapless partner's move was to *try* for airtime, but what puny high-school male could lift a heavyset girl like me?

A blue-eyed, blond fro-sporting member of the swim team, it turned out. For Musical Man to lift me in that audition—without contracting major injury—was the kindest thing a guy could have possibly done in those days. And our onstage audition chemistry (him doing his thing, me flopping around surprisedly at my unexpected aerial) proved winning. I was cast as the clumsy pianola girl, his main squeeze and partner in a rousing chorus and dance number called the "Shipoopi." Already a committed thespian, I threw myself into the part by falling for him in real life too.

Unfortunately he had a real-life girlfriend. But that didn't trouble me much—I had anticipated such a plot twist, and I could wait things out till Musical Man realized I could bake him better bread than his girlfriend. After all, that was Etta James's main selling point in "I Just Want to Make Love to You," and in those days she was my guide on all things romantic. Considering "At Last" immediately followed that rousing torch song on the Etta record I owned, her approach seemed quite successful: she offered to bake his bread, next thing she had her man. The album was no doubt "based on a true story," right?

I'd discovered Etta not long after my parents made the television plunge in 1993 . . . shortly after I had to watch a neighbor's TV to complete a homework assignment. Part of the excitement of finally having our own "boob tube," as Dad called it (as if to diminish his ownership of the dubious appliance), was the joy of watching commercials. Sometime between 1993 and 1996, Diet Coke ran a series set to classic songs I was guaranteed to melt for. There was the masterfully subtle pairing of a honeymoon suite ad with "Makin' Whoopee," the bubble bath set to Mama Cass's "Dream a Little Dream of Me," the waitresses who sunbathed to Bobby Darin's "Beyond the Sea" . . . and the anchor spot: Lucky Vanous as the shirtless construction worker behind an office's 11:30 "Diet Coke Break." Soundtrack for their lust-fest? Etta James and "I Just Want to Make Love to You."

Not only did I call up Coca-Cola to ID every song used in the series (especially Lucky's), I even splashed out for his calendar—to date, the only beefcake calendar ever owned by Anna Broadway. My parents forbade neither the purchase nor the display of the calendar, nor even the purchase of an Etta James CD, but they intervened at audible playing of the song . . . at least when they were around. Since I was still, in those days, considering law as a possible career, I tried lobbying for the nonsalacious nature of the content. As a well-versed reader of romance novels, I was well-nigh an expert on more historic forms of the genre. And in these literary specimens, I argued, use of the phrase "make love" applied to scenarios we might today call "making out" (I had yet to hear Shirley Horn ask, "For what is dancing but making love set to music playing?"). Since Etta had recorded this song circa . . . 1960 . . . it was a clear—dare I say prima facie?—instance of that usage.

Alas, I was outdone by the arguments of a certain opening sax riff. But if Etta couldn't be played aloud, she was certainly played on frequent rotation through the musical umbilical cord connecting me to the stereo where I stationed myself for home-work and my letter writing to Musical Man, once he went off to college. Since this was my first major case of unrequited inter-est (though he was a kinder crush than some to follow), Etta gave me crucial emotional tools for learning how to relate to him. From the heartfelt "All I Could Do Is Cry" (about the woman who sees "her" man wed another) to the woman who knows what she wants from men ("Tough Mary"), she gave me songs for every relational phase I could think of—including sev-eral I still have yet to experience; it's good to know they're there for me in the future.

Most importantly, Etta taught me that the longings in my heart, exposed when an unkind phantom wind found cracks in the boards around my soul, were always due to trouble with men—especially their absence. "Don't know why there's no sun up in the sky / Stormy weather / Since my man and I ain't to-gether / Keeps raining all of the time / Life is bad / Gloom and misery everywhere / Stormy weather, stormy weather / And I just can't get my poor self together."

Though the lyric overstated *my* sense of inward ache, it came in handy for guiding my thoughts one night while waiting for a parent to pick me up from the curb outside the Sears where I worked. This restless ache must be just my heart missing Mu-sical Man! The problem explained, I settled into escapist pining until a parent arrived to suspend my reverie. *How wonderful if my crush should magically drive around the corner, see me sitting there alone, and collect me to ride home beside him in the cab of his pickup truck . . . instead of this Ford Country Squire.* I opened the faux-wood-paneled passenger door of our 1988 station wagon and sank onto the chocolate-brown velour seating with a melo-dramatic sigh as my fleeting daydream slipped away.

Though most Harlequin plots would bore me by the time I

started college, they gave birth that night to a far more potent fantasy it would take years to relinquish. The thought of a man's attention became the tonic that soothed almost every private ache. I was always careful to never imagine having sex with real-life men—since I knew Jesus equated lust with adultery, thought with action—but I spent much of my adolescence and early adulthood turning to thoughts of my crush du jour whenever sadness struck. It was years before I saw that such longings showed deeper needs than the love of a man, or realized the world had bigger problems than individuals' loneliness. But life was still mostly free from pain then; in those days I had no experience of more than emotional "suffering."

THE GOD CONNECTION

Although I shared Etta's dream of finding "A Sunday Kind of Love—a love to last," I didn't expect much help in this from either God or my parents. Given Mom and Dad's silence on matters of sex, I doubted they could be relied on to aid my find-a-husband campaign. And as for God's help . . . sure, He'd created Adam and Eve, but how could God possibly know about sex? I'd read those romance novels . . . and they were so enlightening! Men who'd slept around weren't man-hos; they were *sexually experienced.* And clearly every one of the other women they'd been with had liked exactly the same things I would want from a man. So, really, a man who'd been around was like those toys that come with the battery. He already knew what to do! In fact, he basically came with the Anna Broadway's Perfect Lover software kit preinstalled. He could even teach *me* how I liked to have sex best.

With this valuable lesson learned when I was barely into

high school, I came to believe that God, who apparently lobbies for virgin-to-virgin marriage as the ideal (which rendered my parents' otherwise happy marriage some sort of second best), was a bit like the elderly aunt who thinks a great, fun, educational Christmas gift is a subscription to *Ranger Rick* magazine. Isn't that what every thirteen-year-old girl is dying to read?

Despite these profound suspicions about his advice on some of life's most basic issues, I still thought myself in relationship with God. Relationship: my parents had always been very clear on this. We were not "religious" people, we were not like the Catholics and Mormons and Jehovah's Witnesses in our suburban western Washington cul-de-sac; we were defined by our relationship with God. I later came to see this as the difference between doing good as some spiritual barter with God that earned me blessing, and doing good just out of love for Him, no gain expected. But in those days I understood the stress on a relationship mostly as an accountability thing. If we kids had to deal with our parents when bad deeds were done, Dad had to deal with God when he dealt with our bad deeds badly, lost his temper, or otherwise did bad deeds of his own—which he did not out of fear for the relationship, but his love for God and desire to restore their peace.

Mom had this relationship with God too, but she had always been a model child in youth and never evidenced the rebellious streak that led to Dad's adolescent acts of mischief. These included major misdeeds like having long hair, smoking pot and cigarettes, trying other drugs, and sleeping with women besides our Mom (long before her, of course, but still: I was growing to think of sexual sins as the very worst kind possible). Since Mom's infractions seemed much smaller than Dad's, her need to deal with God was something we didn't see as often. It was Dad with whom I butted heads the most. Dad, who always took time post-disagreement to go have it out with God, then came back to apologize for the way he'd lost his temper or been a less than good dad and human.

That transparency and humility always bugged me. Wasn't it easier to just have a fight and leave it at that, winners and losers being who they were, than to suck back pride and apologize for ways we'd fought unfairly? As the inevitable loser will, I often "cheated" and tried to exact as much pain as possible in my ill-fated daughter–father skirmishes. But if Dad was going to own up to *his* cheating and unnecessary harming, that left me the implicit bad guy (or girl) for being too stubborn to recant my cutting words. I learned to survive those awkward post-argument talks such that no one questioned my relationship with God.

Though I was the only child whose "date of conversion" didn't make it into Dad's brown leather Bible, I knew the script. Everyone's "relationship" began with a dramatic change of heart. If you'd had the bad luck to be born into a Christian family where few acts of major rebellion were likely before age six or whenever you and God attained a treaty, you did like Mom had done and had a less dramatic but equally specific moment of prayer. Say the key stock phrases of repentance and submission and things were a lock. You and God were now friends, which meant he would do good things for you . . . like providing a husband and a happy life.

At least that's what I *thought* the agreement entailed—and by those terms God and I had reconciled once (which was all it took), during a disciplinary confinement to the gold rocking chair in our living room. Based on our truce, I now had some kind of afterlife insurance, which left me free to live life as I pleased, as long as I kept the Ten Commandments—or something like that. Sure, there was also this talk of *loving* God—which I knew I did *not*—but somehow I never thought the relationship contingent on this feeling. It was merely a major failing of faith that I kept as a shameful secret.

In retrospect, this secret may have explained my reluctant apologies to Dad whenever he came to make things right; not loving God meant I cared less what He thought of my conduct. And God's interest in our behavior was the main reason Dad always chose to work through his displeasing feelings and then reconcile with me. Not loving God also explained the ease with which I chose romance novels over God. Maybe that's how I knew I didn't love Him, in fact—because I chose other things instead. That was a conscious choice, all right.

By the time I discovered my first explicit novel, I'd fallen into a habit of praying myself to sleep at night—well, at least praying before I delved into the ongoing odyssey of Hoped-for Husband's pursuit. Prayer in those days was basically a settling of accounts for the day, heavily interlarded with pleas for God to save certain prominent figures like Madonna and maybe Prince (hard to say how many celebs I knew from reading magazine covers in the grocery store checkout lines). But when I started reading those novels, I knew doing so was wrong. At minimum, it was wrong because my parents said so as soon as they found out, and therefore more wrong when I kept reading in a secret, determined defiance. But even if my folks had not forbidden the novels, their content was something I would have shied away from years before.

Once during late childhood, I stumbled upon a tween or adolescent novel from the library in which the characters went skinny-dipping. Something about that scene disturbed me so much, I wondered if I should stop reading the book right then. What better place to ponder such an early ethical problem than the back bathroom where Dad changed my little brother's diapers and dodged his errant urination? In a house overflowing with four small children and the odd mouse that hadn't yet died in our slab-floor pantry (the cause of a stench unexplained until we found its milk-bottle tomb), privacy was hard to come by. But the showerless bathroom/laundry room where outside light filtered in through the high, small window, with a green hue that matched the washer and dryer-cum-changing-station, had a certain security.

In its dim quiet that harkened to the stained-glass windows of church, I asked God to give me a sign if I should stop reading the book. But it had to be something unlikely, right? Because I had not yet reached the chronic messiness of later years, it seemed unlikely that much could be found underneath the bunk bed I shared with Sis. That was it, then: if God wanted me to stop reading the book where people swam naked *together,* I'd find a hairclip beneath the bed.

If shown an accessory lineup today, I could still ID the small white clip I found after frantically searching the bedroom floor. It wasn't that far beneath the bed, and it provided all the courage I needed to go tell Mom about the skinny-dippers. That book got returned to the library unfinished even though, for some reason, I sometimes still tried to imagine what sex entailed.

In the end that curiosity won out. By the time I read a real sex scene a few years later, the allure of the exotic overcame the catch of my conscience. Besides, by this time my three-year-long habit of reading the Bible through in a year was getting a little dull. I sensed that it was becoming mere dry ritual—which even the brief excitement of a new, grown-up, leather-bound Bible could not overcome. Since rituals were religious—which was not what relational faith in God was supposed to be—I decided something had to change.

Right around the time I picked up Harlequins, I put away my Bible. There were brief attempts to carry on with a "devotional" guide that would help me read it differently, but as a precocious if somewhat lonely preadolescent whom men wouldn't notice for nearly another decade, I couldn't relate to lessons involving teenage dating, peer pressure, and youth materialism. If the Bible was the main way God chose to "speak" to folks He had relationships with, I settled for eavesdropping on the conversations other people had with Him. Finally I even stopped talking to Him myself. (I probably started having my dream about sex and the Apocalypse around then.)

You see, the Harlequins were something I'd have to talk about if I wanted God to hear the other things I had to say to Him. Sure, there was the option of making a stock confession each night, but God wouldn't fall for that. He'd know my fraudulent repentance straight out because of all those Catholic hypocrites He dealt with (I thought of them as folks who confessed their frolics weekly, then merrily returned to the bed of the neighbor's wife for seven more nights of sin). Well, I was no Catholic, by God; I was Protestant. Nondenominational, maybe, but Protestant nonetheless—and therefore bound to a code of fudge-free honesty. If Harlequins provoked no true remorse, I couldn't repent. And without repentance, God wouldn't hear my prayers.

As when friends don't yet know about your recent breakup, this distance from God was a secret that quietly gnawed at my insides. When other Christians mistook my intellectual gifts for spiritual depth, it only increased my guilt. *I'm not a very good Christian! Can't you see that?* I yearned for someone to point out my fraud and tell me more was possible, but not even Dad—the one who was always so willing to call me on disobedience, to both him and my heavenly Father—seemed to notice my hypocrisy. If he did, he spoke only to the symptoms without recognizing the root cause.

Not that it should have been his job by then to be my spiritual guide. If anything, it was how much, not how little, Dad involved himself in my spiritual life that would later make things so complicated. But as my years in high school reached a close, Dad was increasingly consumed with work and preparations for making an overseas move with Mom and my three younger siblings. No one noticed when I snuck in late one night from an after-party during the week we performed *Fiddler on the Roof*. No one seemed too concerned about the boys I'd met online (bear in mind this was 1996), Stalker #1 and Midwest Ivy Pen Pal, both of whom I progressed to trading occasional phone calls with. So of course no one noticed that I'd stopped reading my Bible and talking to God.

The terrifying reality was that my spiritual life rested more and more on my uncertain shoulders, not just on awkward bouts of conviction when I clashed with Dad again. You see, over the years I'd gotten the impression that while God provides the power for your salvation, spiritual growth is up to you—like a series of classes and electives you string together, depending on which degree in piety you want. And that didn't hold much appeal. I wanted to be saved, all right, but more than that I wanted to be loved, something I thought God could never provide as well as a human.

By the time I set foot on campus at a tiny midwestern college, it's little wonder I barely made it to church at all that fall. The God I thought had saved me seemed as relevant to my life as the flip-flops I'd worn back home in Arizona were to a winter-ready wardrobe—this was Iowa: you needed boots. And for my heart, I needed a boyfriend.

CHAPTER 2

HELPLESSNESS 101

You're nobody 'til somebody loves you,
You're nobody 'til somebody cares.
You might be king, you might possess, the world and its gold,
But gold won't bring you happiness, when you're growing old.
The world still is the same; you'll never change it—
As sure as the stars shine above.
You're nobody, 'til somebody loves you,
So find yourself somebody to love.

—RUSS MORGAN, LARRY STOCK, AND JAMES CAVANAUGH,
"You're Nobody 'Til Somebody Loves You"

O ne thing I never figured out from the *Sleepless in Seattle* soundtrack was Jimmy Durante's urgency in adjuring listeners to just "make someone happy." Perhaps if I'd listened more closely, I would have found the answer in the very next line: "Once you've found her, build your world around her"—he was singing not to everyone, but to men (well, at least in his day he was). Apparently it's harder for them than us to give love away. But at first I didn't get this; I thought with everything I had to offer, I should be the sort of "catch" men fought over—especially now that we were in a stage where marriage, theoretically, was possible.

Instead the problem of how I could get a boyfriend if I hadn't been kissed—not even in playground play—became the topic around which conversation revolved that fall of 1996. In these deep philosophical bull sessions, my most sympathetic partners proved to be a string of fraternity brothers at the tiny private school in rural Iowa I'd settled on. I planned to use my scholarship money swanning around their many study-abroad programs, stitching together a degree without much time spent on campus. The first year had to be spent stateside, though, so I got stuck in the dorms, amid the cornfields and midwesterners.

In an environment where I suddenly saw that all my "friendships" were products of mere circumstance, where there were no advanced-track classes where I could find the other smart kids, it seemed no one would care if I left the school or died. None of my fellow students seemed to value the life of the mind or my curiosity; no one in my life seemed to prize me much at all. Not even the love of my family, recently moved to Singapore, was much comfort. Of course they loved me: that's what family does! But there was no guarantee they'd care if we were not bound by double-helix ties—did not my frat-brother friends agree?

One of them was a shorter-than-me Asian football player from Cali whom I'd bonded with as a rare fellow West Coaster. Finally one night, after a long conversation about relationships that started in my dorm room and ended in his, in a geographic progression I somehow never questioned, California Kid broached a question couched as carefully as if he were proposing.

"Can I kiss you?"

It was the last thing I expected. Sure, he hailed from the right state, but it was the northern part! Hoped-for Husband and I were supposed to meet near L.A. And then there were practicalities: I was five foot eight, he was somewhat shorter—how could *that* work? Perhaps we could just remain sitting on the floor as we were, but certainly our knees would get in the way if we tried to solve the height problem this way . . . And then I realized this might not be the time to ponder kiss logistics. It was just a simple peck, was it not? Just like jumping off a diving board, which I'd done at least once a summer into our backyard pool in Phoenix.

"Okay."

I closed my eyes and waited to feel dry boy lips (surely they'd be dry, after all, weren't lip moisturizers unmanly?). Except they weren't dry, everything was wet, and—oh my God! That was his *tongue!* He was giving me a *French* kiss! The very thing my parents had said led straight to sex (in one of their few remarks on the subject). But I didn't feel a thing. Not the slightest stirring akin to what even a mediocre Harlequin might produce. The physical, it seemed, was much less connected to the emotional than my parents had implied. In fact I felt decidedly clinical—as if privately taking notes for a subsequent lab report to be graded in one of those force-feed science classes you had to take for the liberal arts requirement.

The experiment ended and he asked if I was all right.

"Yeah! I'm fine. But I should probably go."

It was 3 a.m. I couldn't imagine what more there was to talk about in the wee hours of the weekend. We hugged goodnight, I walked calmly down the hall and out the door, then down the steps to the ground below . . . where I ran all the way across campus as if the devil himself were chasing me, my rotund body as much in shock at the unexpected exertion as at having just been kissed. I sucked in air with the gasping breaths of an infant expelled from the womb—*Oh my God! Oh my God! Oh my God!*—all the way to my dorm, where I saw my R.A. and said it aloud to her a few times, either for her benefit or general entertainment (the thespian in me was not quite dead).

But a kiss did not make him my boyfriend, thank God, or

help me discover my mojo. I somehow scored one date that semester, but this one barely counted, though it was a chance to dredge up the long, size-twelve red dress I'd worn to my high school's homecoming the year before. Barely counted, you see, because my date was none too slim. Oh, he did his best to treat me right; in objective terms, I've probably had few dates that were quite as romantic . . . in intent. College Date #1 had borrowed the chaplain's apartment downstairs so he could fix me dinner (served to the soundtrack from *Phenomenon*) before escorting me to our homecoming dance. But I was a fickle date, more enthralled when I discovered Abba that night—it was like "Dancing Queen" was my *song!*

Truth was, blond, blue-eyed men like College Date #1 were not good enough if not hot enough—and preferably musicians like my Dad (that year my major crush was a sax player whose lips I thought were surely adroit on more than just his instrument; I learned to tie cherry stems with my tongue in case he ever returned my interest). Denied in the quest for such a physical paragon, my longing for love persisted—and continued without satisfaction until I turned as a last resort to the only remaining "man" in my life, that God who supposedly went for relationships.

THE PURGE

I could barely call myself a theist the first time I cracked open that long-forgotten Bible. *Like this book—or this God—could actually do something for my loneliness.* Perhaps because I was so at odds with my own emotions, I couldn't imagine a God who was anything less than distant in His. But something was certainly missing from life, and I was desperate enough to give God one last try . . . in which reading the Bible was fairly unavoidable. It was supposed to be His *word,* after all. And since scenes worthy of that Harlequin I might someday pen had become my favored segue to sleep at night, I didn't expect I could start by telling God a whole lot about me. If sin was like debt, I wanted to keep mine outstanding, thanks very much—just like the credit-card balance I was already slowly building (isn't that what they mean by "building credit"—debt?).

Instead I started by listening to things God said to other folks—one of whom turned out to be this prophet called Jeremiah (he was like his era's pundit or something). Talk about a guy with a lousy calling! In the middle of times so bad most folks would be apt to curse God, he got the swank job of being His personal publicist and prophet. But for those who were listening enough to get bummed by his message, there were also words of hope. I recognized one of these passages from long-ago verse-memorization marathons or a sermon heard once. " 'For I know the plans I have for you,' declares the Lord. 'Plans to prosper you and not to harm you, plans to give you a hope and a future.' " *Blah, blah, blah.* I remembered this. But that was where most people quoting the passage usually quit.

For some reason I kept reading. " 'Then you will call upon Me and come and pray to Me, and I will listen to you. You will seek Me and find Me when you seek Me with all your heart. I will be found by you,' declares the Lord." *That was interesting.* So God promised to be found by the whole-hearted seeker, did He? I sat there a minute. I remembered how this promise thing worked. The Bible had a lot of 'em, and because God was the same "yesterday, today and forever," I could expect that He would keep a promise made through that guy Jeremiah all those centuries before. The formula couldn't be clearer.

"All right, God," I said with not a little hauteur. "You're supposed to keep Your promises. This sure-as-hell looks like a promise. And it looks to me like if I seek You with all I've got, You will be found by me."

I looked at the page again, skeptically. It sure seemed like a long shot. But if this God was real . . . Well maybe, I'd just try seeking Him for a bit. It didn't say I had to change my life to find Him—just seek Him with my whole heart.

It was the first time I began to grasp, ever so slightly, the notion that God saves not on the basis of our virtue but by His compassion and the sacrificial righteousness of our substitute. Not even Hoped-for Husband could promise, "If you seek me with all your heart, I will be found by you"—just God. And while Hoped-for Husband probably would be turned off by my weight, God didn't seem to care about such things. His presence was neither contingent on beauty (and slimness) nor character, just . . . seeking. Wholeheartedly. It said so right there in the passage.

I did try seeking Him over that winter—and though there was no dramatic moment of sudden joy, it was not long before I knew without question I finally loved this God I was once more talking to.

Things started changing. The Bible that had once been so opaque to me—just another book to analyze the way we did in English classes—now had a lot of relevance. Whereas *Moby Dick* was misery to read through and I skimmed a highly symbolic chapter all about blubber without seeming to blunder in class discussions, the Bible I began to read as a life guide. How might aphorisms in Proverbs apply to my life? There sure were a lot about drinking. New to the underground party scene on a campus supposedly dry, I vowed not to drink to drunkenness and maybe not even till I turned twenty-one (except in places with a lower drinking age).

And I started seeking God in communal settings. I quit the

crap-tips waitressing job where they scheduled me to work most Sundays, and started attending church more often. Tiny town or no, there were tons of them to choose from, as midwestern religious zeal goes; I braved a Dutch Reformed church that was popular with students.

Once I got past the denominational weirdness, I found that God was still at work in this setting. One day the pastor challenged us to go home and throw out an object of sin in our lives—the TV, a mirror, or what have you. Immediately I thought of a long-contested white T-shirt whose snugness Dad had never approved of. *Well, I'll think about it later when I'm at home.* Not a prized possession like that! Surely God would be content with something I cared less about. "Baby steps" and all that—right?

That night while praying before my now-regular Bible reading, I asked God to help me be willing to serve Him "no matter what." Then I remembered the T-shirt. That little garment I was really hoping to weasel my way out of sacrificing. It was only the sole source of power I had to attract men. Since no one I found worthy was ever attracted by baking or brains or the other, less sexual parts of me, that left me to wield my lackluster looks for what slight attention they could get me. Most men, it seemed, would accept your whole self only if you had enough beauty to sweeten their tongue—like sugar and cod liver oil. Since I hit 175 that winter—the same weight as my healthy, six-foot father—I might no longer be pretty at all. Between my girth and the feeble appeal of integrity, how could I attract a man without exploiting what meager resources I still had?

But how could I expect God to answer my prayer—which had been genuine—if I wouldn't even give up one little shirt, love-life amulet or not? Slowly, reluctantly, I went to open the drawer. And then I saw the other shirts I'd been wearing with the same intent—a veritable rainbow of midriff-baring, low-cut, or tight-fitting tops calculated to emphasize my supposedly greatest asset in myriad ways.

When I slowly counted out all the shirts, there were more than I expected. Provoking men's lust was a futile campaign for control I'd been quite committed to even though I knew the Bible called all lust sin—and presumably, all cultivation of lust as well. But if I wouldn't give that up for God, why would I later sacrifice bigger, harder things as I hoped I could? Now that I finally loved Him, I didn't want anything to interfere with our intimacy.

With sadness I dumped the shirts in my plastic waste bin, but it was the kind of sick feeling the heart knows deep down to be sham, the fraudulent threats of a nonessential thing that claims you too will die if it departs. *You could always wash them later and take them back for wearing again,* a helpful thought interposed. I was weak enough to do it, too, no doubt. But there would be no half-hearted obedience this time. It had been at least four years since I chose Harlequins over God—and look how long it took to finally restore that relationship! No way would I make the same mistake this time.

Resolving to burn my chances to recant, I marched the pile of shirts down the hall to the big floor dumpster I knew I'd be too grossed out to retrieve them from. Then just one more task remained—though not even I knew it then.

A few nights later the weekly Collegiate Christians meeting provided a rare chance for public confessions. Though Dad was not there to start off the making right, I was for the first time willing to own up to my sin. When the bolder folk at last grew silent, I gulped down my nerves and wobbled to my feet. Somehow the purge would not be complete without confessing and asking forgiveness for my deliberate attempts to provoke lust from some of those very men.

Public confession is not a biblical mandate, and probably

something that could be abused or misused, depending on the motives of those involved. But that night it was a way of learning to cast myself on God's mercy. For most of life, I'd tended to think of myself as pretty righteous, assuming this purported virtue was connected to both my status as a Christian and acceptance by those who shared the faith. Fess up to or get caught in certain failings, I thought—especially if they were sexual—and risk being shunned by both God and fellow believers.

Ironically, the Bible holds just the opposite. In one of His parables, Jesus contrasts a very self-righteous religious leader with one of that day's most despised figures: a collaborator with the Roman oppressors. While the first man's prayers are full of his own virtue, the latter cries out to God: "Have mercy on me, a sinner." To our amazement, Jesus says it is *that* man, who makes no attempt to disguise his sin (though neither does he glory in it), who "went home justified before God." I had always known this intellectually, but not until that night in the chapel had I begun to experientially comprehend what it meant. Rather than putting my shame on full display, that public confession freed me to go home clean and forgiven. It marked a major turning point in not just my commitment to God, but trusting that the whole He made me to be could somehow prove lovable, sin and all.

At the time, it seemed like throwing out those shirts amounted to flushing down the toilet my chances of ever having the husband I so badly wanted—a frightening prospect, but somehow not quite as bad as life apart from God had been. Little did I know the much-harder things I'd one day have to give up and perhaps would only have the courage to sacrifice because of that little wardrobe clean-out.

If God had asked for my shirts, he promptly gave back with a "honeymoon" stage in our relationship and dramatic success in losing weight without even starting to exercise—the third major change that spring. Over the course of six months, I dropped thirty pounds not by following a multirule regimen, but by learning to eat when hungry, to stop when satisfied. By early summer I'd dropped from my all-time high to a moderate 143—only seven pounds more than my freshman-year-of-high-school weight! It was by no means the final battle with my weight (which reached a lasting stability only in my early twenties), but it was one of my first lessons in the goodness of desire.

Always before, my tactic for dealing with weight gain at least implicitly condemned the desire for food without distinguishing between eating for unhealthy reasons (coping with things like loneliness or a loss of control) and eating that was legitimate and healthy. This time, though success came with eating less, it brought a pleasure to the cycle of being hungry and then satisfied with good things like I'd never known. And my lessons in letting God distinguish good desires from legalistic or sinful motives didn't end with food.

As the school year wound down, I faced an unexpected crisis when it turned out the year-end Collegiate Christians retreat occurred the same week as the jazz band trip I'd already committed to. Canvassing friends was little help: all fell predictably into the jazz or the Jesus camp. But I hadn't been taking a poll; I wanted advice! Which trip should I go on? Only my favorite uncle—a pastor famed for his car-repair expertise and hairy chest, so unlike my Dad's—said I might not need to choose on religious merits, but by principle.

Although this defined my recent weight-loss success, it was still a foreign concept. What sort of standard could help me here? He suggested I think about the Bible's advice—especially on commitment. After all, Jesus said we ought to let our "yes" be "yes" and our "no" be "no."

That was it? I could choose to take in the secular, more adventurous trip just because I'd already said that I would go? That choice would please God as much—if not more—than breaking my word to go on the retreat? My uncle left the decision up to me, but his advice began a quiet revolution in my notions of God's character. Who knew? He might actually be in favor of some of the things my heart desired. Maybe then, the key to finding a husband was going *with* God's program, not against it.

HOW TO LAND A SUGAR DADDY

It proved to be a momentous summer: not only did I take the ten-day trip to Mexico, turn nineteen, learn how to drive stick shift, and finally get my driver's license, I found myself struggling to deal with the attentions of my Sugar Daddy.

A South Asian engineer, he first entered the picture as a coworker of my father's in Phoenix, where we'd moved from the Northwest when I was eleven. My parents have always befriended "internationals" through a combination of Dad's natural gregariousness and an affinity for so-called "relationship evangelism," so Sugar Daddy was one of several workmates we shared dinners with over the years. Because he was single, got on well with us, and had no family in Phoenix, we invited him over for at least one Thanksgiving dinner. It gave Dad access to deeper conversation than work afforded and helped to fill the void felt after leaving behind Mom's close-knit family in western Washington. Sugar Daddy returned the kindness by taking us kids to whichever Disney flick was big at that time (such outings were a rare and exotic adventure for a family of six surviving on just one income).

He later took a job in Iowa, but remained fond of the Broadways, calling us occasionally. I think he always had a certain liking for my sister—pervy or not, I couldn't say. She didn't think much of him, though, and always refused to talk when he rang up. I, however, had always listened closely to the maternal Broadways' talks around the holiday dining and picnic tables, just waiting for the chance to enter adult conversation. This made chatting up Sugar Daddy no trouble at all—and frankly a kick. One time we talked for nearly an hour. Mom was probably too busy fixing dinner to notice, and glad to have me off the piano, which I played incessantly in the pre–public high school days (usually sight-reading romantic hits from the twenties, thirties, and forties in compendiums from the library). Dad, who was commuting to a job an hour's drive south, wouldn't have been home yet anyway.

Though his calls were infrequent, Sugar Daddy kept in touch with us, up through my high school graduation in 1996. Two weeks later I waved good-bye to my kin and found myself crying the requisite tears quite naturally—thanks, perhaps, to hormones—as all immediate family put the Pacific Ocean between them and me. (In those days I was not known to be that emotional; just *zehr* romantic.) The rest of the summer I proofed wedding-invitation copy for an Arizona printer and prepared to enter college in the fall, coincidentally in the state where Sugar Daddy now lived.

That was the summer of Matthew McConaughey, whom I saw three times in *A Time to Kill*. I think I sighed every time he came on screen. The obsession was so great I tried to track him down on the Internet. The address I found was in Malibu, California, so I had keen hopes it might be right. Surely he was too new a star to think of keeping his address private! Optimism at full strength, I crafted a letter suggesting we had great potential for a relationship . . . or at least a penpalship. After all, I wasn't your typical love-struck fan. How many women in his life were prepared, as I was, to bake him homemade cookies? True, this ruse had never shown much success with high-school crushes, but Matthew was a different sort. I could tell. He was the first celebrity I actually got the hots for! Not for me the clichéd fixation with Axl Rose or Keanu Reeves. Puh-leaze! I had a more discriminating heart (though gaydar-less: in summer '97 I fell hard for Rupert Everett).

But back to Sugar Daddy. You see, if not for his generosity, my letter to Matthew never would have happened. Sometime early in the summer of pre-nup typography, Sugar Daddy called to have another of our chats. I must have disclosed that I missed the dial-up access of my parents' home (we might not have gotten TV till '93, but we were progressive, dammit: Internet in '95!). Sugar Daddy wouldn't stand for this privation and swiftly promised the money for dial-up for *the whole entire summer.* Not long after, a check for $100 arrived. *Sugar Daddy payout = $100 + movie.*

Three months of Web leisure later, I moved to Iowa with a pared-down romance library and my trusty Mac LC II. (At some point I'd decided owning eighty-odd Betty Neels novels might be slightly excessive—especially since her plots relied on two or three worn but satisfying tropes: the mousy English nurse, the heavy-lidded doctor, usually Dutch, and the stunning English nurse of "Junoesque" proportions, usually the alternate heroine.) Since I, the novel and music obsessive, could never be bothered to save for such an appliance as a *stereo* to play all my impulse CD purchases, the computer was my stand-in for a jukebox. Well, the computer plus my external CD-ROM drive.

Sugar Daddy and I were once more living in the same time zone, but initially little came of this. For spring break, however,

I went up to Des Moines to visit other family friends. Informed of my visit, Sugar Daddy decided Des Moines was drivable distance from his eastern Iowa home. Our two dates sort of blur together, but I know the first evening concluded with a leisurely dinner at Olive Garden, including appetizer, entrée, dessert, and maybe coffee. In my book this was lavish spending; the Broadway clan barely ate out at all, and then with great frugality.

The outing also included predinner shopping, because I'd somehow managed to mention my lack of a stereo—this couched in the innocent lament I couldn't exactly drag my desktop Mac down the hall to the common dorm bathroom and plug it in outside a shower stall, which was essential for coping with the tubless facilities. Sugar Daddy wouldn't have this hardship either! Off we went to find a portable stereo. At the end of spring break, I returned to faux-Dutch Small Town with a $130 Sony boom box subsequently praised for quality of sound. *Sugar Daddy payout: $230 + movie + at least one dinner.*

And then came summer. Before starting my internship with a one-femme PR firm, I went off to the Yucatan with the college jazz band. Somewhere along the line I'd acquired a basic camera, but found its 35-millimeter lens less than adequate for documenting my fortitude in climbing up and down the ruins outside Merida. Wasn't it quite a feat for a woman who not long before had tipped her pops on the scales? Alas, my camera failed to convey this Olympian accomplishment. My pique persisted through the early weeks of summer until July rolled around, along with my nineteenth birthday, which meant it was time for another of Sugar Daddy's visits.

By this time, I confess, I'd begun to wise up to his "generous" attentions. When he kissed me on the cheek in familiar greeting, my heart sank. But despite that first real kiss the fall semester before, boys still were not lining up to date the romance reader nicknamed "Betty Crocker." (The wall-length desk in my dorm room proved an ideal "counter" for kneading dough and rolling out pie crusts I took downstairs to the basement ovens to bake.) How could I pass up this dynamite trifecta of attention, conversation, and electronics? I mustered my gumption, smiled up at the "family friend," and prepared to enjoy my birthday outing.

Sugar Daddy first took me to the Des Moines botanical center, a biosphere-like structure whose vibrant foliage reminded me of my camera's meager talents. Next we lunched at Schlotzsky's, a modest treat I associated with those occasional family meals out. This was just refueling for the afternoon's shopping, which resulted in the purchase of a $270 Samsung zoom-lens camera with lots of features. The evening concluded with yet another trek to Olive Garden, where we had cocktails Round 1 (a bloody Mary I didn't much like despite its presumed sophistication), appetizers, cocktails Round 2 (a smooth drink that induced my first real buzz), entrées, coffee, and the Olive Garden birthday-girl dessert. *Sugar Daddy payout: $500 + movie + lunch + 2 dinners*. Since he later refused repayment of a supposedly short-term loan of $200–$300, total payout was actually closer to a grand.

I guess he was that rare man who truly prized my conversation. My parents, however, had alternate theories. When they heard of his generosity on a birthday phone call "home" to Singapore, Dad's suspicions were finally aroused.

"Do you want me to talk to him?"

"Oh, no," I answered breezily. Though battling moderate guilt at the strange affair, I was far too attached to the camera and stereo to plead affront. Besides, by this time I'd realized how disenchanting Iowa was.

On the return flight home from a cousin's Dallas wedding, a

crushing realization had enveloped me: I was miserable at my college. Not even my newfound love for God and new friends in the jazz band could overcome my loneliness and loathing for Iowa winters. If the thought of returning to Des Moines was painful, my school's small town was well nigh unbearable. How had my four-year plan gone so awry?

Two months of soul searching followed, my first exposure to major but largely unstructured decision making. Initially this was quite terrifying. But as I struggled to rethink a suddenly, scarily blank-slate future, my prayer life changed from the sort of laundry-list confession-booth prayer that treats God as a magic-endowed personal assistant, to something far more honest, gritty, and conversational. Many times I didn't come away with answers or instant fixes—in fact almost never—but I learned that life with Him could be more real and nuanced and all-encompassing than I'd previously experienced; one's spiritual life could truly be *relational*.

Eventually I decided that while I wanted a better school paper to work for than the miserable monthly at my present college, I couldn't wrack up the debt out-of-state tuition would mean (money had been the primary reason I passed on NYU's debt-laden offer the year before, though even then that city held out the whiff of adventure). My deciding principle resolved, I thought through the few remaining options, all of them happily warmer than Iowa's face-searing winters.

By the time Dad and I had our little love-life conference, transfer plans were already in motion. It was only a matter of weeks before I left Iowa, conveniently eliminating the Sugar Daddy problem . . . if not my religious, rather manipulative tendencies of dealing with God and people.

CHAPTER 3

SWOON SURVIVAL

Give me a kiss before you leave me
And my imagination
Will feed my hungry heart
Leave me one thing before we part
A kiss to build a dream on

When I'm alone with my fancies
I'll be with you
Weaving romances
Making believe they're true

—BERT KALMER, HARRY RUBY, AND OSCAR HAMMERSTEIN II,
"A Kiss to Build a Dream On"

I n August 1997 I made a last-minute application to call myself a Sun Devil, established an oral agreement to room with an international student from Taiwan, and shipped my boxes off to an unknown address in Tempe, Arizona. A few weeks later I walked through the palpably sunburning heat of a southwestern midday to a small, shady table where I met the people from College Students for Christ.

Almost immediately I was connected with a social network that launched me into the lowest grades and best social life I'd ever known (in that pre-hipster boom era and such a suburban pocket of the almost–West Coast, nerds such as I rarely acquired voice mail or required cell phones). I did the Labor Day retreat and the fall retreat and contrived to bake for every attractive guy I fell for. There were many in those days, including a lazy but blond musician majoring in religious studies. Maybe God didn't want me making men lust after me, but surely I could use their other hungers to my love life's advantage. And now that things with God were going so well and I'd learned so much, wasn't it time I paused to enjoy life a bit?

One of the classes I ignored that first semester at ASU was a dismal Calc. III class. I had no real obligation to take it other than a persistent if casual interest in math—the subject had not yet "licked" me, hence continued study—so the dismal part was solely the bland professor. At least that's what I recall. I didn't really attend the class so much. In fact, I got the first and only D of my academic career and had to retake Calc. III the following spring. By that time I was cursing myself for wasting all those chances to see the Winner, who had been, miraculously, enrolled in the *very same section* as me.

A friend introduced us fall semester, at which point the Winner's face matched up with a hazily recollected profile from my calculus class. Clearly I was not just dense but in fact quite blind at the time, for the impact of his Jude Law–like features and manly, rugged jaw did not sink in until the spring, at which time the Winner became the object of regular giggle-fests with various girlfriends (much later he went into modeling, but that was long after college). There was a certain business involving a newspaper photograph of him, reproduced on a Kinko's color copier . . . but I'm sure I threw all that stuff away long ago—with the letters from Musical Man, of course.

The Winner was still living in a dorm *just down the street* from my housing at this point, but I wasn't clever enough to request math tutoring until the semester's end, when I got up the nerve to call him and ask for help "studying" for the final. He was willing enough to do it, but somehow we never got around to meeting—probably because, ultimately, the test was nothing a little hard work and focus couldn't conquer. In fact, I was such a glutton for math "punishment" I later went on to take Differential Equations, earning a B that would be the first of several belt notches, including the brake pads I changed myself and the eyes—I would boast to Poster Boy—that had not seen and would never see *Titanic*. But Poster Boy was still unknown to me then; the concept of someone who could eclipse even the Winner was unfathomable. Besides, this was the summer before my junior year—wasn't it about time Hoped-for Husband made an appearance?

If anyone seemed like a candidate, it was the Winner. Sometime that May or June, he attended a Bible study organized for CS students sweating out the Phoenix summer. He was a zealous student not known to hang out post-study like the rest of us coffee-and-convo addicts, but this time we persuaded him to join. A "trade" was proposed, whereby two of us girls agreed to attend a 5 a.m. World Cup soccer game viewing the next morning—an equal hardship since we were such night owls.

These terms accepted, the Winner came along for ice cream, and ended up giving rides home to me and one other person in the dark turquoise Chevy sedan he drove. It was humbler in looks than he, which disjunction seemed to bode well for my chances with him. While I was inclined to think people rarely dated those "below" them in attractiveness, his car gave me hope the Winner might not think his looks deserved a lovelier woman than me.

Whether thanks to his car or not, I scored the second drop-off slot, securing two or three minutes alone. While I had all the giddiness of the hopelessly infatuated, I was wise enough to recognize such precious one-on-one time could hardly lead to deep and intimate dialogue. But unexpectedly, casual chitchat *did* turn into "deepcon" (as my brother later termed such sharing). The upside: the Winner candidly told me of struggles he was wrestling with; the downside: they foreshadowed a midsummer move and college transfer of his own—to a prominent Christian school in the wacky South.

For maybe half an hour, we sat there in his car, in the parking lot behind my building, talking as it felt two adults would— as two people whose lives might romantically intertwine would speak. No guy had ever let me into his world the way he did in that brief conversation. When we finally said goodnight, I went upstairs elated God had given me such an unexpected connection with the Winner. Obedience was paying off! And I was going to see the Winner a second time, in less than twelve hours. With that he moved from boy-I-giddily-giggled-over to full-on Major Crush.

Hours later I dragged myself out of bed and made my bleary-eyed way over to Macho Guy Friend's all-bachelor pad for the early-morning soccer game. Determined to show off my cooking prowess, I volunteered to make pancakes for the mostly male crew. When the Winner arrived and joined me in the kitchen to mix up orange juice, I was so overcome by this boy-time double-header—plus the fact he overdiluted the juice— that I spilled flour on the stove while mixing batter.

Too lazy to clean up the mess, I started frying the pancakes, flour still on the burners. This filled the apartment with so much smoke Macho Guy Friend still razzes me about the roommate who woke up thinking the house ablaze. So much for wowing 'em with my mad Betty Crocker skillz . . .

Fortunately I had a chance to retry my other strategy for alluring him: neediness. A few weeks later, my family was due for their first return visit to Phoenix since moving to Singapore. The older of my two younger brothers was moving in with me to start college, so the five Broadway travelers had considerable baggage. Though we had many friends from our old church in northwest Phoenix, I, the carless college student, was unsure how we would haul my kin—and all their stuff—from the airport. The welcoming party, I decided, might need a little help. And who was a possible, car-possessing guy friend, around for the summer, of whom I could ask this generous act of service?

I spent a suitable interval working through the faux algebra to derive the legitimate reasons I could ask this favor of the Winner. After all, God might want to "see my work" in light of the bigger ends I had in mind for this request. But I had legitimate reasons, didn't I?

Heart beating madly, I called the Winner up with one or two days' lead time. Was he free? Would he mind? Was he willing to do such a thing?!! He was. And so I managed to show up at the airport with a handsome, suitable, and eligible young man at my side. A paragon of courtesy, kindness, and casual conversation, the Winner parlayed his engineering major into talking points with my engineering lecturer dad. Visiting friends from yonder Northwest even managed to snap a photo of the reunited Broadways, Winner at my side.

Yes . . . friends. Thanks to church folk enamored of my parents' pluck at moving overseas in their mid-forties, a more than adequate welcoming party had turned out at the airport—an occurrence I certainly never could have anticipated. Was it like me to concoct a flimsy excuse merely so that the one time my parents were in town—much less in the country—for the next two years, they could meet my current and highly promising crush?

Noooo. That coincidence never crossed my mind. Until right this minute, of course. (I can't imagine why Sis always accuses me of overanalyzing things . . .).

Sadly, soon after this Significant Meeting, the Winner went home to Oregon, from which he would depart to a new school in Texas at summer's end—a harbinger of the bumpy year that followed.

FRIDAY MORNING COMING DOWN

For many years if you asked me what changed junior year— especially spring '99—I would have told you I didn't know, but surely there must have been some secret sin, some sense in which I was gradually drifting from God. Was there? Sin is certainly always in the picture, but it's not quite the Christian's karma—why then all the Bible's barren women: Sarah, Hannah, and John the Baptist's mother? Why then Job and Jesus? This is where some shift the problem to God. But even despite these suffering righteous ones, Jesus Himself—who constantly predicted His own death—insists that God is good. Evidently that doesn't mean He can't ever "break up" the party you think of your life as, or push your relationship past the honeymoon.

As summer 1998 gave way to fall, I adjusted to living with a sibling again. Although I never backed down from treating Bro like he'd moved into *my* home instead of becoming an equal-rights roommate—a major source of tension in our occasional fights—I enjoyed the sense of community he afforded me. Other than the possibly retaliatory blow-dart holes with which he peppered my much-beloved Miles Davis and John Coltrane posters (hung prominently in the living room as part of *my* decoration scheme), Bro seemed fairly content with our setup.

On the whole, that year we lived together was the beginning of adult friendship and a sweet reprise of the family life and sense of home I longed to re-create. Sometimes I even joked that my perfect man would have Bro's laid-back manner, servant's heart, and dry, funny observations—plus slightly more intellectual depth (he always winced good-naturedly at the latter part, though his later letters from boot camp were certainly witty enough).

It was good for my heart to live with a male relative less inclined than Dad to deny me beauty, especially as I still struggled with my weight. Though friends' perspectives were often much less critical, it wasn't hard to downplay their views as less than familial "honesty." My brother, then, had a crucial role in being both friend and family, and a voice of more moderate views on everything from the modesty of my clothes to the attractiveness of my appearance. Such regular contact with a man I trusted also did much to meet the needs I often blamed on singleness.

But while I was enjoying restored community in one sense, I was losing it with my circle of friends from College Students. During the first year I was involved with the group, the core included a handful of older students who went on to jobs in churches or other sites of creativity and service—a bunch unafraid of intellectual topics and reflection. Whether their graduation had any impact on the changes during my junior year is hard to say, but by the spring semester it was clear my taste of heaven had been brief. Nowhere was this more evident than the post–CS meeting coffee hour.

As with "clubs" of that sort, we had a formal weekly gathering that spilled over into a casual but habitual migration to a coffee shop nearby. This was, of course, where the biggest laughs and best conversations happened—or at least where they *used* to happen. Each Thursday night of junior year I went, same as always, nourished by hope and fond memories from the year before, but somehow I always left disappointed and empty.

Conversation had always been my life's blood. I would try to replicate the high in one-on-one friendships, but nothing could replace that early childhood taste of vibrant, lively dialogue around the Broadway clan's dinner table. Talk of this sort required skill—a gift for inserting words, jokes, and anecdotes just as musicians reply to and echo each other in deft variations on a theme. Not until that first golden year with CS had I found consistent access to such music again. But junior year they gave it all up for the muzak of romance and movies, as the weekends once spent talking or playing games in someone's apartment slowly gave way to regular sit-downs at the cinema.

Maybe it was just an easy way for newly formed couples to still enjoy group outings. And yet, perhaps because I'd never had a very close peer group before, that movement to the theater was the first time I really realized how much my interests and zealous analysis of everything stood to set me apart from others. I had romantically pictured college as someplace where philosophical dialogue passed as the local dialect, but it turned out my native habits of thought were mostly a classroom exercise for my friends at ASU. (Don't laugh: they have an honors college, party-school rep or not, but I ditched class too often to make the grade requirement.)

In a desperate bid to stoke the old conversational flame, I tried to make my friends discuss the movies we saw. Perhaps if I played "conversation god" long enough, eventually a community would evolve in which, like the deists' God, I could retire and simply enjoy the system capably running itself. But nothing can replace an honest question, asked in earnest, and none of my friends wanted as "deep" a conversation as I sought with my leading questions.

Well, at least I still had God . . . or did I? Right around the same time, my now-familiar devotional rituals started to wear out the same way the read-the-Bible-in-a-year program from childhood had. This time I didn't give up so quickly, but "meeting God"—feeling as if I'd encountered Him in Bible reading because somehow my heart was touched or the words really resonated with a situation in my life—became a spiritual/emotional ecstasy I was increasingly desperate to experience, and equally unable to produce.

True ecstasy always has that crucial aspect of dependence and surprise, but I had lived too little to see that yet, so I tried to push and prod myself into some reaction to each particular reading. Mostly the deadness inside me just increased. Not that I noticed then, but when God granted a sense of His nearness, it often proved dependent on whether I had a demanding spirit or waited patiently on Him. If I sought God Himself, He met me in sermons, prayer, and Bible reading; if I sought just an experience, He let that comfort wither like the plant that sheltered Jonah outside Ninevah.

A DATE TO BUILD A DREAM ON

As was my escapist habit, I coped with my growing disappointment in God and friends by stoking the long-lived, now long-distance, crush on the Winner. Styling myself his reporter on the lives of friends left behind, I maintained an occasional flow of e-mails he sometimes replied to. He even talked of a spring break visit (a success for my e-nostalgia campaign?), which tidbit I managed to forget when planning my own mid-semester trip.

It was nearly two years since the break with my first school, and I had enough frequent-flyer miles from trips to Singapore to splurge on a zigzagging cross-country jaunt. Since freshman year of college, when I spent many a lonely Friday night trying to find something fun and social to do, I'd been obsessed with inadvertently missing what could be the best time of my life. Sam Cooke's "Another Saturday Night" might as well have dictated my overscheduling of breaks and social outings.

Because this was the first spring break in college when I'd been able to get away, I squeezed three visits into my one-week vacation. The result was a cockamamie itinerary that started with a one-way ticket from Phoenix to Seattle (via Salt Lake) departing early Thursday night the week before spring break and put me in Seattle some three or four hours before a 1 a.m. red-eye connecting flight to Des Moines. In those days inconvenience seemed a small price to pay for maximizing travel time, frequent-flyer miles, and therefore, of course, fun.

Only after I'd committed to this madcap, multistop trip did the Winner e-mail with *his* travel plans—for a break that inevitably fell the week before ours. Because I was skipping out early to squeeze three stops into one week, I'd conveniently blocked myself from all chance of hanging out the one major weekend during his visit. And as the Winner announced his visit respectably in advance (but after my booking), I had time to foresee and thoroughly rue the horror invoked by my travel plans. I knew, somehow, that if the fragile connection between us weren't strengthened by this trip, it wouldn't survive beyond the Winner's visit—and he was my best, if not only shot, at finding Hoped-for Husband on schedule!

When the long-awaited week arrived, the Winner and I promptly made plans for coffee Tuesday night. Since he was now carless in Tempe, I volunteered—over his hesitation—to borrow a car from friends and pick him up. Tuesday came, and the clever lad tracked me down by phone at work to confirm we were still on for that evening. The transit question came up once again, but I cheerfully assured him that I'd arranged to borrow the car and would call him from my friends' place. But somehow as I was standing in their cozy kitchen two hours later, making the promised call to the Winner, yet another transportation talk transpired. Finally something registered in my woefully thick head.

"Well, which would you prefer?"

I drove the half mile back to my complex and settled into the apartment to await his arrival, happily mulling ideas for our not-quite-date. *We'll discuss which coffee shop to frequent, and I know just the place to suggest: that cozy spot housed in a former bank where you can sit and drink inside the vault. Or there's that equally decent place across from my pad—serving drinks we could linger over . . . back at my place . . . where I could bake us up a yummy apple crisp!* Surely that would blot out memories of a hapless Betty Crocker fanning smoke away from burning flour . . .

The Winner arrived amidst these musings. He greeted me sans hug, to my disappointment, and led me down to a sporty little Mazda.

"I see why you wanted to drive!" I fished, teasingly.

"That's not why," he said, but no further explanation was provided.

I climbed into the car and conversation continued so smoothly that not till we were nearly to Mill Avenue (Tempe's main strip and later home to Irish Pub) did I realize there'd been no discussion of *where* to get our coffee. He parked the car but still did not address the potentially tongue-burning question. A few minutes later we queued up at the coffee shop CS people always flocked to after the weekly Thursday-night meeting. Though he had rarely gone along on such jaunts, I guess he hadn't thought of any other coffee shop. Still chatting away, I ordered a non-sleep-disrupting mug of hot chocolate and turned aside to rummage in my purse. But as I started counting out money, I realized he'd already paid for both of us.

Paid?! Dates were still the stuff of movies, Harlequins, and other people's lives for me; how could I be expected to sense I might at last be on one of my own? He was a boy I greatly liked, after all; surely he could not *return* my feelings enough to buy my drink! But a date it seemed to be, confirmed when we settled outside to chat.

Still assuming this was merely friendly catch-up time, I thought to "gently" guide discussion to some preconceived topics—no sense letting talk dry up and allowing the night to derail! Instead the Winner had thoughtful, probing questions for *me*. He asked if I was really happy, in a way that didn't invite a superficial answer, and got me to talk about my struggles with money. He even suggested taking lunches to school, and dispensed financial advice I never would have accepted from my parents (the only other party generally on such intimate terms with my spending habits). Since these tips came from him, I listened well, covertly scrabbling around on the ground for the other half of my jaw.

Until that night, I'd not realized my dominant tendencies. Although I was an oldest child, my siblings were all stubborn and feisty and not that much younger, so we mostly balanced each other out in the clamor to win adult attention—no doubt exhausting our folks in the process. That was the scrappy community I was used to: a group that valued me yet held my ego in check, among whom I could be small in importance and talent (compared to my own self-assessment) but not too small to serve or listen or even sometimes chime in aptly.

From this I grew up wanting to be an ensemble player, not

some lonely soloist whose mistakes were all out in the open. That's why I took up piano, in fact—you had more collective performance options than with the guitar. (At eleven, I had no knowledge of this thing called a "rock band." When my brothers found one of Dad's old Beatles tapes, I hid it behind a speaker because of my current obsession with classical music; to call their little ditties "music" seemed almost heretical in those judgmental early days of high school.)

But as things had slowly fractured with the CS crowd, and I'd desperately thrown more energy into keeping our music going, I'd forgotten what I longed for: a chance not to be the leader, but to respond to someone else's leadership. I guess most guys were too cowed by my vocabulary—or too content to let someone else take control—to show initiative themselves.

Not so the Winner. For him to expend so much effort meant I could relax and slowly remember how to follow another's cues. Tonight the volume of words exchanged was not dependent (solely) on my thoughts, my wit, my energy. It wasn't just me who wanted community. And the night wouldn't end if and when I fell silent, just when the hour grew late. When it did, he drove me back and we parted ways on my doorstep, still hugless.

Though I had not thought it possible, the crush had gotten much worse. If the kindest act of Musical Man was lifting me without injury, the kindness shown by the Winner was giving me access to a community I didn't have to sustain all on my own. But given this rare gift, I'd basically thrown it away in advance. The Thursday night I was ducking out so early (two days later) was our weekly College Students meeting—the Winner's attendance guaranteed. Here I was, just returned from a coffee date that possibly was *in fact* a date (though for years I still feared that label was merely wishful thinking at work), and I had just said what might be my final good-bye to the Winner, who might be my last, best shot at a husband.

That wasn't a romance-novel ending! But I could find no hope of redemption in my utterly miserable, totally self-appointed fate.

By the time a friend picked me up for my ride to the airport Thursday evening, I was almost inconsolable over the loss of this final hangout time with the Winner. Oblivious to all signs of this looming emotional apocalypse, my chauffeuring friend made cheerful inquiries as to my travel readiness. I mustered a wan smile for his daughter, then muttered a glum reply to her father. Even the slightest mishap, I feared—a stubbed toe, perhaps—would launch a major crying jag (unusual for me, in general, but increasingly a hallmark of that less-than-placid 1999).

I got to the airport 30–40 minutes before departure, as one could still do in those days, and walked sadly to the ticket clerk, toes mercifully intact. As I began the check-in process, the woman confirmed that my baggage should be checked through to Seattle.

"No, actually Des Moines."

At her confusion, I showed my red-eye ticket and sketched the strange itinerary.

"Hmmm." She seemed to be looking into something.

What was there to ponder? I knew my fate. I might as well have been Juliet, just waiting for the poison to take effect. Hope was not an option! There was no escaping my travel debacle. It could not be fixed; I'd researched that.

For someone to have said otherwise at that moment would have been as absurd as Jesus's assumption that a few loaves and fish could feed several thousand people. Only, like His deeds, those of the ticket woman disproved such a fatalistic perspective. The next thing I knew, she was looking into direct flights to Seattle. She started with flights near my original departure time, but then my brain caught a whiff of sudden hope. *Wait a minute . . .*

Since I wasn't scheduled to leave Seattle till the wee hours anyway, I had no reason to make an early exit. And since a non-stop flight was just over two hours at the most, what if I could catch a later flight—late enough to still take in the 7:30 CS meeting?

It started to feel like I was in one of those hopeful, frenetic scenes that are a chick-flick conclusion cliché. Even with an hour layover in Seattle, I could leave as late as . . . as 10 o'clock that night! Plenty of time to catch the meeting and see the Winner one final time, which gave me one more chance to save our romance and, therefore, possibly even my hopes of marrying. Heaven might not be completely lost to me!

It was like that moment when the viewer of *Sleepless in Seattle* spies the child's abandoned backpack and realizes Tom Hanks will have to *return* to the tower, catching Meg Ryan before she leaves.

The woman got me onto a satisfactory flight . . . then gave me a *$250 travel voucher* to do it. She had just reversed my fate in the most miraculous way I'd ever experienced in my twenty years, and she was *paying* me to do it! Never had I known the kind of high I felt that evening, the complete elation as I numbly left the ticket counter, boarding pass and travel voucher in hand. Never have I since.

It was a moment of redemption, yea resurrection of a dream, felt firsthand. Something that meant more to my life and happiness than I realized or than it should have—but which I'd started to accept as permanently lost—had just been returned to me as if raised from the dead. Returned to me though it was I who'd pissed away that chance, who'd consigned my own hope to this fate. How could anyone but God own the gracious hand behind this? Perhaps He was less opposed to this fierce desire of my heart than I'd feared.

I rang up the friend who'd first introduced me to the Winner and sheepishly asked if he could pick me up from the airport. Returning to campus after a quick dinner I barely ate, we met the Winner before the meeting. He took my unexpected arrival in stride and even chose to sit beside me.

He was wearing these athletic-type sandals (fine by me because they were not Tevas), and as the praise music started his bare toes caught my eye. To my delight I saw they were toes I found attractive. I've always had this weirdness where hands and feet are concerned, and while I'd never reject a guy for having substandard nail beds (which he could likely pass on to our children), it's always been like a small "confirmation" when I like the look of someone's fingers and toes. Which I did the Winner's.

This thought must have overheated me, for I soon peeled off the utterly dreadful big blue sweatshirt I was wearing, stripping down to the shirt beneath.

"Take it all off!" he teased.

Ohmygod, flirtation! From a boy I liked! The evening was just about perfect.

At meeting's end, I had to depart for that now-happy trip to the airport. This was it. The good-bye. I could almost hear the schmaltzy music they play just before the credits.

I'd been hoping for a hug, but none was offered. The best I could manage was a clumsy side hug I stepped into before walking away to the car. Nevertheless, the orange-tree blossoms that night sent me off on the scent of hope that I had a soul mate whose destiny was bound to mine by no other matchmaker than

God. Not that I planned to leave all the work of producing romance up to Him, but still. Was this miraculous happening not a sign to end all signs? God had finally remembered me in my singleness. Maybe I'd find a husband by graduation after all, vanquishing loneliness permanently!

CHAPTER 4

INTO THE CANNON

Always dreamed of flyin'
and now the dream comes true
I'm not afraid of dyin'
so I will fall for you, all for you, baby
This is your big top, baby
Yeah you've got all your clowns
around it's true
Why are you just smilin' at me fallin'
Oh maybe this is keeping you amused

The sound comes 'round
now I wake up
with my ear to the ground
I rise surprised
so this is how a fool gets wise, oh

—DAVID WILCOX, *"Human Cannonball"*

As I waltzed onto the plane that balmy Thursday night in March, it was easy to think God was good, to want to submit to His will for my life and to trust He surely had good things in store—was not the Winner likely to be part of that?

In the days that followed, I couldn't help myself retelling what an amazing miracle God had worked, described to whatever hapless person indulged me with patient ears. In fact, the story over-shadowed all the rest of the trip. One of these listeners was the wife of a couple I knew from my church in Phoenix, whom I visited in Seattle. My weekend sojourn as their guest afforded a chance to ride the ferry beloved from childhood memories of the city, buy a giant Starbucks coffee mug from the original store at Pike Place, and then like any girl so inspired by sea and coffee, indulge in trading lengthy stories.

While the wife's might have been shorter, they were invaluable for their clear resolution and their genre. Even if she hadn't guessed their future then, the history passed between her and her husband now described a story of courtship. I couldn't resist this chance to apply her retrospective wisdom. When I probed what her first hint was that her husband might be "the one," she mentioned something about how he just "felt like family."

Aha! *Had the Winner felt like family to me? Had there been a rather unusual sense of comfort with him?* I sifted through impressions and recollections, as if these tea leaves would prove prophetic.

The problem, of course, was that she could see what made her tea because she was now drinking it, whereas I held leaves that might steep nicely or wind up in a drawer sachet . . . or even hand-rolled clove cigarettes. Should this remarkable episode with the Winner be understood as part of the story I always thought my life told: the tale of courtship and marriage to Hoped-for Husband?

During the first few days and weeks that followed, I scarcely imagined an alternative. But once my spring-break high wore off, I couldn't escape a growing awareness of one flaw in my childhood plan for life: I'd never imagined anything interesting *after* the vows (except, of course, sex).

Now granted, probably no child has the foresight to dream big dreams for her forties or fifties . . . but I started to see that a life whose point was wedlock might leave something—even many things—to be desired. As I looked around at most of my friends, some almost in sight of my greatest dream, their shadowy Ghosts of Marriage Future held out visions of bland suburbia and tepid middle-class lives.

My parents, by contrast, had always conveyed a subtle but definite sense of momentum—life hadn't ended when they got married, had kids, and turned thirty; it reached new levels. Theirs had not been a gradual spiral downward from the peaks of college and courtship, but a steady progression onward: Dad's education, plans to move overseas, the initial departure southward to test the trials of separation, then the eventual move to Singapore.

Were they just adventurers? Perhaps. But if so, those two, who spent their honeymoon backpacking in the Canadian Rockies and planned each summer's vacation as a camping trip, were unlikely candidates for a midlife move to a bustling city in Southeast Asia. More likely, it was because of their submission to the routine of rather ordinary obedience to God that my parents wound up living a life somewhat extraordinary.

This sense that God, not marriage, led to a life of meaning and purpose—even adventure—was like a subtle whiff in the breeze, whose fragrance the other, more clamorous smells of college never completely overwhelmed. Ever beneath the sweat and the coffee, the greasy lunches and midpriced body wash, was that mysterious tang of something like the pines and creosote bushes in the desert beyond the city, whose scent was sharpened by the occasional rains.

Perhaps it was this elusive invitation that drew me out more and more nights that spring to walk around an on-campus track near my apartment to pray. However they had started—maybe a study break late one night, half thinking a paper through aloud, half running certain ideas past God—those laps eventually became one of the highlights of my spiritual life that spring. To my surprise, involving God in things like that week's writing assignment didn't feel weird or forced; it felt more like the sort of dialogue one might carry on with a spouse at each day's end.

When you have frequent contact with someone, whatever love they have for you is apparent—most unmistakably face to face. However much my father's lack of attention sometimes disappointed me when I lived at home, there was the frequent weight of a tender hand on my shoulder, the care he took in sugaring a weekend cup of coffee for me, that quietly counterbalanced the pain of imperfect words and too little time to simply talk and enjoy each other. He could not make such small but consistent gestures of affection and fail to love me. Thus it is with God: the more time together, the less I doubt His love's veracity.

And so one night, when I kept feeling like God wanted me to chat up a fellow sitting by the fountain near the student union, I gulped a bit then slowly headed over. It certainly seemed slightly reckless to chat up a stranger late at night, but if this was God's idea, shouldn't I survive intact?

Trying to look casual, I wandered over and somehow thought of an opening line. It wasn't long before we wound up discussing spiritual reality—whether this was just an energy, or connected with an infinite personal being like the Bible describes. Some might have called our conversation "evangelism," but unlike how uncomfortable I tended to get when trying to bring up Jesus with other people, that evening chat felt natural, even relaxed. This was fairly shocking.

ADVENTURES IN JESUS MARKETING

For as long as I could remember, talk about God with people outside the church almost always felt like trying to sell a vacuum cleaner, to someone who might not even own a carpet. Whether you'd been accosted by some door knocker on the weekend, or invited to church, it was the same. And when we moved to Phoenix, it had become an annual problem: every summer the church's week of Vacation Bible School included a day to bring friends. It was like being forced to report how many voice mails or e-mails you'd gotten, how many people liked you—except in this case my failure to bring the requisite friends symbolized not just my social but also my spiritual shortcomings.

Once in early youth, I'd taught a neighbor girl John 3:16—"For God so loved the world, that He gave His only begotten Son, that whoever believes in Him shall not perish, but have eternal life"—but later such open-to-Jesus friends proved hard to find. For a long stretch my closest "friends" were books. But you couldn't quite tote a pile of pulps to visitor day and proudly proclaim this your "potential-convert posse." Instead I'd desperately size up the neighborhood trying to think of someone I'd talked to, let alone someone close to my age (I don't recall that adult "friends" were ever an option at VBS). Luckily my sibs were no more successful at this than I, so that removed a bit of the heat: we were, as a family, blighted with some peculiar allergy to evangelism.

We kids, anyway. Certainly not Dad. An adult convert to the Jesus freaks, he was known for early proselytizing zeal and the sort of boldness for God I'd later cringe at . . . until it became my chief criterion for a husband. As the years went by, Dad mellowed into a man who befriended colleagues and invited them into his home more frequently than his church. Not that in doing so he cared any less for their souls; indeed, when he and Mom moved the family to Asia it was just this sort of hospitality-based evangelism they hoped to carry out.

The idea was that in living for God and being restored to His family, their quality of life was so radically altered that people would voluntarily ask what made them different. And since these people would know them in relationship, such talks about God would not be a pressurized, special, one-time event but a series of hopefully natural dialogues. In Dad's case, these often started with his story of rather remarkable transformation.

I still remember a conversation in Singapore, when he explained to a colleague what sort of person he used to be. The man looked at my father—clean-cut, friendly Mr. Broadway, so well respected and liked by his peers—and struggled to grasp how he had once been a long-haired, unruly, selfish teenager. From what my father told him, it was clear that more than inevitable maturing had happened. How had Dad's life been changed from the course it started out on?

The answer was probably as shocking as Dad's portrait of his former life: one day not long after boot camp, he was invited to a Tennessee church, where what he heard transformed him in a way not even the navy's discipline could. There he heard that he was a sinner: not just a reckless nineteen-year-old who'd already broken a few laws (and some hearts, perhaps), but someone who'd broken the laws of the Being who made him. Regardless of how Dad might distinguish one sin from another, all his deeds flowed from the same motive of a naked grab for power, an unflinching determination to get his own way no matter what.

This was treason of the highest order, and nothing Dad could do could restore the peace, for himself or anyone else on earth. Their rebellion was comprehensive—it drove everything from petty selfishness to the war Dad would soon fight in—and its penalty was death. But because God loved all people and longed to live with them in perfect relationship again, He sent His own son to make things right. So, like an artist stepping into his own painting, Jesus took on the form of a human, coming to live and to die a traitor's death as a substitute for Dad and anyone else who would accept that path to peace.

However much of this Dad had heard before, and no matter what he might have objected to in earlier years, he caught a glimpse that day of a beauty that was worth accepting his own condemnation to discover. I guess it seemed too simultaneously glorious and severe to be made up.

You see, as much as all of us at the table that day in Singapore would probably agree Dad's life changed for the good, he certainly couldn't have foreseen the benefits of his walk with God when turning to Him years before in Tennessee. If anything, conversion soon made his life as a sailor harder. While their cruises through the Pacific might have eased him into the Christian's life of chastity, Dad couldn't share his shipmates' relief when they docked into port. Only when you love someone deeply would you give up so much. Only when you realize how much *you've* been loved does such love even spring up. And that love—it has a perfume to it, which Dad's colleague must have scented.

I always preferred my parents' approach to explaining their faith, but that never fixed the problem of having so few friends to share my own with. The best I could do was single out acquaintances or work colleagues with whom there seemed a smidgen of real connection, build a friendship, and hope I'd someday get to ask leading questions like "If you died tonight, where do you think you'd go?"

I never got to probe that far, but then again, maybe how

many folks I could have asked that question of wasn't as important as I thought it was. Was saving souls supposed to get me an upgrade on spiritual blessings? The scandal of the gospel, as one friend once put it, is not that good people go to heaven and bad people go to hell, but that "bad" people go to heaven, "good" people to hell. Those human distinctions mean nothing to God—we *all* fall short of His standards. But because so much of the problem is that we live by human standards and in search of human approval, all but the most unabashed sinners are too proud to ask God to save them from their sins. So used to, though enslaved by, others' opinions of us, we simply don't think we're that bad. Even once we've agreed with God that we *are* so corrupt, it's mighty hard to remember, easy to slip back into old, legalistic ways of trying to relate to Him—evangelism included.

And yet, despite how borderline disingenuous much of the proselytizing I'd seen appeared, I couldn't shake the sense that lurking beneath the often self-serving and religious was something God Himself desired and delighted in—if not commanded. Although I'd certainly spoken as His ambassador to the student by the fountain that night, it wasn't all that burdensome; instead my goal was sharing the joy I'd just had in my prayer walk around the track. And while I didn't walk home feeling I'd just "saved a soul," my ease in talking about the one I loved left me more hopeful about my forthcoming trip with College Students.

Every summer, coeds around the country trekked off to join one of several projects reaching various cities (often tourist hot spots), where they typically found jobs in the area and did a lot of evangelism. Several of my friends had done such a project the year before, but I'd been convicted by debt and other factors that this might not be the time to seek such adventure. Hence "deepcon" with the Winner, my pancake debacle, and his meeting with my family.

Then I started my junior year. And when the brochure for summer '99 came out, I couldn't forget one tantalizing write-up. It said College Students sought "radicals for Christ" who wanted to learn about postmodernism and research how to reach a new generation with Jesus. Interested parties should apply to the project slated for Berkeley. Well, it would be radical to spend a summer wearing less than 45 SPF sunscreen and not sweating away half my body weight each month. And though I wanted to take a stab at giving my life more wholly to God, I couldn't shake a growing unease with how College Students shared Jesus with people.

Since its founding in the mid-twentieth century, the organization had been known for trying to win people over with this tool called "The Main Principles." It was a small tract discussing basic reality (per the Christian view), the chief thing wrong in life, and how to fix it (a message similar to what Dad heard that day in church). While this presentation worked fine in the fifties and sixties when the Christian world was still responding to Scopes and all that modernist monkey business, it doesn't do so well today.

It wasn't doing so well in 1999, either. If I had tried to use the tract with the guy from the campus fountain, I doubt we'd have gotten that far past point one. Like many in our generation, his life revolved around different questions from those the Main Principles presumed. And frankly, perhaps there's even been a shift in whether we're open to some stranger asking our time to learn about his product or idea. Somehow the traveling salesmen you read about in fiction like *Caddie Woodlawn* sound like they were more welcomed in their day than today's seller of Amway (then again, maybe I'm just burned because the one time Mom bought stuff from a guy at the door, it sparked a rare ruckus with Dad; their compromise on the encyclopedias was that she returned the new ones and got a 1978 set, which we bought at a King County Library auction).

Regardless of whether the issue lay with the tract or its typical use, there were those in College Students who were troubled by this problem with their sales pitch—maybe not so many in 1999, but a few nonetheless. And not just skeptical students like myself, increasingly turned off by much of Christian culture's spun-sugar "substance" (in those days I scored the newly hip WWJD bracelets). At least one College Student's staffer shared our concerns and reservations and had guts enough to ask if he could run a summer project devoted to looking into CS's flagging God pitch. Given my spotty history of evangelizing, nothing seemed a better way to ease into talking about God more freely than researching ways to best do so.

After the stories friends had told of their experiences last year, it seemed a splendid summer awaited. But as late winter gave way to spring, and the Winner made no reply to a series of casual postdate follow-up e-mails, I couldn't shake the growing premonition of a difficult season ahead. That thought first hit me in prayer one night, during one of my laps at the track.

As I pondered this sudden sense of foreboding, the stroll of habit became a vaguely uneasy pace. *Was I soon to lose a loved one? Would someone get sick or die? Had the Winner found a girlfriend?* While the author of Hebrews says we know we're God's children when He disciplines us—that this is a mark of His love—I thought such troubles only befell those guilty of major sinning. And I was still a virgin, still not drinking till twenty-one! As long as I wanted good things and was a fairly righteous person, why would God need to perform corrective action?

Owing to this immature grasp of the Christian life, the gradual spiral downward that defined the rest of the year remained an inexplicable mystery for some time. And yet life in that final year of the millennium did not have the feel of incidental chaos. Though much of what transpired came as a shock to one so otherwise unused to pain, there was a peculiar sense of deliberate progression. My life unraveled gradually, and primarily in a social sense—as if, in fact, God were weeding out the sin my fear of loneliness was driving me to: the same old problem behind those long-gone T-shirts.

The upshot of this, as confusion left me vulnerable to lies that explained my pain as proof God wasn't all that good, was an almost total destruction of faith He could be trusted with *anything,* much less my love life. Except . . . except for the faint hope that lingered, nourished by memories of that inexplicable miracle with the Winner, which I could never fully make sense of but could neither deny God's role in. The heart remembers things the mind has forgotten—and through all the pain, close calls, and rebellion that would define the next five years, mine held to the hope that God's best for me might not be so opposed to my heart's desires.

I wonder now if the main reason that hope survived was not the night when God seemed to smile on His daughter's attraction to things like leadership, character, and kindness. That, perhaps, and the prayers I soon forgot in Berkeley.

AN INVITATION TO QUESTION

One sunny weekend late in June (then three months into the Winner's postdate silence), I set off from Tempe with two other friends: Girlfriend #1 and her future husband, Family Friend. A few hundred miles and no speeding tickets later (though I'm sure I hit a buck during one of my stints as the backup driver), we arrived in Berkeley, three of eighteen students who made the pilgrimage from around the country. Evidently "radicals for Jesus" were hard to find.

Though Berkeley is hardly known as a bastion for churches, the big Presbyterian one in town ran our home for that summer—a large, rambling structure we came to call the W-House. Situated as it was in a place where ideological turf is so hotly contested (that summer the local radio station prompted protests and marches that shut down one street for three weeks), the W-house was not exactly immune to the rebellious spirit that permeated Berkeley.

Our project director had only rented enough rooms to house the eighteen students and some of the staff—along with access to the kitchens and bathrooms we'd need. Since he had a family and lived in the area year round (unusual for most projects), our director was only on-site for meetings and training. However, in an attempt to foster some kind of project unity, he tried to keep us separate from those we shared the house with— mostly long-term student residents, with whom it turned out he had a contentious history.

This effort to divide the house into "project" and "off-project" students and zones went so far as restricting their access to "our" common space. Unbeknownst to us, these ongoing tenants—whom we came to know as some of the "Project Pals," local students who befriended us—had been barred from the heart of their long-term home. (And also from the big meeting room on the ground floor, except for some occasions, like the worship service they held on Sunday nights. That might have been the only time we were truly sanctioned in mingling with the others in the house.) I understood the desire to keep us focused, to try to foster some group identity. But considering all of us soon had to track down jobs and buy groceries and locate cheap eats for meals we didn't cook, it was natural we would turn to the Berkeley "experts" who shared our house. And that's without even considering the gender dynamics.

It turned out our bunch of "radicals" was overwhelmingly female and upper class, by which I mean, almost ready to graduate. There were two of us for each guy on the project, and almost as many third- or fourth-year women for each of our freshman peers. The six guys split fifty-fifty, single or dating, with the single half all freshmen. All. That's not to say we had come there to find boyfriends, but when the project guys were compared with the mostly male, upper-class Project Pals, it was going to take more than a door to keep us women from forming friendships with the latter crew.

But as Hippie the Groper would later recall the divisions of the house, they went exactly that far: a new door splitting the hallway my bedroom was on. Hippie was, of course, a Project Pal, so separatist measures like that made an impression. At the end of the hall, by the stairs to the big ground-floor meeting room, was the closetlike space that one of the Pals called home. In my mind that wasn't an issue unless he planned to share a bathroom with my roommate and me. But our director—committed with typical Christian zeal to separation of sexes—wanted a very physical barrier between the project women (who shared private, same-sex bathrooms) and the male, off-project resident down the hall. Hence the newly installed door enforcing his summer housing zones. The rest of our women lived downstairs off the meeting room, while the men were in a building known as the Annex, that jutted out back from the main house. As far as I know, their housing did not require any construction.

Such was W-house geography 101. Not that we got this introduction that summer. But we *were* supposed to be learning a similar kind of mapping as part of acclimation to Berkeley. Our project was, after all, more research than marketing—and one of our leader's hunches was that people promoting Jesus had not (recently) thought through secular demographics. Which should include looking at the milieu of one's target audience. Since our leader worked in Berkeley year round, he wanted what further insights we could glean in a summer. Our early training focused on ways to observe the social geography of a place. How do people use it? Where do they meet? What are intersections where decisions are made and people are more likely to read a poster? When one is foreign to a place, the reasoning went, you sometimes see those patterns better than you would in your own home—though the aim was that we would take these analytical tools back to our campuses in the fall.

Although we were learning to look at our new city newly, we were slow to pick up on more obvious key features. Had we practiced such observation by asking the house's long-term residents how *they* used the space and how our presence affected them, we might have been more prepared for some of the tensions we encountered. Not that any of this anger was directed at us personally. But as the summer went on, we would learn that conflict had been brewing between some of those students and our director—not just over his division of the house, but over other issues in the Berkeley CS chapter, which he ran and they'd been part of. Once some of the project women formed friendships with the Project Pals, it was only a matter of time before they were pulled (at least emotionally) into that quarrel. We were there to question, after all. Whoever said that posture of skepticism couldn't also subject our very own leaders to suspicion?

No one thought it would be our own faith that tripped us up, much less its adherents. If anything, those more anxious about our summer had feared that contact with Berkeley locals—with their many, atypical faiths—would be what led us astray, should there be any fallout from the project. But in aptly postmodern fashion, our inquiry turned more and more from *who* we were trying to reach to how we'd been reaching them— how *we,* or more generally the church and groups like CS, were really the problem.

In many ways, the critique was certainly called for—no doubt the reason CS had even approved such a novel project. But from the start, its promotion was guaranteed to attract those "radicals" most primed to revolt against much of Christian custom. The challenge for our leadership was encouraging a questioning, critical spirit that could distinguish between resisting corrupt or misguided authority and rebellion against all authority in general. Teach people to interrogate, and there's no guarantee they won't eventually turn those questions on the very one who sharpened their bite.

Living in a house still steeped in the residue of more than one upheaval between authorities and those under them, and living in a city where, that summer, radio station workers mutinied against their corporate bosses' interference with budgets and threats to sell the station license, such a response seemed natural. We were not immune to an inflammation of well-intentioned questioning into willful, myopic revolt. It was almost as if the city had drawn those of its rebellious temper to itself. As the summer progressed, we all increasingly chafed against more than the aspects of Christian culture that rang false to us; we chafed against the very structure and leadership of our project.

Raised in a happy, stable home where my parents rarely fought, I wasn't equipped to cope with such building conflict on top of all my internal drama. When, in the middle of all that confusion, a boy appeared who slightly resembled the Winner in face and voice—albeit a boy then rather embittered toward women—how could I help but to choose the man at hand over the man afar and the conflict at hand? It wasn't as if I could face the summer without some sort of romantic escape—and this one seemed safe enough. A guy with wounds as raw as his was unlikely to like me back, ideal for a surely short-lived summer crush. Besides, it had been a while since I'd fallen for a musician. True, the last such crush went through me like an enduring case of food poisoning, but this one talked of things like Bertolt Brecht and somehow I didn't think he had the last guy's passivity.

After the conversational wilderness my Jesus freak social circle had become, a man unafraid to wax even remotely intellectual was hot stuff, especially when he had a small cluster of like-minded friends. Whereas the ASU College Students crowd was reluctant to opine more expansively than "good, bad, or boring" on most topics—much less talk *ideas*—this guy was not only willing, he was better read! Brecht was someone I'd barely heard of until the new crush explained him to me one night. A smart guy who might be even smarter than me, who might make heady remarks without me even steering the topic that way?!! Hot stuff indeed.

Add to this that said smart musician was one of the only people around whom I wasn't forced to socialize with, and who hadn't been picked off among the choicer Project Pals (perhaps since he lived off-site and only came by the house once a week for the worship night), and it's no wonder I have no memory of *not* liking Poster Boy that summer.

CHAPTER 5

MY FAVORITE ESCAPE

*We listen and we are aware of . . . a sigh. And under the sigh is
something dangerous, something that feels adulterous and dis-
loyal to the religion we are serving. We sense a passion deep
within that threatens a wild disregard for the program we are living; it feels reckless, wild. Unsettled, we turn and walk quickly
away, like a woman who feels more than she wants to when her
eyes meet those of a man not her husband.*

—BRENT CURTIS AND JOHN ELDREDGE, *The Sacred Romance*

Although he was mostly aloof and less than kind, I had
remarkable luck in hanging out with Poster Boy and
his posse over various weekends and even a few weeknights that summer, a blessed escape from the project-crowd
drama. Compared to them, both his friends and his pain were
simpler, more straightforward things to process—not unlike the
somber solos from *Kind of Blue* (Coltrane work I *had* heard and
owned, though for years I only knew it as Miles's album) and
the *Blue Train* record, which I hadn't yet but would later hear
and own. Just as I suspect I liked more of Coltrane's earlier work
than his later experimentation, I was drawn to something more
solid and stable in Poster Boy's crowd than the Project Pals,
though all of us were fairly cynical Christians that summer.

Perhaps the critiques of Jesus-freak culture I heard from
Poster Boy's friends made me less uneasy than those of others

for the love of God that seemed to lay beneath it. The others seemed to love righteousness—as they defined it—just a little too much, a concern that can foster obsession with purity, and intolerance for the impure. Though I loved God quite poorly, and my trust in Him was even worse, the questions I started to face that summer came more from a longing to know Him better than to unravel the ties that kept me obeying Him (no matter all my complaints about the rope burn). I sensed a similar passion in Poster Boy's friends.

One of those weekends with Poster Boy's posse—the one just prior to that of my birthday, the marathon, and a rather strong Long Island iced tea—was July the Fourth. For any woman who has never progressed beyond the high-school stage of liking a man (did Freud have a term for this, I wonder?), spending key holidays or other events in the company of The Crush is a major coup. It doesn't matter how long you've liked him or if it's you and The Crush and many others . . . it's still a coup (although separately attending the same homecoming or other high-school dance doesn't count).

So, somehow or other, I managed to join Poster Boy and his friends on the Fourth of July. It probably helped that the holiday fell barely three weeks into the project: my new-groupie status had not yet worn off so my presence was borne. I have almost no recollection of the fireworks (oh right, because there were none . . . between us), but I do remember showing off my domestic skillz, taking care not to spill the flour this time.

As I recall, my baking took the form of an apple crisp that night . . . but there's a reason Poster Boy's not called Boy Who Ate Apple Crisp. You see, the minute I walked into his living space that night, I noticed a poster of John Coltrane. The *very same* poster in the *very same* size that I had hanging in my living room at home—except without the blow-dart holes. *Come to think of it, he did resemble Bro a little . . . Did he, too, spend ages in the bathroom getting ready?*

Sometime during my freshman year of college, I'd acquired two subway-sized posters of jazz musicians—more for visual appeal than because I idolized them over any other musician or band in my CD library (though I did take a jazz improv class that year and started learning to transcribe solos from my limited listening library). The posters were great, and they were big, and I liked for people to see them when they visited my living space. I had never, however, encountered other people or stores that had those same posters in that particular size.

But Poster Boy had my Coltrane! In the *exact same size*.

"Oh my God!" I exclaimed, in typically overdramatic Anna fashion (probably the kind of yelp I had perfected as Fruma Sarah). "I have that exact same poster!"

As I stared up at it, in awe of this peculiar sign, I continued. "I have another just like it, but it's of Miles Davis and he's sort of pursing his lips . . ."

"You mean that one?" Poster Boy pointed to a wall I'd not seen.

"Oh my *GOD!* Yes!"

The very same poster, in the very same size. Who knew the printer had run such a shockingly large edition of my two posters? For a minute it felt briefly like being back in my own living room with Bro again. To this day that's the only time I have ever encountered such remarkable similitude of taste. It took seeing *Serendipity* to teach me that the real sign is whether the money someone gave you with his phone number written on it comes back to you. While Poster Boy never offered me money that year, he did buy my drinks almost every time we hung out that summer.

His first chance was the following weekend, when it was *my* turn for a birthday (his was the day right after the holiday, and my reason for baking the crisp). The Sunday I turned twenty-one, our project worked or ran the San Francisco marathon, part of a weekend research requirement. There are limits to how much you can test the culture of the group that's sponsoring you, and College Students was known for sidewalk proselytizing. So, although my famous quote that summer was that "Sharing Jesus too quickly with someone is like groping on the first date" (like I knew), we still sought to chat up strangers. The sales-pitch twist was that unlike our peers on other projects—who mostly used the "Main Principles"—we tested a different type of tool each weekend.

At the marathon we went propless: some volunteered to help the runners, while others formed four-person relay teams like the one I joined in a madcap burst of optimism. *"I don't exercise! But hey, how bad can six miles be? It's not like you can die from that."* I didn't die, but I wouldn't have made it through my run without another student who felt so good after running his team's Leg 1 that he chose to join me as I ran my team's Leg 2.

This was such a feat that after Sunday night worship was over, Running Buddy and a few other of-age students and locals took me to a nearby "publick house" to celebrate my milestones. Although it turned out that Running Buddy had never gotten to buy a friend a twenty-first-birthday drink and hoped to finally break that streak with me, I hadn't felt that loved on a birthday in a while. Cursed to be born in the middle of summer, I'd gotten used to opening presents while on some family vacation camping out in the wilderness. With all the marathon hubbub, I figured no one remembered my birthday, much less that it was a big one.

Instead the group proved touchingly eager to celebrate; some girls had even bought a cake. More remarkably, without any planning on my part, or work to include him, we were joined by the most coveted guest a girl like me could have wanted: her current crush. First we shared a major holiday (and almost his twenty-third birthday), now we were celebrating my entry into adulthood?! Incredible.

After we'd begun my celebration, Poster Boy even bought my second drink of the birthday, a Long Island iced tea so potent it effectively finished me off for the evening—no buying rights for Running Buddy. When I asked if this was unusual, Poster Boy flashed a devilish grin and said he'd told the bartender to make it "extra strong." I stifled a moderate swoon. *Could it be he was good boy and bad boy at once?* Such a man conjured up the prospect of being pursued both for one's character and one's beauty—a rarely seen amalgam of safe-but-possibly-boring love and the inconsistently pulse-thrilling kind. Surely his eagerness to buy me drinks was a portent of good things to come.

Good things in the long run, that is. Even I could sense that should something ever happen with Poster Boy, now was not that time. In those days, except when talking to me about jazz, in which he'd majored, or helping to get me liquored up, he came across as a classic case of embittered male cynic, though having been deeply and recently betrayed by the girl he planned to marry, he was not without cause.

Instead of warning me off, his "women are the devil" kick only brought out my contrary side. After all, he seemed unmoved by all the compassion other women no doubt gave him—and really, what's hotter than men and women who bicker? Almost every romance novel I'd read (and not a few movies I'd seen) made clear such fights betrayed an underlying chemistry. For Poster Boy to spar with me confirmed my hopes for our future. Because, you know, a man in that state is surely looking for the next Mrs. Poster Boy or at least the next Poster Boy girlfriend candidate . . . right?

The chance to negotiate my standing came roughly a week after my birthday, one Tuesday night at the video store. As the posse weighed the script-light aggression flicks on display, women's taste in movies came up. Ah, but here was my chance! What movie was still a recent mass phenomenon of weepy women, bad taste, and wimpy male leads? The very movie I had not seen as a point of proto-hipster honor. Even against the disagreement of my *family,* who claimed *Titanic* wasn't half bad, I had stood firm. Not seeing that movie was a notch on my belt I made sure Poster Boy was informed of. That and how I shared his fondness for *Swingers.* Was this not ample proof our tastes were much the same? Surely he'd have to like someone so much like himself—we'd even both been *homeschooled.*

For a moment I seemed to be winning. Then he moved to other female clichés, namely the musical, and I was doomed. True, I own fewer than ten videos (and not one made in the eighties), but one was indeed . . . um . . . *Sound of Music.* In Poster Boy vs. Broadway, the battle was over: Broadway guilty as charged, just like all the other women are the devil. Brought down by my cursed romanticism.

To be sure, going after another's approval as zealously as I had sets you up to be judged and defined by his standards rather than on your own merits. But in those days I wasn't spunky enough to pull off the snappy dialogue I aspired to. The key to all those feisty heroines' sass was that they truly didn't care. I, on the other hand, rose and fell by Poster Boy's standards, misogynistic or otherwise. And fell hard. Indeed, he would later recall me as quite "nuts" that summer because my liking for him was so poorly concealed.

GOOD-BYE TO THE HEART-FAKE HOTEL

Ironically, this transparency was just the thing I was going for. As I struggled to cope with the Winner's perplexing silence, the last thing I wanted was new heartbreak on top of old. It was all I could do not to find God's mysterious letdown after that oh-so-promising miracle a caprice of the cruelest kind. Days into the project, I wrestled with these old and new predicaments my heart put me in:

Why can't I get past the Winner, Lord? Why does that silly, al-most (now) meaningless name still haunt me? It's like what they talk about in The Sacred Romance: *"the message of the ar-rows." I want to stop the feeling. I want to wipe him out of my mind, stop wondering about him. Why is the thought, the ques-tion, so deep-seated that someday something might happen— someday he might be the one?*

It's like this whole thing with Poster Boy. Not parallel or analogous, actually, but . . . I don't really want to like him. I see so much potential to repeat the mistakes I made with Musician Crush #1. He's pining over this girl . . . How could he possibly be ready for another relationship even?

I want to reason myself out of interest, out of whatever my heart might feel. I guess it's not the liking I fear or loathe—it's another misplaced or unreturned affection . . . I've so many times been wrong in whom I've liked, why should I start to feel again?

If ever there was a case where liking would surely be a waste of time and emotion, this was it. My heart must be accursed! And yet, there was no denying Poster Boy did hold a strange attraction: he had most of the Winner's good points (except a scorn for dancing), plus a thrilling hint of adventure, even danger, about him. I often worried he'd kill himself in reckless, sleepless drives on the treacherous switchbacks to his home along the coast. At least he didn't ride motorcycles!

On the whole, though, it was more than a rakish appeal. I had spent most of my life as some kind of outsider—first as a homeschool kid, then a Christian, then an out-of-state student, a transfer student, a girl who liked ideas too much . . . But Poster Boy seemed to share much of that, most importantly my passion for an honest, wholehearted faith. It wasn't just that he was a pastor's son, either. Some people's lives bear a sense of God's hand upon them, no matter how bleakly hope sometimes flickers in their gaze. Even behind the barrier of his bitterness, I sensed a work of God in Poster Boy that made me want to be there when the construction was further along.

And yet . . . the bitterness. And that wasn't even including the unlikelihood we'd keep in touch beyond the summer! Fall for a guy like this? Here was trouble, indeed. It was tempting to run away from the nearly certain pain of liking a man too good—and too badly wounded, at present—to be meant for me, but how could I expect to give my whole heart to someone— chief of all, to God—if I ran from caring and feeling just because it might hurt? Maybe one couldn't brand all desire as bad. After all, God had blessed that desire to leave my first school, to see the Winner once more—even to come on a summer project. Which I had applied to in a quest for more authentic faith!

It didn't seem very honest to deny my feelings, risky and troublesome or not. In those days I still mostly believed one psychologist's adage (once tacked to my dorm-room door) that "feelings are neither right nor wrong; it's what you do with them that causes the trouble." Maybe I needn't squelch my feelings so much as accept they couldn't be satisfied now.

Reluctantly I left things up to God and decided not to block, stifle, or deny my attraction to Poster Boy though it was almost sure to be ill-fated:

> *I guess I can't manage my heart here, Lord. I'd like to, but . . . I'm not convinced that's right. So . . . please do Your will, whatever that is. Help me to submit to that. "Not my will but Thine, Oh Lord." I ask only—no, I beg—that You guard my heart, for my desire is not to keep expending its passion on disinterested boys whom You have not selected as my husband. Maybe that's not Your plan, but that's my desire.*

While that settled the matter of my nascent attraction to Poster Boy, depending on God's wisdom did not provide quite the protection I'd hoped for. That summer I had a nightmare more vivid and frightening than any I've had before or since. In the dream, our project was scattered over a hill near Berkeley, paired off in search of a lost student. My partner was a friend from school not actually on the project but (in real life) acquainted with Poster Boy's good friend, Posse Pal—who turned out to be the dream's missing student.

When we found him just inside a forest along one side of the hill, he was unstable and self-destructive, waving a gun we feared he would turn on himself. Instead he turned on us in the midst of our pleading with him, killing our friend in front of me. Just then the rest of the group rejoined us, accompanied by police who took him away. In the next scene, I was for some reason led in to see Posse Pal, alone, in the jailhouse waiting room where he was bound to a chair with heavy chains around his arms.

The minute I looked in his eyes, I saw hatred for me—a murderous rage so terrifying I woke up crying and calling aloud to Jesus for help and protection, so loud I awakened my roommate. She crawled into bed beside me to calm me down, but even after she prayed with me, returned to her bunk, and fell back asleep, I didn't dare doze myself. Posse Pal was actually sleeping right down the hall from me! And the dream had been so vivid it was initially hard to separate from reality, too real to dismiss as simply a troubled psyche letting off steam. I stayed up in a tense, fearful state the rest of the night, until the faint light of dawn grew strong enough to banish paralysis.

Even though the Bible describes a number of meaningful dreams, some of which are connected either to very important decisions (like the flight of Joseph and Mary with baby Jesus) or the impact of future events (like the famine foretold to Pharaoh in a dream only Joseph the slave could interpret), I grew up in theologically conservative churches where such dramatic works of God were all believed to be past tense. I had certainly never paid much attention to my own dreams, much less pondered whether God had any influence on them, but in the first hours after my nightmare, I couldn't shake a strong sense that it had somehow been supernatural. At first my dream spawned hushed conversation with a couple of women who vaguely spoke about spiritual attack, but all such talk receded soon enough.

Although we were ostensibly doing "spiritual" work that summer, the spiritual part was increasingly taking a back seat. We might have talked a lot about how to discuss God with others, but I don't remember much time spent talking *to* Him. My own walks to pray had been almost completely forgotten, and if we ever prayed as a group, except for meals, it wasn't a memorable part of that summer. With our own God's nature so increasingly overlooked, a dream like mine was little more than a passing, if briefly terrifying, blip. Before long it was back to the strange, confusing routine besetting our project.

We were failing that summer; maybe that's how a psychologist would have explained the nightmare. Instead of making much progress on our mission—either in research or evangelism—we were self-destructing beneath the weight of escalating conflict and the clamor of our eighteen increasingly selfish, self-righteous, voices. Our stated (if totally vague and equally unattainable) goal had been to each find a local "subgroup"—the goth crowd, the jocks, the stoners, and so on—somehow get to know them, and by the end of the summer write up a research paper on how to compellingly tell that group about Jesus. All that in eight weeks—well, seven weeks, since the last week was left for writing. And really, not even seven weeks, since the first week was spent learning the city and supposedly finding our not-quite-full-time jobs.

When exactly we were supposed to have time to *meet* such people was somewhat unclear. We all worked nearby during the days, which left our evenings and weekends "free." Except that every night was reserved for something. Monday was our weekly meeting, Tuesday our small group Bible study. Wednesday was our "date with God" night (set aside for Bible reading, prayer, and so on), Thursday we had "ministry training," and Friday we ran a coffeehouse as "outreach" to the community. Saturday night was the mandatory group social, since the planners must have thought we wouldn't see enough of each other the rest of the week. Not even Saturday morning was free; we started with cleaning, then launched whatever ministry "research" project was the day's assignment (these ranged from passing out slickly packaged Bible excerpts to sharing leftover food with the city's many homeless). Only Sunday was really open, but of course we were supposed to spend the morning in church. It was a happy coincidence that the one day Poster Boy usually came around (he lived some thirty miles away) was that Sunday-night stretch I finally had to myself.

Friends who'd been on other CS projects said ours was much less restricted than usual, but I found that inconceivable. Having so much of my schedule and social life set for me felt oppressive—and it was here, more than in friendships, where my own rebellion took root. Torn between the demands of living in such a structured community and the thrill of spending a summer away from home and the heat in a *city,* I gave little thought—much less time—to meeting and infiltrating my subculture. Even my target group was chosen based on a naive hope I could somehow give God my summer without much threat to the swing dance habit I'd nurtured the last two years.

It seemed, at the start, such a grand and clever idea to pursue my passion using the pretext of research and ministry. I didn't think God would mind if I tried to serve Him by serving myself. Instead we learned to our shock when we went out dancing once, on a weekend, as a group social that San Francisco's swing scene did not presume men dance with women.

Ideally, I suppose, we all would have found jobs that furthered our research. Only one or two people managed this. But how could you find even *a* job, much less such a socially specific one, in your first week in a totally foreign place, moreover a place whose summertime crowd was very different from the school-year set our director knew and could have given us pointers on? You couldn't. And because all of us signed up for the project assuming we'd still make some kind of income that summer, we focused on finding jobs.

Mine was a few stops north on BART (the region's form of mass transit), helping out with accounting in a small business, where once again my presence played into larger, preexisting tensions at work. In this case it was the bitter, post-hippie accountant who was my supervisor, and the oblivious but well-intentioned CFO above her. Because the office was located in a somewhat unsafe Richmond neighborhood more than walking distance from BART, they had to pick me up and drop me off at the train each day (eventually I got a bike). At first they promised to share the rides, but the CFO usually flaked, making my safe arrival and departure the accountant's concern.

I must have been a good listener, for those rides turned into a chance for her to vent a lot of the anger brewing inside—especially the end-of-day rides to the BART when I could sit there in her car while she fumed another ten or twenty minutes or more. The Thursday night after my birthday, she went on for *three whole hours*—so long that when I finally alighted, the trains were coming at latter-evening frequency and I missed most of that night's training session.

I didn't much mind. It was almost a relief to be late, and when I came home, it was to the twilit silhouette of Poster Boy's car out front. First I got to hang with him and his friends the last two weekends, now he was stopping by on a Thursday? Such frequent encounters with a crush were completely unheard of.

When I found him in a lounge reserved for off-project folks, Poster Boy wound up convening a foursome that went to the "publick house" for pints, the same place we'd gone the weekend before. We were probably just into the second round when the training I should have been sitting through ended—but given my patience through three hours of the harrowing chauffeur harangue, had I not earned some off-project downtime?

Surely his surprise appearance showed God's blessing on our clandestine happy hour. *When in Berkeley, do as the locals do—rebel.*

We had no lack of models that summer. Local papers were full of an ongoing protest outside the Berkeley radio station, which shut down a nearby street for nearly a month. The board that owned the station had fired its well-respected manager, prompting employees to break a "dirty laundry" rule and start disclosing the conflict in their broadcasts. When a member of the embattled board accidentally leaked by e-mail—to a station ally—possible plans to sell the station's license (in a naturally lucrative business deal), the ally announced the news. Station employees who broadcasted the press conference were yanked off air mid-program. (For weeks tensions had been so high that the board hired private security for the office, intended to quell the employees' mounting resistance.) When listeners heard the fracas disrupt their news that day, they trooped en masse to the station and filled the building in a sit-in that resulted in mass arrests.

We outsiders didn't quite "get" all this drama, but for the locals—proud of their city's long-standing protest tradition—such defiance was a matter of course. Eventually we, too, came to understand it all too well. For those students who hung with the Project Pals, their new friends became our version of the station workers—airing dirty laundry that prompted their listeners to join in condemnation of the overlords: in our case, College Students and our project director. Somewhere along the way, our questioning had ceased being something aimed at seeking to know and represent God better. It became, instead, a way to merely one-up those bad "religious Christians." We might have thought ourselves moving beyond their glaring mistakes—salesmanship and judging people—but we became just as zealously self-righteous in condemning first their hypocrisy, then our leaders', then each other's.

In each case of acting out, one's own sin seemed much less unrighteous; we even convinced ourselves we were behaving virtuously. Since I reacted more against our schedule than against concrete entities like people or institutions, I hardly noticed the spirit in which I began to resist the demands on my time. For Poster Boy to drop in that weeknight seemed like God's short-term salvation for my weary soul. I felt little guilt at ditching the end of the training I'd mostly missed through no fault of my own. Surely my postwork conversation did more toward the spirit of our goal that summer than sitting through more teaching!

The outing I took to reward myself wasn't altogether happy, however. Though I was thrilled by bonus time with Poster Boy, he took the opportunity to sketch the details of his still-in-process breakup, including the almost-fiancée's betrayal. And she wasn't the only woman intruding that night. Our fourth, since Posse Pal chaperoned things, was the small, cute Asian girl—much closer to PB's stated "type" than I—whose pages and phone calls had disrupted the previous Sunday hang. Perhaps to make it up to me she bought my second drink. Perhaps to draw on some ancestor's Polish courage, I drank it down like I was used to strange, frequent, intimate outings with men I liked who were so good at rattling my confidence and testing my liver's fortitude.

I was getting reckless then. Skipping training, and doing so at a bar, risked not just affronting our leader but drawing ire from peers as well. Reprimands from men have never affected me much, but female anger is different. Maybe since my father and I clashed frequently when I was growing up, I take male drama in stride—but my calm, even-keeled mother never gave me a chance to face an estrogen-fueled tirade. Every one I *did* face, therefore, felt like a profound injustice, a violation of how I thought women should behave with each other. Beginning when I left our homeschool, each female outburst I suffered seared itself on my memory, as did the confrontations with women that summer. For I didn't just face my supervisor's anger toward her boss and life in general that Thursday, I risked further condemnation from one of our project's younger women.

She'd been affronted when I turned twenty-one and drank to it. Not recklessly, not noisily, not drunkenly, but actually rather quietly—almost privately. But just the mere consumption troubled the nineteen-year-old, who chewed me out not long after. Now, granted, CS may have had a dry-project policy, which I'd agreed to follow when I signed up. But I was hardly the only one imbibing, as I would learn—and probably one of the most quiet in so doing.

When self-righteous anger surfaced a couple days after she confronted me, I deemed the others' flagrant, less legal drinking more deserving of her wrath than my moderate, perfectly legal birthday bash. The gall of a younger student's unfair attack only stoked my growing defiance. I might not have planned to drink much more that summer, but after her words that all changed. All the water the seeds of my rebellion needed was condemnation from a "religious" person. And who better to guide me than my newfound drinking master?

CHAPTER 6

REBELS AGAINST THE CAUSE

Your aspirations glew like flies
You took the planet by surprise
You truly believed
But of course you'd been deceived

In a drug infected haze
You attacked the bourgeois ways
And felt so relieved
But consider what you leave

It's an age of your creation
Of a disunited nation
So much for your invasion
It looks like rain to me

—TAL BACHMAN, *"Looks Like Rain"*

When Poster Boy and his friends came around one Friday a couple weeks after the birthday outing, I tagged along, dragging two friends who were visiting for the weekend, one of whom had long-standing ties with Posse Pal. It was planned as a less restrained follow-up to my birthday, since, as Posse Pal later told me, tipsy Anna rather amused them. Blissfully ignorant then that our bender was planned half at my expense, I gleefully followed them into the city.

After parking the cars on a hill steeper than you'd ever find in Phoenix, we went to some loud two-room saloon they knew of, just steps around the corner from a row of brightly lit sex shops and strip clubs I later learned was infamous as the porn strip where North Beach and Chinatown meet. Though Poster Boy bought my drinks that night and taught me the proper way to take tequila shots, he started to wane in my favor.

Why would a man this bitter toward women be the one buying my drinks? Why not Posse Pal or one of the others, or *me?* It surely couldn't indicate what I longed for but didn't expect from him—which made it feel almost cruel in the end. *Don't give me attention I know you won't follow through on.* Add to that an ongoing joke in which they compared me to a stripper, and even my emotional martyrdom was exhausted.

In retrospect, it's hard to see why a few drinks chased by a joke another woman might take in stride were the things that got me over Poster Boy. Perhaps it was latent anger that the men most suited to intellectual engagement with me instead gave more attention to my body or sexuality. It felt like Poster Boy was using me for what little salve my attentions gave his ego, though largely distrusting me since I belonged to the class of person who'd hurt him so badly.

It wasn't like I needed to hear his life story, or forge intense emotional bonds; I just wanted more talk of things like Brecht, jazz, and theology. Instead they let me perform the stock anecdotes I later built a blog readership from: mildly sexual and acerbic but told with tinges of secret dismay that were masked when they encouragingly laughed in response. I'd hoped that I could jam with them, but I'd wound up being the evening's guest entertainment. *Did being a girl really have to matter that much?*

The following day I wrote grimly in my journal:

Girlfriend #2 wasn't terribly impressed with him. My folks would be DECIDEDLY unimpressed. His intentions are probably fairly questionable.

Those objections my head musters. You're going to get hurt. This probably isn't a good idea.

And my heart responds that his actions might be less heinous given the context of his heart and struggles. But am I just defending him? I feel like there are better things in his heart, and that several months from now things would/will be different. If he were in a different place emotionally and spiritually, I think the exotic dancer joke wouldn't have been as long running. But where he's at now, I don't think he respects women much. I don't think he respects me *as much as he would under other circumstances.*

It was late July, just shy of three weeks since this Poster Boy hangout marathon started, and barely halfway through the project. For someone used to the less frantic pace of liking a man from afar, it was quite exhausting. More wary than ever of letting God guard my feckless heart—especially since it seemed Poster Boy would rebound with that other girl who'd gone drinking with us, the one who was his "type"—I gave up hope for the present. He was, perhaps, my shortest crush on the books.

If there were a reason I liked him, a reason I'd met him (as my foolish heart quietly speculated), I'd have to solve that riddle later. *This too shall pass,* a small voice whispered. *He's the one. You'll see.* Recounting this in my journal, even I wondered if I had really lost my mind: "What am I jettisoning here? Reason? Ration?" How could Poster Boy be "the one" when God had performed such a miracle with the Winner? Surely I was not meant to have *two* husbands! Besides, I wouldn't see Poster

Boy ever again; we had no connections between us except for God, who was unlikely to give me his e-mail address.

More likely he was, like other crushes before him, too out of reach for the likes of a transparent piner like me—too cool and too canny, too great and too gifted, too broken, too bitter. Served me right falling for such blue-chip guys as him and the Winner. Little wonder my favorite single that summer was Tal Bachman's ode to resignation, "She's So High." It seemed to be playing everywhere, those distinctive opening chords and Bachman's falsetto. I'm sure I heard "She's So High" in the defiant little Gap store clinging to the top of Telegraph north of all the locally owned—and hence more respected—shops south of campus.

Once Poster Boy was lost to me, I turned to my standard fallback escapes to get through the rest of the project: music and shopping. You might say they were my therapy, which meant Berkeley was my shrink. I liked Tal enough to buy his record that summer, on some trek to the vast, mysterious innards of Amoeba Records, a curious East Bay amalgam of gritty record racks and sunny high ceilings. One left feeling slightly warm and dirty all at once—a testament either to the store or the druglike nature of consumption. I bought seven pairs of new shoes in Berkeley, almost one for every week we were there. But nothing could staunch my misery—and what few protections I had were stripped from me, one by one, as my unrest slowly increased.

THE DAWNING OF AN AGE OF INQUIRY

It was getting to be a pattern of losing what I most loved: my girlfriends, the Winner, my brother (as roommate), this crush—

not to mention how my communities kept failing me . . . What exactly was going on? How could the God with whom fellowship had briefly been so sweet let me go through this? You'd think that since I was there to advance His cause that summer, at least He could have defended my comforts and me.

But no. God hadn't stepped in once, so far as I could tell. Not against my nightmare, my fellow student's unfair condemnation, or the inevitable failure of our research. Indeed, except for my strange, inexplicable calm about Poster Boy and the tagalong, God seemed almost totally passive. I had a hard time getting in touch with my anger toward other people, much less anger toward Him—He was *God,* after all—but the reason I was in Berkeley, the reason I chose to stay in that pain, was because God and I were in relationship.

I rarely put the issue so explicitly then, but that was the bedrock reason. If not for knowing Him, and for knowing Him the way I did—such that honesty was paramount—I would not have found myself in that place of confusion and disruption. So where was I to turn now that He wasn't providing the comfort I thought He should? What was I to think now that trying to work on our relationship had made things with God worse instead of better? Committing two whole months of my life to God and God alone was supposed to take me dramatically deeper with Him, not leave me on the brink of failure, afraid that since my piety had stopped working and God was not stepping in to mentor my spiritual growth perhaps there was no God involved at all.

Although once that summer my Bible study discussed how Berkeley could change our lives, at the time it seemed a preposterous prophecy much like the "true love pact" Sandy claims Danny pledged with her. *If* it happened, such change was not expected to hurt so much or to make us question so fiercely.

Like all well-schooled Jesus freaks, I thought myself equipped to face the intellectual zingers a hostile world lobs at one's faith. My parents' training and later church instruction were quite comprehensive on answers to those questions you get from hecklers and other folks as eager to change your mind as you ostensibly are to change theirs. (Except, of course, that only you, the religious zealot, might be seeking conversion; the secularist merely wants to open your eyes to the truth.)

When I met such a man on my final "date with God" at the much-beloved coffee shop next to the W-House, his zeal to challenge my thinking and change my mind was novel and strangely attractive. Few men cared that much what I thought, and such heady talk was swiftly replacing swing dance as my chief passion. The conversation proved so lively—and I so starved for attention and escape—that we swapped e-mail addresses and briefly stayed in touch even after I returned to Arizona. Perhaps my growing obsession with sex created intriguing mojo; not like he needed to infer from my thousand-word e-mails of intellectual searching that I was hungry for a man who wanted to *talk!*—I told him that flat out.

The plan was that we'd both read *Atlas Shrugged* then have an e-mail discussion about it. (I pretended such a means of acquaintance could not be written into my meet-the-husband road map.) This was supposedly a means of seeking truth, but also of sating a burgeoning hunger rekindled from my childhood by things like Poster Boy's talk about issues of faith and serving God. When I was small, Dad's obsession with creationism and that favorite uncle's discussion of car repairs and theology had taught me that one rarely found intellectual engagement with other women. Both our project director and, to a lesser extent, Poster Boy and his friends had reinforced that by showing me men talked of things I cared about. Not that I wanted to be *like* them—I just wanted to talk *with* them, be admitted to their world though still a woman.

Deprived of such conversation partners, I settled for Aryan Atheist's attention (he'd not just learned German but looked it, in a dangerous, dirty frat-boy way, thus making him über-hot). In my opening e-mail, I gushed:

> I've been realizing how surrounded I am by people who have the same answers as I do; all we really discuss is shades of meaning or semantic differences. But when I can talk to people who don't accept those answers, people who challenge me to think differently, or even open up new vistas in my mind . . . wow, that's a kick! :) It is such a good feeling to be challenged like that, even if it makes the struggle harder.

What I didn't know how to say in those days was that men and women talking deeply have, because of our major but complementary differences, a unique capacity for that vista opening. Thus men were my sought-after conversation partners.

But Aryan Atheist wasn't sure my curiosity was so genuine. He responded:

> Are you prepared for any truths that might subvert your beliefs or are you just trying to understand other arguments to build up a defense of your a priori true beliefs? Are you looking for mere affirmation and a defense strategy?? Most are.

A man that attentive to my ideas was hot stuff. I'd never met someone so unafraid to challenge me! Why, it almost seemed as if he *cared* what I thought.

Not that we were dealing on *romantic* terms of course; this was pure and honest intellectual talk—if I were truly being honest, that was. Had we been talking a few months earlier, or merely walking through the points of debate so well laid out in all my apologetics training, I might have been the insincere girl he expected. But everything I'd learned presumed the line of argument on which the failing CS God pitch was based. Supposedly, there were five or six main questions: *Does God exist? How can He be good and still allow suffering? Did He create the world or not?* And so on. My dad was really into this stuff, especially scientific "proofs." Though what process God used to make the world had never affected *my* sleep at night, I never doubted that people still threw these "basic" questions at Christians. I didn't realize they largely defined the difference between the audience CS had always presumed and the postmodernists we were there to understand.

Ironically, it didn't take Berkeley's Buddhists or Hindus or atheists for me to get it finally; it only took my growing confusion with God. Then I realized why the questions I'd been taught to answer—framed in response to modernist skepticism—held so little resonance for me. They didn't matter because they weren't my questions. I didn't care about things like the literal origin of the earth, but about the origins of *knowledge,* especially within my received tradition. *Where did the things I'd been told about God all my life really come from? How could I trust what others said about Him?* This was the paradoxical fruit of Berkeley: I'd gone there to learn about postmodernism, only to learn how postmodern I myself was.

For a brief time my Berkeley e-mail buddy was the perfect sounding board. And because it didn't hurt that he had the look I'd always liked, I mistook the vigor of our debates for an early taste of intellectual compatibility—something I would for years deem essential to potential husbands. Not until much later would I realize such intellectual "fizz" was there with *every* semi-smart freaked-by-Jesus man I met just because philosoph-ical differences gave us ready-made points to argue. But Aryan Atheist wasn't the one to open my eyes to this faux *frisson*; our e-mail dialogue was an early casualty to his grad-school schedule.

Considering my openness to lip-to-lip exploration, after our first meeting at the coffee shop, it's not surprising God saw fit to separate us. As I once told a longtime girlfriend who did not stay sexless long, the difference between her life and mine was not that we wanted different things but that she got her wishes and I did not. Plenty of times I wanted things like whisker burn (a goal my senior year, in fact), a boyfriend, or even sex, but op-portunity never coincided with my moments of greatest reck-lessness. It seemed God had no qualms about playing the heavy-handed father, and unlike my dad, He had the power to really interfere. Apparently He'd been doing so most of my life, for which I started to hold a grudge.

As this anger festered, the gulf between us grew so profound that sometimes I opted out of not just training, that one night when Poster Boy came around, but the Saturday outreach as well. There was almost no way to talk credibly in glowing terms about someone with whom I could barely connect myself. Why pretend? Wasn't honesty the point of all this?

I recall no repercussions for my absence. Though it was a major act of defiance, we had only student leaders by then, since the CS staff had left at the halfway point (a standard procedure for summer projects). Only the director, who lived in a neigh-boring community, would return at the very end for a debrief to discuss our research findings. The student leaders appointed to run things in place of the departed staff carried on for the rest of the summer. Unbeknownst to me they were just as confused about things as I was, which might have explained their silence on my absence.

Besides, though somewhat experimental in nature, the Saturday outreaches technically weren't part of the research we were supposed to report at summer's end. Other than a guy I met in the post-marathon massage line, weekend outreaches bore almost no immediate fruit—in either us or the people we met. I still remember one awkward conversation we had with a guy who played the drums or something. He seemed to have some genuine spiritual interest or reflectiveness, but it wasn't like he was puzzling over the Bible when we found him. Of course he wasn't that open to our rather leading questions.

As much as we tried to take a different approach from the normal College Students sidewalk pitch, we really weren't there to deal with that man as a whole person—we just wanted to engage the spiritual side of him, on our structured timeline. We might have used different, more audience-sensitive tools than our peers on other projects, but nothing displaced the centrality of *message*.

But what if the issue was not so much our words but that we were viewing the unsaved as "fragments," people whose needs we only hoped to meet in a spiritual sense? I think we sensed this instinctively in moments of some discussions, but we were crippled by our project's reactive nature. Because our critique was more concerned with the *content* of evangelism than how it compared to Jesus's work with the disciples, we never addressed the real issue. But then, we were maybe too full of ourselves and our "radical" take on ministry to recognize the problem as not message but a man-centric take on evangelism.

Ironically, the Bible was one of the books we read the least that summer. We spent some time in John, but I only remember discussing Jesus's conversation with the woman at the well. As I recall, we focused on how He took her from concern with temporal, earthly things like literal thirst and temples to the spiritual and more ultimate. And you might say that of their topics, sure. But what else was going on? She was a racial and social outsider—both to Jesus and her community, in the latter case because of her sexual sin. In both their terms and ours, she'd be known by these prominent fragments of identity. So how did Jesus treat her? Like a person. Like a *whole* person—with needs and thoughts and wounds. He certainly took her spiritual needs as most serious—and didn't avoid her sin—but He didn't address that till He earned her trust and showed He cared about not just her scandalous parts but her whole life. If we'd seen that part of the story, it might have challenged our very emphasis on subculture and the core aims of our project.

In retrospect, I wish we'd spent more time studying Jesus's ministry than learning to decode Berkeley. If we had, we might have understood why the one exception to those discouraging, frustrating Saturdays was the time we paired up not to try the latest pickup line for Jesus, but to give away leftover food from a banquet the night before. That day, my buddy and I found a homeless girl with the same first name as mine, to whom we talked for some two or three hours, there on her square of sidewalk along Shattuck Avenue. We may not have talked about Jesus, much, but we sure learned a lot about her.

For someone who spent most of her days enduring the worst I could imagine—being ignored by almost all—that may have been the greatest gift we could have given. And surprisingly that fairly minor sacrifice was one of the best gifts we *received* that summer. But like other things, that wasn't apparent until I left Berkeley for "home" and realized I now saw the homeless not as the statues they'd once been but as sometimes smelly, sometimes crazy, always needy humans much like myself.

FAILURE HAS A MANY-SPLENDORED STING

The banquet whose bounty led us to the streets that day marked the end of our seventh week on the project. Our time was up. We entered a grim, final stretch: the week set aside to write up our "findings." As even denial slunk away at the reality of the failure most of us felt, we eighteen took on the pallor of resignation. Except for one student whose research earned academic credit, we had no outside guidance on how reports such as ours should look, much less how to organize or explain our lack of findings. Some cobbled together what few observations they'd made ("my presupposed subgroup proved to not be a 'community' after all"), while others made last-ditch redefinitions of the population they'd studied. I took this route, attempting to profile the lonely, middle-aged staff at my Richmond office even though such "data" wouldn't help those bent on finding better ways to tell bohemian Berkeley that Jesus saves.

Most controversial was the report of my post-birthday-drink confronter, who chose to write about the conflict between our leader and the Project Pals, in a direct assault on our organizational sponsor and local leadership. It was practically insurrection. When all our reports were sent to the printer (long before most were satisfied with their rough drafts), her paper was bound under a separate cover from ours. The printouts came back, we had a final debrief dinner with our director, then it was off to our mostly eastward homes to sort out where the hell our summer went.

Though I left there strangely optimistic that someday Poster Boy and I would meet again in a different place where he'd finally appreciate me, I soon forgot the moody, jazz-playing preacher's kid who shared my taste in posters. The project as a whole was more than enough to process without some trifling crush on one more musician. As I returned to a new, cramped apartment and three roommates I couldn't boss around the way I had my brother, I wanted nothing more than the space and calm to make sense of Berkeley and figure out how to cope with Hoped-for Husband's perplexing delay.

Summer's end brought senior year, which meant I had nine months left on the timeline that had guided me all my life . . . supposedly to marriage. When that ended, the future loomed—not unlike the Communists who took over Hong Kong's keys in 1997. Sure that's putting it melodramatically, but what's not to get extreme about when you've nearly run out of the guidelines hope and dreams provide for a life? If I couldn't imagine life as a single college graduate, how would I know how to live it? I'd never thought past marriage to other things; what better fate awaited? Even heaven seemed a bore, which must be why it comes at the *end* of life—when you're too old and dead to really care.

God didn't consign me to heaven that fall, but neither did He bring a husband or the calm I thought I needed to process the rather rocky recent past. Instead, within a dizzying span of days, I was stripped of things whose departure made the previous "losses" seem slight by comparison. I came back from Berkeley feeling as if trapped beneath a high-pressure storm front that clung to me like a leach. That should have been my first warning that the tornado was just forming, not losing strength. But I thought, you see, that all the increasingly painful moments I'd had during junior year and my time in Berkeley were merely some especially discordant pebbles in a string of otherwise randomly ordered stones that made up my life. The only time God intervened to establish a certain pattern was when arranging things like my miraculous second evening with the Winner.

That my various losses and social griefs should follow so shortly after one another seemed not a light version of Job's suffering (which the reader knows full well God has permitted Satan to inflict) but proof that like the Baals Elijah taunts on Mount Carmel, God had left the office or fallen asleep, allowing all this to happen. Soon enough, surely, He'd awaken or come back to work, resume our talks, and set my life to rights. What purpose could God have for pain?

Apparently more than I thought. One week into my postproject funk, the local College Students chapter organized a retreat for student leaders like myself. Under the leadership of CS staffers, we led Bible studies for peers, ran the weekly Thursday night meetings, and staffed a position required for formal recognition by the ASU student government. The mini-retreat reunited me with Family Friend and Girlfriend #1, with whom I had not yet discussed our summer.

As far as I knew, my depression was just an isolated reaction far different from what they took away from the project. But once we started catching up at dinner that first night, we realized the heaviness, disappointment, and vague but potent sense of failure were fairly true for all of us. Discussing our feelings so frankly not only validated what had seemed like merely individual perceptions, it affirmed the value of honesty often discussed on the project—redeeming at least one aspect of the summer's learned wisdom as actually useful and true. Encouraged by the connection our candor produced, we three left dinner emboldened to face the leader meeting that followed.

Other topics were on the agenda that night, but somehow

the CS staffers in charge felt we should continue the predinner debrief on everyone's summers, since most had done some sort of project. Given the pioneering nature of what we'd done in Berkeley, all were especially keen on hearing about *our* summer. Before dinner we had described it somewhat vaguely, each unwilling to be the lone voice of complaint. But now that each of us knew where the others stood, Girlfriend #1, Family Friend, and I felt strengthened by our new bond of shared confusion to speak more frankly about our less-than-perfect experience. If honesty over dinner had done so much good for our hearts, would not equal candor with fellow leaders continue the same trend of deeper connection? We shook off clichés and insider jargon, all pretence of unspecific joy, and fessed up to our disappointing summer. We even acknowledged a growing lack of certitude, a feeling that we didn't have much relationship with God anymore.

We were talking, of course, in human terms—of that sense you sometimes get when communication with someone has mostly broken down and it seems the relationship that once was is nearly gone, at least for the time, at least in the form you'd grown accustomed to. But to the ears of our hearers we were not speaking of a hopefully short-term distance from God; we were saying we weren't sure we were Jesus freaks at all. Family Friend is a pastor's kid like Poster Boy, as steeped in tradition as I am. But during one of the prayer times, he told God, "I'm not even sure if you're really there to hear this." To the rest of the gathered student and staff leaders, it was a nearly heretical scandal that promptly derailed the meeting for good.

I don't recall that we were all that rebellious in that meeting—just honestly searching. But we were no longer with a group where it was safe and even normal to question. To them it was not a signal of seeking to know God more (which all three of us desired), but of challenging the foundations of our faith. In the lengthy session that followed, some downplayed our feelings as the mere "doubts" most normal Christians face from time to time, while others rushed in to reassure us with how great their own experiences of God were. It was like they thought they could somehow talk us out of this, dissuade us from asking questions. Almost none understood how desperately we needed to be persuaded that God could bear the weight of our faith and questions alike.

It didn't help that many relied on precisely the opaque insider clichés of Christian health I was so eager to move the talk beyond. How could such words be honest when no one bothered explaining what the phrases really meant? Such language encouraged a kind of hiding, in which you never had to spell out the sort of experience your words stood for. For all the understanding I'd just discovered with my two friends only hours before, I started to feel quite alone.

A few got where we were coming from, cared enough to stay part of our lives, but our honesty had major repercussions. Family Friend and Girlfriend #1 stayed on with the group, at the cost of a demotion to a less visible leadership role. For me it was the beginning of a sudden, unexpected coda; in less than a month I dropped out of CS altogether. Just weeks into what proved to be my most academically demanding semester, I found myself almost completely alienated from what had been the social center of my life at ASU.

Around that time, but for unrelated reasons, I also parted ways with the newspaper job I'd had for just as long as I'd been a part of CS. Between them, these two worlds had mostly defined my identity as a student and given me some measure of on-campus prominence (my weekly editorials were read by more than forty thousand and I was a frequent announcement presenter at CS's weekly meetings, known for my frumpy librarian shtick). It was the first time in almost ten years that I'd been without an audience to write for, the first time I'd felt so abandoned by community.

It wasn't the first time I'd been pushed into the alley between the church and the world I was supposed to avoid, but last time such spiritual homelessness was short-lived. This time there was no one to reinstate me from the alley. Senior year was not supposed to be the time when you had to make friends all over, but within a few bleak weeks, I was suddenly groping around a lonely world where nothing made sense and places to turn were vanishing faster than tickets to opening night of the latest Epic Trilogy movie. *Where was God? How could this happen?*

CHAPTER 7

THE QUEST FOR ECSTASY

When people defend their world view, they are not defending rea-
son, or God, or an abstract system; they are defending their own
fragile sense of security and self-respect. . . .

   Given the nature of belief, it is no wonder that the reflective
Christian will attract the displeasure of any subculture in which
he or she is perceived as a threat to the ruling orthodoxy. . . .
Questioning the institution is synonymous, for many, with at-
tacking God—something not long tolerated.

—DANIEL TAYLOR, *The Myth of Certainty*

told myself the questions that now prompted regular weeping were just honest philosophical angst that could have
arisen for any person of thoughtful bent. But my search transpired against a backdrop of rebelling against conventions of
youth and faith. Just as my confronter's words of judgment on
my twenty-first-birthday drinking incited subsequent trips to
the pub, the outcry of my fellow Christians set me in search of
ways to explore my newly libertine streak. For Halloween, I
went to the CS party dressed as a stripper—the only condition
on which my brother and King of Pseudo Dates would go
dressed as two Chippendales (for the record, my costume was
their idea, not mine, though I'd been lobbying them to go shirtless).

Another night, two fellow Jesus-freak girlfriends and I all

went to a bar and did a round of one of its more provocatively named shots—to much male-patron attention. No one got drunk; what harm could there be in "casual" fun like that? Sin to me now had less and less to do with failing to meet God's standards, more with failing to hurt yourself or others—at least in a palpable sense. I'd thrown away my T-shirts as a freshman because I didn't want any hindrance to my intimacy with God. But with God now so hard to find, what difference did victimless exploits make?

When a newfound kindred spirit that fall spoke breezily of masturbation, I decided to give it a try again; maybe this time it would "work." It wasn't as if the Bible really forbade it—most scholars agree that the infamous story of Onan is not about "spilling his seed" but about refusing his family duty to give his brother's widow a child—a baby in the line of David, even Jesus. In my one conversation with Mom on the subject, she'd even hedged that masturbation might be okay for widows or spouses enduring brief separation. Well, I was practically a widow, considering how long Hoped-for Husband was taking. And besides, my fellow-virgin friend was convinced the practice better prepared us for future, unsolitary sex. Was it not a way to actually love my husband beforehand? At least I couldn't get pregnant or get STDs from this. Other friends said it was not really sinful unless you fantasized, which was then lust since even looking with lustful thoughts was sin in Jesus's book.

I recognized that none of these answers made for a credible Christian sexual ethic—this just the latest of many faults I could point out in my fellow religious folk—but I was too angry with God for withholding marriage and sex so long. Too angry and too obsessed with finding whatever would sate my now-clamorous soul, whose yearning I sought to quench with whatever it took. Conflating the sexual with my spiritual hunger, I kept trying to figure out what all the fuss about sex was about. Was it not a likely candidate for the ultimate thing my soul was so parched and hungry for?

Though I soon concluded that the ecstasy induced by music was much better than any other kind, I was nowhere near seeing the lie that sex is heaven on earth for what it really was. The seeds of fragmentation had gone too deep; it was all too easy to blame the pain of a broken whole on a part so clearly unsatisfied. Once I had mistaken this false cause for the real source of my misery, it launched a spiral of slaking thirst with something that only worsens it—like alcohol when you're dehydrated. The further inside I welcomed the lie, the more it reinforced a sense that God was cruelly bent on letting me stay dissatisfied in *every* way, despite even the claims of his very scriptures.

Not just in the Psalms—which are filled with depression, yes, but also ecstatic ravings on how great God is—but also in many later accounts of faith in Him, there is this theme of extravagant satisfaction, a satisfaction I'd once had dim glimpses of in my mid-college honeymoon with God, but which was now almost unproduceable. The Bible that once brought tears of relief when a passage seemed to resonate with my troubles of the day now brought only tears of weary frustration at its opaqueness. The longer I found myself in that wilderness, the more I effectively shook my fist at God, demanding, "Rend the sky and come down, dammit!" The longer he stayed unresponsive, the longer it seemed there might be no God at all to answer.

FINDING A SAFE HOUSE

It was with great reluctance that I went to a final fall retreat with College Students. I hadn't wanted to go, of course, but our campus director—who also went to the church I was still attending—invited me since he thought I'd like the speaker. I had too much of a history with C.D. and his wife—who'd so often given me rides to the airport or from church, invited me over for dinners and holidays, loaned me their spare car whenever I asked, and whose children I babysat weekly my junior year—to simply ignore his appeal flat out. And his attitude was different.

C.D. didn't seem to get our struggle any better than most of the students had, but I felt no self-righteous judgment from him, just genuine, fatherly concern for my relationship with God. The church connection helped too. Though my sermon notes now looked like a dialogue, if not debate, with the pastor, I still found life and nourishment in that community. Like my parents had always been, the people there were less committed to slogans on T-shirts and coffee mugs, more defined by thoughtfully hewing to the Bible's instruction—the one authority I did not really question. It also helped that services were mostly free of the syrupy praise songs I'd once sung as part of the CS worship team.

Praise songs I *couldn't* avoid on retreat, where the words were hollow and superficial on my tongue, rife with the taunt of a love now cooled to something heavier than the buoyant joy of before. But all was not as bad as I feared. If the music was a taunt, it was the speaker's words that haunted as he echoed the few disciples' response to Jesus when most of His fans have disappeared: "Lord, to whom shall we go?"

I hadn't known such a question was in the Bible. All this time, I'd been so concerned with escaping the pain my faith and my God now produced, I'd not stopped to think about what alternatives really existed. When I did—thanks to my major, I knew more about the options than many Christians might—I wasn't impressed with any of them.

"I may not know enough to stay, but I know too much to leave," I told my journal that night.

But stay where? How? After one of his talks that weekend, Girlfriend #1, Family Friend, and I found the speaker, with whom C.D. had arranged a meeting. The speaker taught theology at the well-respected seminary that had trained my uncle, and was less concerned than most about our questions (he even said, casually, that "much of life is quite boring"). Perhaps, he suggested, we had not lost faith in God—as most of the rest seemed to assume—but were merely caught between paradigms.

This term was not standard Jesus-freak lingo. "Paradigm?"

It was how people bounded data, he said, the way that they explained things. Say you do a study, and you start to plot all these entries on some graph. Perhaps you're mapping how far most students live from campus. The paradigm is the circle you draw around those points—to indicate that most students live a mile or less from school. (I think he drew us a sketch.) But let's say as you keep entering data, more and more dots fall *outside* the circle—more students live further away. You can take so many outliers, but at a certain point you have to redraw your circle, revamp the paradigm, even change your hypothesis. Perhaps most students do not live close to the campus at all but commute from various suburbs. In our case, he suggested we were trying to find a paradigm that could account for our recent distance from God and why things had gone wrong on the project. That wasn't so bad—as long as we kept seeking God. While we were, he said we might like to read a book called *The Myth of Certainty*.

That speaker was the first of a small but crucial string of people, books, and ideas that were "safe houses" on our journey through the wilderness. Without them it would have seemed like we were going someplace no person had gone before; certainly we were following no discernible path aside from where questions (and covert rebellion) led us. But every time you found a safe house—always when the storm seemed to shriek its loudest—it was affirmation that others had gone this way and used these places for respite and comfort as we were. Such assurances gave me the courage to venture outside again in the morning when the wilderness winds had died down a bit and were, in their way, a quiet hint that perhaps it was God Himself who was guiding our path, though in a silent, mysterious guise I'd never known Him to use before. ⎯

That retreat resolved one issue: I could not become an atheist. Though my faith was emotionally inconvenient, it certainly hadn't died altogether. There was no change of *mind* about God. In the core of my being, I still believed He was real, and there was no way I could change that. While this resolved the primary question—"If God is silent, does He exist?"—it led to an equally troubling follow-up: "If God exists, how can I know about Him?" I concluded that if things weren't "working" in my faith anymore, if promises weren't coming true the way I'd been told they should—but I could not disbelieve in God—I must have expectations about Him based on promises He hadn't actually made.

For a time the easiest thing was simply to doubt all that others said about Him. You might say I went through my own mini-Reformation—committed to only my interpretation. But it wasn't as extreme as that (I still was going to church, after all), and it wasn't as easy as that. If others' interpretations could be questioned, so too could mine. What about things I had thought before and now rejected—or even times I thought I "met" God somehow? All too easily even my own experience broke down into merely wishes and overreaction. If the problem with others' experience was that they saw life through their humanity—that their sight was subject to the distortions of a flesh-colored lens—even so was *my* perspective distorted. If I was no less human than the others who were so hard to trust, I was no more trustworthy than they. This anguishing conclusion reduced my prayers to simply: "I don't know what to expect from You." In that limbo I languished till Christmas break.

HOME ON THE FRINGE

At last finals brought a respite and the chance to go "home" to Singapore, though I took with me an in-progress paper I had to turn in by e-mail from abroad. As if in divine acknowledgment of the grief that I'd been through, I scored a flight upgrade all the way—first class one leg, business class another. Endless bottles of water, fresh spring greens in my salad, even Bailey's for my coffee. It wasn't as magical as seeing the Winner one final time, but it did help me start to relax—bolstering my hopes for the visit ahead, which was to include a first-ever trip to Malaysia's tea plantations.

After four months coping with a heavy class load, an overcrowded living arrangement, and the pressing matter of what to do when my life's road map ran out in the spring—as if rebuilding my social life and coping with a newly shattered worldview weren't enough!—I was desperate for the comforts of this humid, year-end break and what I was sure would be my parents' accepting embrace.

The first time you really feel adulthood enough to miss your parents must be the first time you get sick—alone—and no one's there to make you soup or bring you water and washcloths for your head. Perhaps the stuff they bring when you're sick is actually all placebo: you just need their hope and conviction this cold thing hasn't licked you—you'll get better even if Mom has to kick the fever's butt herself. Fighting for you when you're down and too weak to fight for yourself: that's one thing I thought parents did best, especially for their beleaguered adult children.

My folks had always promised to love me no matter what, even should I get pregnant while unwed, which had always been the worst we could imagine. How could they fail to take my crisis of faith in stride? Surely my family was the one remaining solace God had left me as this devastating year wound down. Besides, we'd always been mostly in agreement about spiritual things. My questioning even seemed like something they would encourage as part of the honesty with God Dad had always modeled. So, once "safe" in their home, I was honest with them—in my now profanity-salted speech and renewed exploration of form-fitting clothes (angst had been good for my figure, shaving a few more pounds off the stable, healthy weight I'd finally won, late in my undergrad years).

Their response did not affirm my commitment to candor. It proved a difficult visit eased only by our briefly happy sojourn in Malaysia. One night back in Singapore, Dad was so vexed by the overall tension between us he told me the scoop-necked tee I had on made me look "like a non-Christian." And maybe that's what he feared I was becoming. Because I didn't know what to expect from God, I didn't think He could expect much of me—so I was pushing against a lot of what I deemed merely cultural parts of the faith. But neither God nor my parents fought back with hope the way I expected. He was silent; they seemed fearful I might give up God altogether.

I'm not sure they expected me to question so—especially things their categories were able to address (well, Dad anyway).

Ask him about evolution, Dad had much to say; ask him how I could trust the process of transmission—how we know the "truth" about God today is just as true as two thousand years ago—and he didn't get why I cared about that.

Asia was slowly changing him for sure; Dad remarked once how he didn't like to "wave his Christian flag" as visibly anymore, now just letting folks see his life and ask what set him apart from others. And in another twist, he'd stop amidst ardent pleas with me to follow God to acknowledge that his zeal resembled that of equally pious Buddhist or Muslim parents, before saying why his appeal had more weight than just standard parental concern.

But he still didn't get why *my* faith hung on such questions, so he could not give me answers that satisfied. Maybe that scared him. The rest of the kids still mostly were his *children;* I was the first to jerk him into the role of father to *adults*—a transition more difficult since I was not a son but a daughter. Even egalitarian fathers parent us differently than their boys and tend to assert their authority longer. He has always struggled to separate his roles as father and fellow believer.

Though Dad and I were increasingly at loggerheads that Christmas, I still had much respect for my parents' faith, itself so crucial to my boldness in questioning God. Where they feared my faith was dying or under threat, I saw my questions as taking God more seriously. If I was too scared to ask my hardest questions, what God is that? If when your paradigm is broken there's nothing left, you've trusted in nothing all along. But if when your paradigm is broken the thing it was just an attempt to sketch reappears in a form your old paradigm somehow couldn't contain, you trust in something whose existence depends not on you but something intrinsic to itself. Maybe that's what Jesus was getting at when He talked about foundations. He told this one story, you know, about two men who go through a storm. One builds his house on the beach, and it all blows away. But one builds his house on a rock, and it holds firm. I'm not so confident either man was such a great builder; the *real* point seems to be which *man* got blown away and which didn't.

The problem with many Jesus freaks is that we claim to "build our house on a rock," but when a storm comes we have such confidence in the *building* that all our focus is on the house. As if its surety comes from construction, not from the foundation. But if that long, strange year of 1999 showed me my house wasn't all it could be, I was surprisingly sure the site was good, and that no storm could sweep me from it. I just didn't expect to face that storm so all alone.

One had blown up, no doubt. Many in my life were urging me to focus on the house—even to protect it. After all, my parents had invested a lot in helping me build it in the soundest way we knew. But I wanted to indwell the best house I could, even if that meant remaking parts or discarding pieces Mom and Dad and others thought well of. At first I thought I could stay inside the house to make those repairs. The things made right and true would ride out the storm, while poorly constructed parts would blow away—the storm in that sense saving me time by unearthing structural flaws. Why should I weather a storm *outside* a house that needed fixes merely here and there? I didn't count on losing parts of the house I liked rather well, or getting stuck outside it to face the gale. But God's plans did not jive with me staying warm and dry. And my parents proved, ironically, to be what pushed me fully into the very storm they feared most.

Since it was 1999, there was much buildup to the millennium—both in all that Y2k worry (if only we had known how that would pale in two short years), and plans for spectacular celebration. Tempted by Singapore's grander, urban hoopla, I wanted to change my plans for the New Year though I was scheduled to spend it stateside with some friends (I'd finally bonded with a fellow intellectual—and a woman!—whom I knew from a couple econ classes). It didn't hurt that a once-hefty colleague of Dad's was now fit and hot and recently parted from his wife. Surely New Year's Eve would be a chance to hang with him . . . and of course the sibs, with whom he was also on very friendly terms (four- or fivesome coffees with him were almost an annual ritual). Grandma Broadway, visiting that Christmas, was not blind to Singapore Fling's appeal but said he was "out of my league," a challenge no better than when Poster Boy brought up women's taste in movies.

At first I extended the trip just a couple days—perhaps to work in one more group coffee. But when I heard of the New Year's plans my sibs and Singapore Fling had in mind, I started arranging to change my flight again. Then I checked with my folks to okay the extension.

No, my parents said flatly.

No, I could not stay longer than we'd planned. They thought it better for them—and for me—if I went home to the States as prearranged.

It took a bit to come down from my giddy New Year's plans to register what had just transpired. *Not stay.* They were kicking me out? My parents had never refused to meet such basic needs. But because all this took place against such a backdrop of fierce philosophical conflict, the only conclusion was that my parents' long-touted-as-unconditional love had just coughed up an effective condition. They were kicking me out. Because a questioning daughter was too much for them to deal with, they were pushing me out on my own.

In their minds they were simply showing tough love, choos-

ing not to let the strangely selfish daughter their oldest child
had become just walk all over them and presume so much on
their food and housing and time. To me it was like getting
locked out of the very house they helped to build, and left in the
storm to hope and pray the flood would not sweep me away.
Most painful of all, it didn't seem sin had gotten me into this
suffering, but well-intentioned honesty! Why was that over and
over and over again the reason religious folk always pushed me
out? Was truth incompatible with faith despite all their claims
it was absolute? Well, it was all or nothing now. Either in building my life on God I'd staked it on something that would hold
or I was about to learn how well I remembered to swim.

I wept three or four times on the long, lonely flights back
east from Singapore (five or six hours to Japan, another eight or
nine to L.A.), trotting to the tiny plastic bathroom to wipe my
eyes on their cheap, scratchy tissues or let out the sobs I
couldn't silently shudder in my cramped economy seat. It didn't
help remembering the comfort of my departing flight; it made
my constricted regular seat now that much more miserable. Not
even my funk at the airport the week of the Winner's visit had
been as bad as this—and this time there'd be no last-minute
miracle. Each minute I cried sped me farther away from home
and acceptance.

As I journaled, half to God: "I can't go back. I don't know
how to get back in everyone's good graces . . . and to try to do
so wouldn't even be terribly honest. So I'm jettisoned. Alone.
Alienated. Separated even from the God whose intimacy I once
took for granted because I no longer know how to talk to You,
no longer know quite Who I think You are, or where that leaves
me."

In the short term, it left me in L.A., where I stayed a couple
days with a cousin in the snug Pasadena bungalow I'd visited

many times before. It was the third time that year she and her family received me in crisis, but they were no less hospitable than they'd been in May when a visit with a CS friend from SoCali got awkward, or in August when I was quite numb with immediate postproject aftermath. On none of those previous visits, however, had their books meant so much. My cousin had been raised mostly in Asia, the middle child of career missionaries, and, like many well-traveled people, had a vast and eclectic library. A library including a slim little volume all about certainty—the *myth* of it, that is.

Could it be? Did my cousin have the book that speaker had mentioned, but which I'd never purchased, though Family Friend read and recommended it? She did, and I read most of it in just a couple days. Never had I needed such solace more. I began to see in these safe-house graces a mark of divine intent. It was as if for most of my life as a Christian I'd been guided by a bright little handheld torch someone gave me—until one day it got knocked away by the wind and a rock broke the bulb. I was initially terrified in the pitch-black dark of the forest, until my eyes began to adjust. Then I started to notice faint markings on trees as if a phosphorescent moss that grew had been planted there by their maker and mine to guide me, faltering step by step, farther into the gloom ahead.

This latest safe-house respite revived me enough to depart two days later when friends picked me up for New Year's Eve. But the journey proved little better once back outside. I spent the millennium's eve in San Diego, fighting Girlfriend #3 for space at the hotel suite's toilet bowl; she was drunk, I had gotten food poisoning from our dinner—and maybe the whole damn year as well. As I told my journal, "This agonizing struggle of mine is like a dark and threatening journey through a gloomy terrain of stark, wind-whipped tree skeletons and ominous storm clouds. Like a horrifyingly barren landscape in some novel. Indeed, the feel of it is even reminiscent of vaguely remembered scenes from *Pilgrim's Progress.*"

The allegory was more and more on my mind those days. Named for the wife, I now found the book symbolic of how accursedly painful my spiritual legacy was—how deeply my parents had pressed their faith into my life. Not that I resented knowing God, just that it was so hard to separate faith in Him from being part of my family. I only now realized how ingrown was our blood and spiritual kinship and how hard that made it to tell one from the other. To question faith was not just questioning God but even the fabric that bound our clan, in which my much-beloved community consisted.

A grad student I'd been e-mailing with before the break seemed like he could probably sympathize—his name was even more potent than mine and, strangely, found in the same allegory. *How funny,* I'd thought one steamy but bleak day in Singapore, *that I, so obsessed with story, had never imagined a plot where I married a man named like my allegorical husband.* Then again, I'd never thought my name would be so full of pain.

"What is it like, having a name like yours?" I asked in an e-mail. My friend didn't write back immediately, but once I returned from the New Year, we renewed talks about getting together for coffee.

We hadn't actually met yet. One of my professors that fall—the first in my major I'd really felt connected with, especially since he shared my religious roots and sympathized with my new uncertainty—had mentioned his former student to me. "You might find a lot to talk about," he said with a puzzling hint of smile. No prof had ever set me up with friends before, so I noted the student's name, tracked down his e-mail, and sent a message while trying to swallow a faintly ominous sense of excitement, which only increased when the student wrote back.

From the very first exchange I was intrigued. He was in the photography M.F.A. program, and fall semester I'd started to read lots of scholarship on images—Roland Barthes' collection *Mythologies* among them. Those readings had been one of the semester's few bright spots, actually. Though I was nearly done with my college career, I started to figure out my intellectual passions—enough that I'd begun considering grad school. In this phase of self-discovery, an M.F.A. student in photography seemed like the perfect new friend.

We both were working on campus during the week or two left of winter break, so he told me to just stop by the photo building. The first day I tried he'd already left, but somehow we wound up talking by phone that night. If finding *The Myth of Certainty* had been like a night in a safe house, our talk was like stumbling on an oasis. The Atheist's e-mails were cursory compared to this feast of ideas. Not only was he at least my equal or more in intellectual terms, my new friend knew all the books I'd been reading and shared a large part of my spiritual angst. After more than a year with few friends who wanted to form analytical thoughts, much less discuss the latest ideas to set my brain afire, it was like finding someone who not only spoke one's language but one's own dialect—this after an eon with strangers who spoke only a foreign tongue.

About an hour into this epic chat, whose liveliness set me to pacing the kitchen in excitement, I remembered to follow up on my question of names.

"Oh, my parents were Catholic . . ."

I was stacking cans in the pantry then and started to zone out until he said something that stilled my hands.

"You know that book?"—he meant the one I was named from—"I'm like that guy. I'm him."

I came out of the pantry to lean against the counter as if this could still my suddenly thudding heart. *He was talking about my allegorical husband.* No leading the witness, I swear. He brought it up all on his own.

If I'd thought sharing taste in art with Poster Boy was weird, this was downright spooky. On top of my new friend's equally promising phone voice, I took it as proof that sometimes you could fall for someone sight unseen. There was just so much to like about him! When had I ever felt such connection with anyone? Forget finding someone who spoke your dialect, this was like finding a tongue you'd previously thought just your own in the mouth of a stranger—hearing thoughts you'd imagined private and inscrutable in the casual words of another.

And yet as I set off to meet him finally, not long after, I had a bad feeling. Too much had gone wrong of late for this one thing that meant so much to actually work out well. My inner dramatic narrative expert did not believe I was due for a break after such a season of loss. He'd be fat or ugly or bald— *something*.

Sure enough, when I finally got to the photo building, the first guy I saw was post-hippie enough to be sporting a long, graying ponytail. *See, that's probably him.*

Only when I asked, it wasn't.

"He's upstairs in the darkroom."

"Oh, okay. Thanks."

My heart racing slightly, I headed down the funny-smelling corridor just as a striking-looking blond man with piercing blue eyes and gray-flecked sideburns stepped out of one door.

"Hey, I'm looking for—"

He nodded in recognition.

It was him! Not fat, not bald, not ugly. My phone-voice instincts hadn't been off at all. We eased smoothly into conversation while he looked at some contact sheets he'd printed. So smoothly that not until almost twenty minutes had passed did it register—as if blood were flowing through brain cells filled with slowly thickening gelatin—that he had a piece of jewelry on. A ring, in fact. Which he wore not on his right hand but his left.

I'd finally met my soul mate, and he was married to someone else.

ACT II

THE BAWD

It seems to me, suddenly, as if I had spent quite some time fixating on sandcastles. All around me, as a child, I saw other people enjoying them . . . Since I never figured out how to get or make one, I started drawing an elaborate design for one. Someday, I figured, I would find or commission one just like it, and then it would be mine.

Then one day I came out of my house, and there it was: my sandcastle. As I leaned closer to inspect the exactness of the exterior, however, a curious smell assailed my nostrils. I realized the castle wasn't sand at all—but rather shit. It felt like a tremendous joke had been had at my expense.

For you see, there was an ongoing contest to submit one's sandcastle designs to the owner of the beach. He was a sort of artist type (though no one had actually seen him), and generous too. And rumor had it, if you submitted your design to him often enough—or otherwise impressed him—he would have your sandcastle made, and present it to you by surprise . . .

It's been here almost a year, my castle. Sometimes the pain of the taunt is as fresh as that first day; other times more dull. But in spite of all that time, and all that hurt, it still has the power to captivate, sometimes.

Until finally, I am convinced this must be a great, grand joke—a part of the artist's kitsch which the stories neglected to mention. I've been sitting here a long time, now, waiting for the laughter to come—the explanation that will make it all clear. Can't they just show me my sandcastle now?

And I sit here waiting for the "gotcha."

Waiting.

Hell. Even some sign of growth in the shit would help to relieve that disappointment. Then, at least, I could pass it off as an artfully sculpted manure pile or plant bed.

—JOURNAL ENTRY, DECEMBER 10, 2000

CHAPTER 8

ANNA IN BLUNDERLAND

We've got these chains that hang around our necks,
people want to strangle us with them before we take our first
      breath.
Afraid of change, afraid of staying the same,
when temptation calls, we just look away.

This name is the hairshirt I wear,
and this hairshirt is woven from your brown hair.
This song is the cross that I bear,
bear it with me, bear with me, bear with me, be with me
      tonight.
I know that it isn't right, but be with me tonight.

—STEVEN PAGE AND ED ROBERTSON, *"What a Good Boy"*

There are things you don't know you believe until you're fighting for them, and things you don't know you *didn't* believe until you wind up dismissing them. It was always implied in the Christian circles I moved in that no deeper, closer community was possible than with those who shared our faith. But for the last six months, I'd been attacked and rejected precisely by those who shared my embattled allegiance to Jesus.

Perhaps it was time I chose intimates based not on their theology, but on how well they understood me. College Students, my family . . . those I couldn't control. But how could I give up not just the one man who "got" me at this lowest point of my life, but the man who seemed to understand me more than anyone before? For that was, of course, precisely the sacrifice Married Man's vows obliged me to make . . . at least in the view of my friends. But I was too lonely and angry to suffer this final attack on community. There must be a way to maintain this one friend and still follow God. There *had* to be.

INTO THE RABBIT'S HOLE

I can't remember how many times we talked the first week, but it was like the frenzied start of therapy—and Married Man was my shrink. Four hours could drift away like the breaks between "Mean Mr. Mustard" and "Polythene Pam" (which album I heard often that spring). There were several long conversations, most in the narrow little darkroom he got as a color photography grad student. Our talks assumed the rhythm of day and night—long stretches in yellow, fluorescent light while he sorted contact sheets or fussed about other errands, then brief spells of total darkness bounding the quick, focused flash of exposure. It was mostly I who talked, unloading my pain and confusion and loneliness while he worked.

Eventually our work-and-talk routine reached the point where he'd clap twice for me to catch the lights while he hovered before the enlarger, waiting for darkness. Once exposure was done and paper safely hidden inside a black box, I'd open the door, step aside, then trail him to the tinier processing room where he fed the sheets into a big machine whose noisy rollers spit out dripping prints two minutes later. We were both a bit like that machine, I suppose: always processing life and spitting out little snapshots that we hoped framed our troubles usefully, or somehow rendered them beautiful—always processing, but never, ever done. Doomed to go on churning and spinning without ever spitting out an image that would free us to cease our labors.

Married Man was haunted too, you see. His mother had died when he was still in high school; a couple years later, his younger brother committed suicide. Now only he and his father and sister were left, but she was an avid Christian whose pleas and exhortations fell on dull and weary ears.

Once through our respective bios, we talked of ideas—things I'd read, things he *thought* I should read. He gave me Roland Barthes' *Camera Lucida* as a present, said I should sign up for an introductory photo class. I did. Perhaps it was time I found a new way to reflect on life, since words had failed to protect me from estrangement with my family and other Christians. Community, it seemed, depended less on love than being understood—and my peculiar way with words, my accursed candor, clearly had not lost its alienating power. I might have at last "become adept at the vernacular"—as I comically bragged to roommates—but that was precisely the problem.

Perhaps not words but pictures were the way to connect with others. Besides, photography had always been more than just a way to preserve adventures and feats like climbing Mexican ruins my freshman year; I fancied there might be something artistic in how I saw the world. When Married Man treated some of my "snapshots" seriously, he transformed me into an artist—more of one than I'd ever felt like as a music student or journalist. Photography became the basis of my new life in the alley I felt I was living in, the common passion with the friends I made there.

But though I slowly met others who knew him, I never met Married Man's wife. She remained a phantom blonde seen only in pictures he'd sometimes show me during darkroom chats. I asked about her carefully, as if treading a ground made sacred by the explosive secrets buried somewhere beneath it. Mostly I followed his lead and didn't probe unless he brought his wife up first.

Although I had not had married guy friends until him, Married Man's reticence seemed peculiar. Surely a happily married man should not have spent an hour and a half on the phone with a strange woman and never mentioned he had a wife. A happily married man should seem . . . well . . . *married*. He didn't. Once he mentioned "compromises you make" when you get married—how later you sometimes meet more like-minded folks than your spouse.

That comment sank into my stomach like greasy leftovers, clenching my intestines in a painfully long digestion. On the one hand it was dismaying to learn that marriage—this relationship I set such store by—could leave one unfulfilled, and on the other perversely hope-inspiring that my friend's might not be so stable. But how could I want something that depended on the destruction of the very institution I hoped to someday enjoy? I tried to make it a mantra: no matter how much he seemed like a handsome single man too careworn for his barely thirty years (Married Man turned thirty-one that March), he was *married*. Off the market. Unavailable.

Except that he wasn't, entirely. He seemed just a bit too *emotionally* available, as if disregarding his marriage was a habit. Too willing to chat for hours, even if he mostly listened. I tried to counter by pulling back emotionally myself. But since I couldn't deny how much I felt, that left few ways to diffuse my passion except by renewing the marriage mantra—scant help to me since he treated his status so casually.

Conceivably, I also should have reminded myself he had no love for God—just a slight issue, that. But when Married Man had mentioned the book I was named from, he planted a thought in my brain I was powerless to uproot. I couldn't disbelieve we shared a fateful connection any more than I could force myself to believe in whatever creed it was they said got you into heaven. *Feelings are neither right nor wrong; it's what you do with them that causes the trouble.* I still believed that too—and I was certain repressing my feelings would be as wrong as indulging them.

If only I could redirect them . . . The week I finally met Married Man, I found an excuse to e-mail Singapore Fling. Dad had decided to work on our shattered relationship by embarking on an e-mail dialogue about questions like "Can love exist if God does not?" I thought not just Dad but Singapore Fling would like to hear my thoughts in response. He did, and an e-mail flirtation began: "What sexy speak" rapidly progressed to "I have wondered what it would be like to kiss you." About as bold as a man that much my intellectual equal had ever gotten. But he was some nine thousand miles away, while Married Man lived no more than nine thousand *yards* away. I needed to try harder at confusing my hopeless heart.

RUNNING FROM SIN TO THE DIN

In March I redeemed more frequent-flyer miles for a five-day spring break in London, full of street photography, pub crawls, and two fleeting dance-floor hookups. It was my first experience of nightlife in a big city. With girlfriends I barely knew enough to trust, I ventured out to various bars and shows and more bars after that. I'd never been one to bounce so cavalierly from man to man, but if I couldn't stifle my heart, surely I could distract it.

My efforts paid off on St. Patrick's Day, when a cute local's hips matched mine twist for twist, inspiring his lips to do dancing of their own—my second snog with an Englishman in four months (the first had been Mr. December, the lead singer of a visiting British swing band). Mr. March and I didn't bother trading e-mail addresses; it suited us fine that our bodies got better acquainted than we ever would. I was just glad for another storied holiday, and proud I'd vanquished my anguishing crush enough to "cheat" on my heart, albeit while dancing.

I mourned a bit longer for Mr. March II—er, Roadhouse Catch—whom I met the next night at a vast club near Covent Garden. My Roadhouse Catch (so named for the club) was all mystery and wit, a slim, dark-haired, self-described "bean counter" I suspected of using a pseudonym. The name he gave sounded Spanish, which he didn't look in the least. Well, no matter. For how bad my knowledge of pop music proved, I should have gone with a code name too. When I couldn't place "Billie Jean" from the opening chords, he gaped at me, then pulled me close as if American ignorance was endearing.

"At least I know the Beatles!" I mustered, dismayed that what I'd thought a decent ear for music was putting me to such shame (then again we were talking mainstream *eighties* music). And then there they were after all, fabulously reunited for our final dance. Roadhouse Catch pulled me close enough to cop a tender feel as we swayed slowly to the melancholy strains of "Let It Be."

I tried to take their advice. But during the cab ride back to my girlfriend's cramped flat, the words still echoed inside as I realized how much his banter had meant. *The man had briefly given me repartee!* Why hadn't we forged a more lasting connection, at least made out? Why was I so slow to realize I liked him and his timid way with my arse? Well, I had nothing but "our" song to guide me—on both this loss and the waiting despair beyond the Atlantic.

The Beatles proved little help upon my return, though. That spring I got accepted to ASU's graduate program, admitted on one of two full-ride scholarships offered to religious studies students. I was effectively given two more years with Married Man, and handsomely paid for it. *Could God somehow have a purpose for this friendship?* Such gracious provision stunned me.

Debt had become the currency of material distrust in God; most of my student loans were procured to pay off credit card bills from numbing my woes with too many trips to clearance racks on Mill Avenue, and never accepting my meager student salaries as really enough to live on. I was convinced such financial sin could not just be forgotten. Forgiven, perhaps, but ineligible for mercy, much less grace.

I knew God commuted my sentence for sin in general when I called on Jesus to save me, but I thought gifts were out of the question. Except . . . He was now giving me free tuition *and* a job *and* a modest stipend on top of it? Such kindness made no sense to my beleaguered, self-righteous soul. It held tremendous relief—that I couldn't screw things up despite sin and mounting debts—but tremendous terror: if God's gifts weren't connected to *my* goodness, I couldn't make demands for a husband or cry injustice when He didn't provide my so-called "needs." Apparently there was far more to this God—and to my ignorance—than I'd fathomed.

Gifts being what they are, you can always reject them. I briefly considered chancing the glamorous perils of London city life over a free-and-then-some master's degree in desert suburbia, but fierce dissuasion from Singapore Fling and others changed my mind. Apparently there was no escaping two more years of learning to be friends with Married Man—a lesson which held no promise of getting easier.

Sometime in April, he mentioned a rare class assignment requiring him to write and submit a paper. Typed. Since he only hunted and pecked and I played "sheets of sound" in QWERTY, we worked out a fruitful swap: I'd type his paper if he made contact sheets from all my pictures of England. (The black-and-white ones I could do myself thanks to Photo I, but the color work was impossible.)

When I mentioned this arrangement to our inadvertent matchmaker, the prof said typing papers was something a wife or girlfriend does. Worse yet, he was confident Married Man had realized this. I'd thought this professor was someone I could turn to in my religious and ethical crises, but what good did such comments do me? He even asked if we had chemistry, as if subtly encouraging my longings for the forbidden and disastrous.

I was aware at all times of the danger, of the preposterous risk it was—emotionally, sexually, spiritually—to keep going back to a tiny, intimate darkroom not much larger than a closet to talk with a man I took for my soul mate. But in every breath of longing was the anguishing stab of betrayal, as if my insides had been slashed from top to bottom and were only held together by a medic's cursory stitches. That pain proved to be my protection, for it kept me from slipping into the moral lethargy of despair. I must always be on guard against our friendship becoming physical, a sin I was sure my fragile connection to God could not withstand. On guard, because I couldn't see walking away—just cutting things off as if I'd suddenly been deported overseas. So I hung in there, trying to find a way to stay friends without committing what I feared would become the adult version of my Harlequin rebellion, except with much greater repercussions.

My main concern was avoiding both sex and bitterness, the self-protective hardening of cynicism, which seemed to mean I had to keep on hurting—feeling the longing to love *and* its denial—until I found a healthy way to rehab. In one of his books, C. S. Lewis says we're advised by different instincts, like a chorus of moral guides. Some help us protect ourselves, some tell us when we should help others. The tricky thing is when those instincts compete—when we see a drowning that both compels us to help and save ourselves (since we might not be strong swimmers, or afraid of the cold, wet clothes, and hungry sharks). What tells us how to balance our instincts toward both self-protection and self-giving, which note to play so our lives make music, not mere noise?

For Christians, of course, it's God and his "word," the Bible. But over time a lot of us have come to rely on a digest of this— like following legal precedent, instead of the Constitution. The main thing my crisis of faith had produced was suspension of thoughtless belief in this common wisdom. Until I worked out for myself who God was and what He asked of His followers, I didn't assume "truths" asserted on church authority could be inherently trusted. Prior to meeting Married Man, the most I'd done with all those uncertain views, assertions, and doctrines was to file them under "Wait and see" while leaving nothing in "Things I believe about God" except that He existed, spoke through the Bible, and usually met His people in church. There hadn't been much reason to do more than such initial sorting of truth claims until this crisis, which came with a timing that blew my mind.

In a sense it was like being a soldier who has for years trained and mastered weapons in the event of probable attack. Only when he finally decides to dismantle his armor for inspection and thorough cleaning does the promised assault finally come— with his arsenal spread on the ground in pieces, the soldier armed with only thin khakis and two soft hands for his defense.

Had I only learned to fight according to script, or had I learned the principles on which the script was based? It was like finding out how well I knew music not by performing a prearranged piece but by suddenly having to play jazz, on stage, by ear.

You might say I learned both religion and music "classically": the mastery and technique of playing each note set before you, in increasingly complex arrangements. (I was lazy, so I became an excellent sight-reader—the champion of cursory reads.) Jazz is different. In high school I lucked out with piano scores catered to the classically trained, and never a chance to improvise. That was fine by me; as far as I knew, jazz solos were plucked from the sky at random by those with a gift for making a totally unstructured sequence of notes still sound like music (did I mention I was even worse at theory than disciplined practice?). Then I got to college. And under the patient tutelage of our jazz instructor, I started to learn that solos were not *entirely* about talent. There was a supporting structure there, which gave the soloist freedom to make unscripted music while letting the rhythm section undergird him. As long as everyone stuck to the sequence of chords, which determined the structure, you maintained simultaneous freedom, conformity, *beauty.*

It may be little coincidence that most churches I've ever gone to favored not jazz as their style of music, but hymns and even classical choral works. In many ways, it's easier to be given a moral score for your life than to learn a set of principles that gives you remarkable freedom within God's structure for life and community. But God, from what I can tell, is far more interested in followers who make jazz for Him than in those who perform rote worship without putting their whole heart into it. It's not a difference between obedience and self-expression—you make music only when you follow the chords with the rest of the band—but between the sometimes mindless and habitual, and a fairly mindful, *holistic* faith. That was the test my friendship with Married Man gave me: could I make music that pleased God if I'd thrown out the standard score we used in church? Would God show up without the structure in which I'd learned to find, then slowly lost, Him?

The test happened not in the practice room but onstage, midway through performance, in a song where I never dreamed I'd have to solo. But now there was this break where the band dropped out and just the drummer and bass were playing, while our director nodded at *me*. Significantly. I sat there frozen and terrified, unable to stop playing the two notes dictated by my heart: *serve God, preserve friendship*. Could there be music in this interval? In the sidelines, I saw friends shaking heads no. We never sang a song in church with chords like that—or was it that we never improvised? The rhythm section kept going. And as I sent up desperate prayers for help, something reminded me that even jazz had structure to it, I just had to find out which chord we were on; I'd have to listen and trust that all my training had been not just for my head but for the heart from which true music comes. It meant taking a risk on God, stepping out in faith that He could reveal Himself in more than just the historic record of a songbook, but in the live setting of performance. And taking that risk meant more than simply listening.

SERVING THE KING OF HEARTS

During the summer of 2000, my church was sending a team of short-term missionaries to India—another taste of "ministry," and maybe a chance to visit Dad . . . and Singapore Fling. I applied. And though my "doubts" had preempted me from leadership in College Students, my church did not think me unfit for short-term missions, nor did their acceptance depend on my silence about the Married Man crisis. Though I probably didn't mention it on my application paperwork, I'd let my Sunday school teacher, other Christians, and even my parents know—a loose accountability. No one spoke up to gainsay my acceptance to the eight-person team.

It was, from the start, a vastly different trip. Despite a wide range of ages and personalities, we enjoyed a remarkable harmony through thirty-six hours of grueling travel and the tightly scheduled ten days that followed. I was the team photographer, which freed me to happily scurry around snapping pictures of all that interested me, and subtly defined my role as more documentary than participatory. And there was a lot to record. Unlike Berkeley, where we'd focused more on the message, the time in India was balanced between several medical clinics and preaching sessions in various churches and villages. But these were not the one-time encounters that Berkeley produced, unconnected to local churches. We were there as part of our sending church in Phoenix, and hosted by small local congregations whose pastors were trained by our Indian host's ministry. Whatever impact it had on Hindu villagers that their Christian neighbors let them see the American doctor before them, the churches were there to explain such sacrificial conduct—and host more medical clinics and preaching and worship services as our church and others kept sending additional teams.

Conversion was part of why we were there, no question. But the reason it felt so right this time, despite my own confusion, was that we were there not on a marketing but a kingdom model—kingdom in the sense that Jesus meant. Our "agenda" was love and sacrifice. Anyone who reads the gospels has to notice that Jesus's work was not just preaching or telling short stories that left many folks perplexed; He always combined His teaching with acts of healing or feeding that met the people's physical needs. Jesus's ministry was holistic. Though our Berkeley project was meant to be fairly radical, it couldn't be to the degree we maintained a lopsided ministry model that focused more on what we were saying than what we were doing. It couldn't be groundbreaking as long as we questioned only the content and not the lack of a kingdom mind-set in the typical Christian approach to winning converts.

To be honest, I didn't make these connections then either. The biggest thing about India (beside the plentiful bargains and the beauty it took some eighty rolls of film for me to capture) was that it gave me hope my God was not just a part of American culture. One of the first days there we arrived at a small two-day conference for all the local pastors our friend and host trained. There were maybe thirty men in this steamy, tiny, whitewashed classroom, all seated at desks and singing in a strange language, in an unfamiliar tonal scale, to the accompaniment of one or two crude instruments—about as "foreign" a setting as I'd been in. But the minute I set foot in that room I thought, *The Spirit of God is in this place.*

I began to cry—not tears of rage and confusion but the gentle rain of new life on ground long furrowed to bitter ruts in despair of ever returning to clay again. Just because God hadn't watered me in the usual times or ways didn't mean He'd forgotten this field altogether or that I'd somehow jinxed the rain. Perhaps He was simply readying me to bear a different harvest; perhaps it took drying out to produce the new clay He planned to make of me. Though I couldn't grasp most of the content of that meeting (despite our translator), I felt an instant peace and powerful gratitude for those strangers in their neat trousers and crisp linen shirts.

God was real, and He spoke more than just Greek and Hebrew, Aramaic, English. God was real—and He was big enough and good enough for the people we met on that trip to be willing to serve Him despite rejection and even physical attack by their families and neighbors, willing to serve Him though, for the single women I met, the marital costs of following God were much higher than they were for me. For them it often meant almost certain celibacy. Though these Indian Christians showed me just how costly our faith could be, they affirmed the worth of the risk it was to sacrifice so much for an unseen God. If He inspired such love in them, how could He be just an artifact of the Founding Fathers' canny civil religion (as some of the readings in one of my classes had suggested about Christianity)? By the time I left the team in Malaysia to spend a week in Singapore with Dad, I was feeling more hopeful than I had in many months about this God for whom I still was forgoing sex.

Because of Dad's job as a teacher, he'd returned to Singapore sooner than my mom and youngest brother that summer (they stayed behind in Washington to help Sis prepare for college life)—which left Dad alone. Considering my greatest conflict at Christmas had been with him, and considering our relationship was still in need of repair, it was the perfect chance to reconnect.

In the days that followed, we cautiously bonded over the dinners I made while he was at work, and the dusty Tiger Beers I rescued from languishing in the pantry to drink with my supper. Some colleague had made a present of them one or even two Christmases earlier, but my folks were too polite to admit they barely ever drank, much less beer. But I did. And sometimes Dad would sheepishly ask for sips of mine, which reminded him of the beers my Grandpa Broadway used to drink. I liked that it was in his children that Dad sometimes connected with such memories of his father. If only it wasn't so hard for us to connect with each other.

Though both of us were committed to repairing things, goodwill alone was not enough to span the chasm between us— a gap made larger by our struggle to communicate. Dad still didn't understand my questions and was alarmed at my plans to get another degree in religious studies, which he blamed for the unraveling of my faith. As a consequence, I didn't let Dad see much of what I was *really* struggling with; if he didn't "get" the things he thought he saw in me, how could he be trusted to learn of the real issues and not tear me down with judgment and exhortation? He'd mean well, of course—mean to be building me up in my faith—but sometimes Dad's meaning well only did more harm.

The worst case was one night just before my twenty-second birthday, when we were dining on the balcony where he and Mom liked to have dinner and watch the sunset (they had a great view from their eighth-floor apartment). Perhaps the romantic setting brought to mind my despair about relationships. Though India had been good for my faith in God *generally,* my faith that He would ever bring me a husband—or could be trusted with my love life—had been shattered by friendship with Married Man, who seemed to have all the understanding I longed for but none of the faith.

As Dad and I spoke, and tears drew near, I longed to hear some assurance that I was a great catch, any man would be a fool not to see it, few must be the men who would be worthy of me, and that surely if my earthly father could see this, God was no less eager to bring me good things in this most crucial realm of relationships. I wanted to believe I was right to trust God despite this season of suffering, but India alone could not reassure me. I needed Dad to be the human voice of my heavenly Father, promising God knew the plans He had for me, plans including hope and a future.

Unfortunately, the best way I could articulate this was by the question of whether a man could desire me. Would God ever bring me a good man who would want me enough to chase me, woo me, marry me? Surely that couldn't happen unless I had some beauty. But Dad was still reluctant to praise the physical in women, much less endorse a man admiring his daughter's birthing hips and hoping they'd cradle his sons! So when I asked if he thought I had what it took (by which I meant, could God bring a man both desirable and desirous for me?), Dad faltered for a way out of this corner.

"You're reasonably attractive . . . I'm sure some man would be willing to marry you."

I laughed—laughed so I wouldn't cry at my foolish hope that he could ever be the doting father I longed for. Laughed because at least one of us had to see the absurdity of his words for what it was. Perhaps that was why I'd feared I would remain a virgin until the Apocalypse—no man would be *willing* to marry me unless he had few options. Well, maybe that was being a bit overdramatic. Still, it was hard to accept this adult perspective on my father. He wasn't perfect. And now that I saw that, I couldn't keep on blaming him for all the ways he had hurt me if I kept staking my self-image and my self-confidence on what *he* said of me. He did the best that he could. It was my job to sort the good from the bad in his parenting, to take to heart the wisdom and the love, leave behind and forgive the failings and the bad advice. I hadn't wanted to think adulthood made you responsible for the impact of your parents' input, but it did.

If I was to keep on fighting for my chastity and my faith in God, I'd have to do it without my parents' help. There seemed only one thing to do: return to finding distraction—and now my worth—with men who were secular.

CHAPTER 9

TEN-SECOND FLINGS

If I knew what I was after, I'd remember where I'd been
If I was sure of something better, I'd go, I'd go
But I am just another picture, and I watch myself like you
I imagine what you're thinking,
I know, I know

Ten cent wings, I'll take two
Pin them to my sweater and I'll sail above the blue
Ten cent wings, tried and true
In another life you are with me, and I'm with you
—JONATHA BROOKE, *"10 Cent Wings"*

A few nights later, I met up with Singapore Fling for a private coffee. Dad had joined us for dinner a couple nights before, but turned the talk to technical topics I couldn't discuss, as if to keep me from getting too close to his former colleague. But Singapore Fling was not a man to be denied, and he had plans for more than a dinner chaperoned by his friend.

Once we were settled into our Starbucks, he got to the point: "Let's have a fling."

I laughed at his audacity, though it was better salve for my ego than I'd been expecting. "And ruin this friendship?" *Not to mention, strain both our ties with my father!*

It was a far more adult offer than I wanted. Still, both of us knew it was an absurd proposition, so I didn't quash our banter completely. I wanted to savor my moment with a philosophically minded man who was neither married (any longer) nor judging nor even inclined to somehow malign my looks, but simply admire them—and me.

It was not without its price. When we reached date's end, Singapore Fling insisted on satisfying one lingering curiosity.

"I'm going to kiss you on the *mouth*," he announced when I misread his farewell intention as interest in a cheek-to-cheek adieu. It seemed to be my new tradition when traveling, so I let him.

And though he was a recent divorcé who didn't love Jesus, though I'd met him that night because I still took my measure in human approval, there was a grace in his brief peck—more like a first kiss than I'd had three years before. That night he showed me some men didn't treat kissing as a timed event in gold mining, or disguise their intent as "friendship." I guess it makes a difference when you're still his colleague's daughter; I just hadn't the patience to wait for a man who views you as his heavenly *Father's* daughter.

HOW NOT TO "GUARD YOUR BODY"

I returned home a few days later to find my upgrade to grad-student status induced a newfound camaraderie with Married Man and his friends. Occasionally we even socialized out of school, in the bars along Mill Avenue. When he poured me a final half-glass of beer one such night, remarking that he did so to not "corrupt" me, I took it as kindness.

"Not much," I conceded to my journal later, "but more than

could be said for Poster Boy, 'the Christian.' How do I get myself attached to these guys?

"Well, I shouldn't hold bitterness toward Poster Boy (for nevertheless being pretty much an asshole). And I'm committed to loving Married Man as I believe God does."

Love: that was the new approach, and the fruit of a realization how selfish and immature my previous crushes had been. Implicit in liking Married Man was a hope that we could someday be together. But this event could only come at the cost of further suffering for him—the dissolution of his marriage, either through brokenness or death. If my liking's fulfillment required such, my problem wasn't that I cared too much for Married Man, it was caring too little! I started asking God to purify what I felt so I might come to desire and seek my friend's true health and well-being.

It didn't suddenly spirit me from the rabbit's hole to realize this, but I started to sense within the music a structure by which to survive this interminable solo. That second semester of liking him, I threw my energy into pleading Married Man's spiritual case before God, imploring Him to save my friend and heal the wounds that nothing seemed to staunch. Then, at last, I could see proof of God's power in His redemptive work in another, that mythic transformation I had yet to see firsthand.

This new compassion for my friend's life was not immune to the subtle corrosion of lies creeping in with truth, however. Though I was learning to play by ear, to follow the chords, my early attempts at improvisation were full of wrong notes—more noise than music. I, so mindful of dodging *sexual* contact, was oblivious to the danger of other intimacies.

While many friends feared I couldn't maintain the friendship without sin, they had no guidelines for the vast gray space between ending contact and winding up in bed. Almost all talk of chastity is on how to guard your body instead of explaining why the Bible so often warns you to "guard your heart."

Typical of this is one popular marriage guide, in which the author spells out "all" physical contact as a series of twelve increasingly intimate actions. He says it's best to take each step in order: not holding hands until Step 4, and saving "face to face" in all its various forms until Step 7. But no caressing of hair or touching of face until Step 8, for "hand to head" contact—which he considers fairly intimate—is perhaps the final stage a couple can safely enter without being married. Steps 9 through 12, almost all defined in terms of advances on the woman's body, are described as "distinctly sexual and private." These steps are mapped out in great detail as if either a guide for the procreation impaired or those hoping to justify virginity on technicalities. All in all, it's like a terror-alert scheme for sex: "This movie is rated CODE RED!" "Was your last date CODE YELLOW? . . . Or CODE ORANGE?!"

As thus far my friendship with Married Man had not left the innocent first three stages, all was, presumably, well. Only if committing an actual sexual act would we be guilty of *major* sin. Sure, sometimes I wished I might just once dream of being with him—since by its nature the dream could not be my fault—but if dreams only come from your psyche, mine never wanted that sin enough to conjure it up. Besides, if the struggle against my desire for more-than-friendly relations with Married Man was such rough going, how would imagining the forbidden ease my task? It would only lead me closer to the very action I feared (as opposed to masturbation which, since I never imagined real men—even Married Man—seemed free of partners in sin, therefore not . . . *that* . . . sinful). That our emotional bond posed much the same risk never crossed my mind.

One night not long before finals, I saw Married Man in the

photo building, and learned he needed a transcript typed, for a class the next day. He was haggard and unshaven, in poor shape for the long night of hunting and pecking ahead. It didn't take much for us to revive the barter agreement; I had lots more film from India, waiting for contact sheets. So a little after eight that night, we packed up for my apartment—my apartment, because he hadn't yet finished transcribing what he needed me to type. The sensible thing was for him to transcribe it in sections while I typed up what he had.

For which task we first had to watch *The Simpsons* together— to bolster our strength, you see, and remind ourselves how similar our humor could be (it was an episode full of art world references). From there the talk meandered to things like truth, false prophets, and dreams—I filled him in on my Berkeley nightmare—and the prof through whom we'd met. We joked that I could take a secret lover during my roommate's long-term absence (she was traveling in Asia), which somehow led to various increasingly personal sexual topics, all touching on an oh-so-mutual frustration.

Perhaps in a subconscious effort to pull us back from the hungry abyss this troubling subtext stood to drag us to, I brought up the previous eighteen months of hell and all the spiritual confusion I'd had since Berkeley. Talk of Jesus had after all saved me when The Swinger (a deft piano man I met swing dancing) had asked if he could kiss me. Same tangent should work here, right? And it did . . . until I thoughtlessly mentioned how all this angst had led up to facing "the most serious ethical crisis" of my life. *Shit.*

"What's that?"

Suddenly I realized just how much had passed between us since our arrival: that if I finally, fully acknowledged the crush Married Man surely had to know of by now, there was no guessing the consequence. We were not talking in the relative safety of the semipublic photo building, but in the privacy of my apartment, late at night, after building all this intimacy between us—and tapping what else, I didn't want to know.

I drew a breath, as if I could inhale guidance on this sudden, awful predicament, pick out from the dreadful silence what the next chord was or should be.

The phone rang.

While I took the call, he got up to use the bathroom. It was a silly inquiry—some quick question from Bro's roommate, so brief that when we hung up, I had a moment to ponder the timing of this interruption—*#@$&!% unbelievable.* I poured more of the coffee-creamed-with-Bailey's we'd been drinking, and exhaled heavily on a decision to let him be the one who returned to the topic.

"Who was that?"

"Oh, just my brother's roommate"—who was engaged to a friend from my economics classes, but sometimes seemed fond of *me* in a way I hoped was just my brother's affection rubbing off. This I played up as pretext to remark, "I hope I wouldn't ever interfere with someone's relationship."

He played along. "Well, it could happen. You might anyway."

It was late-night speculation about my hypothetical impact on my brother's roommate's engagement, so we left it at that. Then I typed and we talked (mostly talked) until he left at 3 a.m. Because, you know, married men can do that when they're in grad school . . . can't they?

And pick friends up for school the next morning as if it were routine. I didn't ask why he was so insistent on doing so—or think if I should have said no; the savings in time alone meant more precious sleep. (Despite the complications I had when letting my Iowa Sugar Daddy provide other seemingly innocent needs, I hadn't yet learned that sometimes "necessity" likewise gives birth to danger.)

Married Man was cocky that morning, all confidence that I'd type his papers next spring for our first class together (a photo seminar), and in his suggestion we jointly embark on a project for which I'd write the grant proposal—"of course."

"Yeah, right!"

I kept my comments casual, rebuffing his silly assumptions with eye rolls and headshakes. Kept it casual, that is, until I huddled with God that night. Why was I still so blind to all that obviously made him wrong for me? Somehow the Hoped-for Husband script had gone terribly awry, to lead me to such a place as this—where I believed a man who was married and did not love my God was the man I was "meant" to be with. What happened to the kindness and character I had once been drawn to in crushes? How was it that all now paled compared to intellectual chemistry? In terrified desperation, I pleaded with God to save me from yielding to my attraction, begged help in learning to love Married Man more selflessly—enough to put space in our friendship, even end it if need be, so that I didn't compete with his marriage.

There was no immediate answer, but just a few days later a picture came to me, with such force and clarity it almost seemed to come from outside me, like a composer might hear a song. *This mess was like getting* not *the sandcastle I had always wanted, but its replica in shit—a gift that was hard to account for other than as some whim of the unseen artist who owned the beach where I lived.* In the picture, I wept and waited for answers that never came, but slowly it dawned on me that shit was at least the soil in which flowers grew—creating the hope of a daffodil castle springing up some Easter morn from what seemed a cruel joke.

I wrote this all down in my journal, of course, but even long after I'd turned the page, the image lingered inside me like some solitary shoot sprung up in hope that sunrise would someday shatter this darkness. And one night as further protection—as if to revive my old idealism—I listed all the men I remembered liking, compared by relational status, spiritual life, and qualities I'd admired.

Only the memory of Poster Boy stuck out as not just a "decent" or "semi-thoughtful" Christian but a "passionate" one, but I recalled him as far too wounded to pin any hopes on someone like him. The Winner, at least, had briefly spurred me on to good spending and study habits, but his inconsistent church attendance troubled me. Despite all my painful experiences with other Christians, I wanted a man with faith in both God *and* His people—a man with the courage to trust that God really did mean us to serve Him *as a community,* failings and hypocrisy notwithstanding.

I started stopping by to catch the end of the Thursday night meetings again, when the College Students crowd was just hanging out. Almost none of our fiercest critics from those painful leadership meetings still attended, and my brother, his roommate, and others I knew always greeted me very warmly, tardy or not.

Then, just as I'd started popping in to see them, Married Man took off his wedding ring. This could only mean one thing: divorce.

It felt like the force of my shameful wish had prevailed despite my best, most anguished prayers. I knew from his passivity in our friendship that I mattered too little to Married Man to be somehow responsible—so why did I feel worse instead of better now? Hadn't my shit castle turned into sand?

No.

At the time I thought it was mostly the now-habitual mourning for what could never be: an "us" unmarred by adultery or the whiff of connection with his divorce. But deep down I knew it was more than an issue of timing. Even if my friend was on his way to becoming single, he still had several major deficiencies—chief of which was spiritual. Before this hadn't mattered because it was hard enough to take his marriage seriously when he didn't. But now his faith *did* matter . . . didn't it?

ASEXUAL HEALING?

There were times as that awful January slowly ground into February that I held on by a thread. I met a cute guy at CS one Thursday, who shared my newfound fondness for classic rock (albeit with a most unfortunate liking for Journey or Rush or one of those horribly high-voiced bands) and seemed to like me a little too. But neither his soul patch nor throaty-engined orange muscle car could match the connection that still tied me to Married Man. If anything, that guy deepened my doubts God would prove good in my love life. Though CS was a different group now, meeting in a different space, none of those changes could restore the scene that once fed my soul. I'd changed too much and still felt most at home in the alley between the Stuffy House I compared such social scenes to and the smoky bars where I sometimes drank with Married Man and my other photography friends.

One afternoon, a number of us decamped to a bar across the street from campus, known for its patio, Coronas, and cheap tacos. I drank with them till 6:30, when I had to go meet with a

prof I was assigned to help. When I joked about my tipsy departure for campus, Married Man said to be careful crossing the
street.

"You mean you actually care?"

"I must chastise those I love," he quipped, as if quoting from
The Simpsons—" 'love' in the godly sense, of course."

I staggered out of the patio in shock. *He did not just say that.*
Sure, he was certainly joking, and we'd all been putting back
beers—but still! *Still!*

When I came back to the photo building later, after my
meeting, he was there along with another student—a raunchy,
aging Popeye with a paunch instead of a pipe, reputedly turned
to art from a job tattooing, with the bodywork to prove it. I carried on with my own tasks and didn't try too hard to insert myself in their talk, but I sensed that Married Man was periodically
checking my reaction to the curious byplay between them.
Eventually I gathered that his friend was egging him on—
perhaps to pursue a one-night stand . . . with *me.* Apparently
my crush was an open secret, just not the anguished part.

Whatever his friend's suggestion, Married Man kept blowing
off the idea, as I worked in horrified silence. But after that early
morning last semester, I wasn't sure how much I trusted him.
Finally I jumped in to set things straight.

"If you're talking about what I think you're talking about,
you're full of shit."

"He is."

We left it at that and several of us kept working till almost
ten, when Married Man and a couple others and I went to one
girl's house for pizza and *Gidget* and access to her bong, which
they all smoked while I tried to avoid a contact high. Married
Man drove me home when we finally broke up the party sometime past two, but the trip passed without event.

Temptation was fairly constant that spring—either pulling on my desire or compassion. One day in early March, Married Man wound up hanging out during my lab time for Photo III. We bantered, maybe even flirting, until I asked him what he was going to do after graduation.

"Commit suicide."

He had a dark sense of humor, but this went too far to be funny as he explained some stupid theory about the ensuing buzz such an "absence" would make for his work.

I looked at him fiercely, those months of longing and weeping and praying briefly unconcealed. "You'd do that to the people who care about you?"

"Well . . . I'd wait until my Pops dies."

Some dark knot inside seemed to ease briefly, at the thought of him. The moment passed. Determined it not return, I spent the rest of the hour doing my best to make him laugh, to find some however-fleeting joy in life.

As the semester continued, it was that sense of purpose, the possibility for a larger, redemptive role in my friends' lives, that kept me there instead of running from the threat to my fragile resistance. Almost two years past Berkeley, and finally I'd found a subculture! Sure, much of the time we made the banal art-school small talk of Cindy Sherman, "found" art, Mary Ellen Mark—and "Isn't Thomas Kinkade's success appalling?" But there were brief moments while waiting for prints to dry or the other students to reach the bar when the talk was more real, even vulnerable.

Unlike most of the Jesus freaks I'd known, these new friends spoke with little reluctance of the griefs or struggles they faced. And there was no lack of heartache; depression was like a disease we all got from the chemicals that spring. Sometimes I thought my new circle of friends was on the verge of imploding.

But as I heard their stories of past and present, of losses, rapes, affairs, divorces, and abortions, I found myself praying in greater earnest than ever before that God would pursue and woo my friends.

I could hardly make a sales pitch based on my life and all the difficulty faith in God was producing, yet somehow I found a desperate hope welling up that Jesus really indwelled His followers as the Bible said He did. Maybe I was the only way they could ever get the most minute, imperfect taste of what He'd been like—and how I wished they could actually meet Him. Not all the religious junk that had left so many of us burned and cynical, but the Jesus who spoke to women like sisters and equals in a culture where courts would not allow their witness as legal testimony. The Jesus who fed crowds He knew would reject Him and never really "get" His message. The Jesus who saved a woman caught in adultery from certain death by stoning because He asked her would-be murderers who among them was sinless.

The Jesus I still was scared to trust but hoped more with each day was really *real* because sometimes when I read the accounts of Him, I glimpsed a love more wonderful than any I'd encountered or ever dared to hope was real outside our more compelling fictions. A love that forced you to face your filthiest secrets, but with a greater Lover beside you than you ever imagined would have the courage to stay with you once all sham of coolness or righteousness melted away. Only that love had the balm for my friends' souls, and I was sure that if they ever tasted it, smelted mostly free from the dross of human failings and judgment, they might actually be freed to live in the joy and beauty and hope for which they were meant.

How had I suddenly gotten such zeal to evangelize? It turned out a lot of heartache doesn't just break your heart, it breaks your heart wide open enough that you finally start to *care* about others. All the fire I lacked in Berkeley had finally been birthed in the ashes of my greatest dreams and my first paradigm of God. A funny place to find it, but when I did, it gave new urgency to my friendships.

And yet even that compounded my anguish with Married Man. My heart still throbbed with both attraction and the more selfless love God was producing; you could not stir up one without agitating the other. The Sunday after the suicide chat, I almost had a breakdown. I tried in desperation to call every God-fearing friend I thought would talk me down—including the Winner, though he now had a girlfriend. No one was home. When I finally got through to a fairly new secular friend, he said he thought I should go for it. I felt about as embattled and weak as I had the day after Married Man stayed at my house till 3 a.m.

That such feelings might in fact indicate a battle for our souls did not cross my mind—although I usually had these frenzied relapses after spells of renewed prayer and zeal to see my friends come to know Jesus. Nor did I ever question how effectively I could "witness" as the only Christian among them. Based on the Berkeley model of subculture outreach, I was doing great (in fact I would write my thesis on how some of those students found their meaning in life). I never questioned that going it alone could change me more than it changed them—and precisely because I was so impassioned to represent God among my friends, I did not consider pulling back to escape the perils this third semester of struggle brought.

A BRAVE NEW GIRL

Spring break couldn't have come at a better time. When Girlfriend #3's sojourn abroad in Paris gave me another chance to escape, I threw all ominous credit-card statements to the warm March breezes and booked my ticket.

France was no London or Singapore, though. Ten days of sharing hostel rooms with strangers and sipping overpriced coffees in my friend's favorite cafés did not dispel my palpable heaviness, a cloak like I'd not felt since right after Berkeley. When I finally returned to the grim, sprawling Charles de Gaulle, it was only to get delayed. Extensively.

As the wait stretched on and on, a cute-ish, friendly bookshop worker from Portland chatted me up. We did the whole West Coast bonding thing, and by the time the airline shipped us all off to a hotel for the night . . . well, let's just say a different woman would've had some company. The offer was clearly made, as we stood together at the counter and I proceeded to get my own room.

"You sure?"

I made some vague excuse about my luggage, privacy . . . maybe stopping by later. A night in some man's arms was certainly tempting—if only to briefly escape my heaviness, to forget for a night the fifteen previous months of heartache and mangled faith. *No one would ever know,* the voice that tried to stop the T-shirt toss whispered. *What better way to forget the man at home?*

But it would take more than two years' depression and one half day of geographic bonding for me to tensely toss and turn in some man's arms—especially when his face did not quite light my fuse. That night I slept alone, saved by my "looksism" if nothing else. I guess God uses what He needs to—sometimes a phone call, sometimes our prejudice.

And God used a book that Flight Buddy had to start unwinding the riddle of my despair. There's something more than a little disconcerting about sitting next to a man you've just met on an international flight from Paris and learning his book is the tale of a man whose romance began on a flight from Paris—but so begins Alain de Botton's *On Love.* I'd barely quit fretting my suitor might make too much of this when I read the opening paragraph.

> The longing for a destiny is nowhere stronger than in our romantic life. All too often forced to share our bed with those who cannot fathom our soul, can we not be forgiven if we believe ourselves fated to stumble one day upon the man or woman of our dreams? Can we not be excused a certain superstitious faith in a creature who will prove the solution to our relentless yearnings?

Was he calling this plight of mine "romantic mysticism"?!! The chapter continued:

> Though the dice may roll any number of ways, we frantically draw up patterns of necessity, never more than when it is the inevitability that one day we will fall in love. We are forced to believe that this meeting with our redeemer, objectively haphazard and hence unlikely, has been prewritten in a scroll slowly unwinding in the sky, and that time must therefore eventually [however reticent it has been till now] reveal to us the figure of our chosen one. What lies behind this tendency to read things as part of a destiny? Perhaps only its opposite, the anxiety of contingency, the fear that the little sense there is in our lives is merely created by ourselves . . . the anxiety that there is no God to tell our story and hence assure our lives.

A scroll unrolled from the sky all right, but it wasn't because I'd found myself a new soul mate: the book could have been cribbed from my journals (albeit with far more posh allusions than I'd ever make; no way I could have parsed Pascal and Marx so lucidly). That was it, then: I'd made marriage my source of meaning, a lie that, once so exposed, I could begin to fight. Perhaps I didn't need to cling to Married Man's now-disgraced vows to keep struggling for self-control and self-giving love.

However freeing it might have been, though, my new resolve wasn't painless. By May Married Man was openly dating someone else from our circle. His seemingly passionless marriage had held little threat to my heart aside from the cold fact I couldn't have my supposed soul mate, but this—*this*. This new relationship clearly was based on desire, based on pursuit. It was too much to bear. As I had done when Poster Boy seemed to pursue another, I started pulling up my emotional stakes; the school year was almost done anyhow.

Yet though I sensed a distance now from Photogirl, the new girlfriend, whatever selfless love I had for Married Man proved far less possessive than any crush I'd had before. He wasn't mine just because I'd liked him so long; I had no right to anger just because she'd known of the crush. What right had I to object? Besides, though nothing had hurt as much as this, it was at least the pain of closure. And now that I'd finally reached the end, it turned out that nothing heals cleaner than a wound through which a love refined by God has poured. Perhaps this was the daffodil I'd hoped to find in my shit castle, watered to life at last by the blood of my dying hope I had a soul mate.

A few nights after their "coupledom" was confirmed, I saw *Bridget Jones's Diary* with a friend. And I, who rarely cried at movies, who staunchly avoided *Titanic* for all its obnoxious romantic hoopla, wept inconsolably at the ending. In contrast to most other chick flicks, which cast the heroine as a strangely undiscovered gem any number of men would madly chase, Bridget was everygirl writ large—and far more hapless. But miracle of miracles, her initially unlikely dreamboat puts up with not one or two but several gaffes (or should I say, debacles). In fact, it's that rare story where the hero approaches something like unconditional love—or at least a love based not on the heroine's merit, but some indefinable something he finds valuable.

It's a charming, British, sometimes off-color portrait of the love we all long to find, and which the Bible says God showed to all humanity through Jesus. But I no longer believed in it, at least as romantic reality. I didn't think God could provide a love like that.

When one of my former roommates married later that month, I came home and took off my purity ring, the symbol of a patience and virtue I'd hoped would someday reward a husband. Now it seemed merely a symbol of my accursed romantic mysticism. Did I really want my life defined by the hope of some man I didn't know and who might not exist at all? Did such a person deserve to so heavily overshadow my life that I wore a ring for him every day until we met?!! *Hell* no. It was time I faced the reality that not just truth or our knowledge of it is uncertain, but even love and marriage itself.

CHAPTER 10

THINKING FORWARD, DATING BACK

Loose ends tying the noose in the back of my mind
If you thought that you were making your way
To where the puzzles and pagans lay
I'll put it together: It's a strange invitation

—BECK, *"Jack-ass"*

When I was small, my folks attended a church in Seattle eventually pastored by Family Friend's uncle. My memories of that congregation and its too-vast building are a hodgepodge of pint-sized perspective: people who laughed that I was "seven going on thirty-five," a woman who used vinegar as deodorant, the girl I tried to befriend who wanted no part of me, and one strange Chuck Swindoll book called *Three Steps Forward, Two Steps Back* that hung on a bulletin board for the library. The last word was printed backward, in a typographic emphasis I couldn't grasp.

I thought Christianity was a nice, steady journey to sanctification, marred only by bouts of backsliding for those whose faith was halfhearted. If you were committed enough, such zigzags were avoidable. Though I knew about David's adultery and Peter's denial of Jesus, these seemed like one-time-only failings intended to show our heroes' humanity. You might say I thought Christian growth was like having a bone set instead of going to a chiropractor. (Bear with me, if you believe the latter does quackery.) If a bone's set right, it heals and that is that. But chiropractors will tell you their work requires numerous visits. Why? Because they're often retraining your muscles and bones, teaching them what shape to take.

When they first start readjusting you, putting everything back where it should be (or as close to that as things will move), their work may hold for a day or two, but twist the wrong way or return to your habitual slump and the bones slide back where they're used to sitting. It takes a lot of time and repeated adjustments to retrain a crippled skeleton. And from what I can tell, our spiritual growth is much the same. When you look at Jesus's relationship with Peter, He's constantly "readjusting" something—training his body and soul in what the new life of faith really means.

The same had been true in my life, too, but it took a while to realize this. Initially I thought God had merely been setting a broken bone, albeit during a two-year surgery. Now, however, all seemed to be on the mend. Was not my ringless state the move of a wiser, stronger, and newly realistic Anna?

In some ways it was. But my new romantic agnosticism carried a lot of risk. Leaving hope alive through the pain of liking Married Man had been one thing; staying open to the pain my deepest longings could yield—if they went unsatisfied—was another. Bit by bit, I gradually edged to the safety of romantic atheism.

INTO THE GREAT WIDE, GROPING

Summer brought a new full-time job at a place where they made rally cars and tried to sell or rent strange foreign vehicles. With the job came high-speed Internet and sufficient downtime for browsing the profiles on a British-owned dating site I'd read about in a newspaper story. Between the blue-blood ownership and the seven-day trial period, I decided it would be a harmless enough experiment, never mind such a service had once deemed Stalker #1 my kind of guy. That was more than five years ago, and surely at the time we were the only two under-twenty users listing Phoenix as home. Now you could upload photos and trade "whispers"!

These improvements notwithstanding, online dating prospects in 2001 still tended to be on the sketchy side. I found a hot teacher in Boston who liked to party, a Midwest perv who treated me like his confessor, and three Phoenix guys I actually braved meeting. None sparked my interest, but after the last two years, I felt a bit guilty about my taste in men. Perhaps I had no idea what was best for me and ought to be more open toward guys I once would have shut down instantly. So the night of my twenty-third birthday, I had a casual meet-up with Udate's idea of my local Christian match.

Instead of surprising me with his in-person charisma, Internet Date proved all too similar to those people you meet in nearly every church, whom it seems the Lord has brought there primarily to refine the congregation's love for each other. Are we kind merely to those we'd naturally bond with in almost any context, or do we show equal interest and warmth to people it takes almost everything not to avoid, cut short, and barely meet the gaze of? To interact platonically is hard enough, but I was supposed to be on an actual *date* with this guy, and wouldn't you know it, the friends who'd agreed to meet me there were late.

While some might have simply laughed off our brief, awkward cocktail as a dating rite of passage, at the time it just confirmed my fear that few of God's single male servants were ever likely to alter one's pulse in a good way. Internet Date didn't put up much resistance when I refused to keep trading "whispers" with him, but it had been much harder to draw boundary lines with my longtime friend King of Pseudo Dates. Since we'd met at some College Students event years before, he'd proven a good friend to both me and Bro, yet he was fond of his Tevas and Saturn in ways I knew I'd never be able to get past romantically.

Not that he'd clearly sought out such a relationship, but in the painful year after Berkeley, he'd started seeking me out one on one for friendly "hangouts" that often fell on Friday nights. Between the time of day and week, and the way he sometimes paid for me, I often went home feeling tricked into a suspiciously datelike outing. The worst was when we wound up meeting his mother one Saturday morning at a book sale—his *mother!* And we weren't even dating! Just . . . pseudo-dating.

Which was the most I would have stood for, anyhow. Though King of Pseudo Dates shared many questions we three from the Berkeley project were asking, his approach was fairly different. Where I turned from the church's songbook to jazz, my friend seemed inclined to flip back through the old scores in case there was something he'd missed. Case in point: our talk one night, when I was still struggling through my crush on Married Man.

We'd just seen *High Fidelity* and were discussing its narrative merits. Although I'd been a fan from the opening song, the story of one man's journey to sort out why his relationships never work out could not have been more appropriate. For Rob, it takes starting to fall for yet another woman—which would mean leaving his present, long-suffering girlfriend—to see that he's spent life chasing a fantasy. Then he has the epiphany: "When's it all going to . . . stop? I'm going to jump from rock to rock for the rest of my life until there aren't any rocks left? I'm going to run each time I get itchy feet?" If the stellar sound track hadn't already won me over, Rob's insight into the cons desire is capable of cementing the film as an instant Top Five in my book.

In many ways, King of Pseudo Dates agreed. But when he objected to something that he said countered the Bible's take on relationships, it reexposed the gulf between us. I pushed him for some evidence of his claim, but he just appealed to a widely accepted truism spouted in wedding homilies.

Instantly my cliché alarm clanged out a warning. "What does that mean? Where does that come from?" I'd gotten very good at shifting the focus from me to him when we talked, good at pushing him toward some thorny theological issue instead of what might lead to intimacy. "There's not exactly a verse in the Bible that says that." I tugged my jacket snug, inched further back into the cast-iron mesh of the coffee shop's outdoor seating and folded my arms to ward off the sudden chill within.

Rather than the spiritual algebra I hoped he'd work out—like talking through the assumptions often glossed over in chats like this, or reasoning from God's character to defend his point—King of Pseudo Dates simply gave answers that glanced off my ears as mere platitudes. He was sticking with the script, though not unintelligently.

As the chair left a cast-iron kiss on my back, still cold from the mild winter evening, I wondered if I'd ever find a man who could stand up to me. It wasn't just that such tension supplied the sparks between Tracy and Hepburn; it was the balance key to respect and interdependence. In marriage you have to compromise, give way to decisions you may not always like. You do it because you trust your mate and his thinking process and recognize that you don't possess the whole truth. But I had no such respect for my friend's reasoning, however right or wrong my own position was.

It took at least a year after that chat for me to develop a full-blown case of cynicism, but Internet Date was too squirm-inducing for me to keep trusting God with my love life. After that night, I did what all too many Christian girls do: throw standards out the window, at least in the short term. Never mind that I might not be ready for whom God *did* have; somehow expecting the worst of my heavenly Father was easier than waiting for His best. While men outside the church might have no love for God or His people, they at least challenged my views about Him, and made no pretense of wanting "friendship" when getting to know me.

They made no pretense of settling for my sexless approach to relationships either, but when I first met men such as the O-Zone King—our server at the pub where drinking buddies from work took me to recover from meeting Internet Date—all that mattered was how their looks, attention, and "coolness" outclassed Christian guys like the one I'd just escaped from.

As we settled into the birthday pints and our corner booth, my friends' banter over my love-life folly and our cute, bearded bartender had the ease of bandmates who know how to trade sly jokes among the riffs and eight-bar solos. Maybe this was what life in the alley would look like: deep commitment to God, but community found more in friends outside the church than within it.

Something about our party's verve caught more than my attention that night. When I returned with a girlfriend on Friday, to find the O-Zone King on shift at the entrance, he started with front-door banter and ended up spooning me on the barstool after we'd made plans to meet again. It was the clearest and most welcome interest I'd had in . . . well, maybe ever! When sprinklers at the park interrupted our "hang-out" the following night, he made the logical offer for a nightcap: "Your place or mine?"

Apparently lanky, art-school grad-student dropouts—who smoked, liked Phish, went rock climbing, and had hitchhiked much of the West Coast—moved rather fast. But at least with secular men like him you always knew where you stood: brazen advances meant they were hooked, not calling you back meant they had moved on. Which the O-Zone King did promptly. But I still pined for several months in hopes my rebound crush might forget I wouldn't put out my bedroom's "Do Not Disturb" sign for him.

I did think about it—quite a lot, in fact. Truth was, I'd always bought God's plan for chastity more on pragmatics—the hope for a better future sex life—than His authority as my creator. But what if there was no someone for me? One night when there was still some hope the O-Zone King would call again, I lay there in bed and wrestled with God.

Somehow I no longer feared that I would lose my salvation for so grave a sin as having sex outside marriage. My fledgling comprehension of grace gave me boldness in asking God to adjust His seemingly unkind standards. Hadn't Jacob wrestled with God? *I want this! I want this! PLEASE.* Finally I sensed a kind of divine assent. That scared me. It felt like God would not stop me if I pursued what I wanted, but I did not sense His blessing. *His blessing.* Could I really say for sure the thing I thought I wanted *was* what I wanted?

No. After everything with Married Man, *no*. I was intent on destroying the childhood fantasy and idolatry of marriage—this in a desperate hope that purging myself of all romantic nonsense would produce a new me, clean and whole enough to finally deserve love from the kind of good man I still longed for—but I wasn't ready for more than the whisker burn O-Zone King's red beard had left behind. Sex was still an ultimate I didn't want to pollute except in my fantasies.

I don't exactly remember what happened after that night—except that nothing more happened with my crush—because all too soon world affairs dragged all eyes to the shocking events in New York City. Dreams like I'd had before and during Berkeley came back, only this time I played a role in averting some diabolical scheme of which I always had prior knowledge. I've always gauged my fear at dreams with a spiritual barometer that goes *Pray, Pray out loud, Call aloud to Jesus.* Those dreams brought a new extreme: *Ask Jesus to come back.*

"Come, Lord Jesus" is one prayer Christians should cry with great longing, but I had always choked on it for fear its answer might shortchange me out of, well, sex. Now I faced more basic concerns: the fear life might end unnaturally and prematurely. Evil had become real. And yet that is the very thing Jesus says we should not fear: "Do not be afraid of those who kill the body but cannot kill the soul. Rather, be afraid of the One who can destroy both soul and body in hell." Fear not pain and death, but the One who is our ultimate judge . . . the One whom Jesus called Father.

But when we ask God to let Jesus's death serve as payment for our sins, the Bible says we become His children as well. The One we should fear most of all is He who gave His son to take our punishment so we might be reunited! For the first time in my life I started to comprehend why fearing the God of the Hebrews was so right and good, even healing. Fear of God alone freed one from the fear of death—not to pour your life out so your enemy's blessing is turned into a curse (as the bombers had done), but so your enemy's curse might give way to a blessing. That is the reason Jesus died, and why His disciples are each called to live sacrificially.

I had no clue what this looked like for one so far from the tragedy's epicenter, so my new courage emerged in minute decisions to choose contact with other people: I cut out all but unavoidable viewing of TV news and deliberately sought communal sites for the hours of grading, reading, and writing my studies involved. Given the price of decaf and hours of business, it wasn't long before Irish Pub trumped Starbucks as my regular place—three or four, sometimes five or even six nights a week.

As talk sprang up with other patrons, I found far more spiritual openness than there'd ever been with the photo crowd. This time, with this subculture, I could do more than listen and pray about things later on; I could chauffeur home drunks who might have otherwise driven themselves and talk to people about religion and their standoffishness toward Jesus. Surprisingly such conversations came with an ease and joy I'd never thought were possible. Sometimes in those moments it was all I could do not to weep. *Who would have thought it?* The place one could talk of such ultimate things as meaning and God and selfishness was not a meeting of other Jesus freaks but a pub full of half-tipsy "sinners."

And yet, since I was still a sinner myself, there were nights my fondness for Guinness or male attention rendered me just as tipsy or flirty as everyone else in the bar. It slowly became a pattern that fall—a dizzying lurch between talk about Jesus one night and meeting some guy or pining for the O-Zone King the next (despite dalliances with Slobberguy, Sgt. Ex-cessories, Invisible Ma(ri)n(e), and the Other Air Force Guy, my rebound crush did not subside).

I didn't exactly go to the pub to meet men, but when I did, I consoled myself with the thought that most came for the Guinness; I figured a man's taste in beer, at least in *that* town, said as much about his character as his face or the shape of his nail beds. Unfortunately, taste was little help when they moved on from idle chitchat to the pickup. Though I rarely felt instant attraction to guys I met there, neither was I immediately, vehemently turned off. And if I'd started by thinking the guy was cool in a general sense, it felt cruel to shut him down when he got flirty, as if he had worth only when I deemed him date or mate potential. Unless the guy was completely repulsive physically, I wanted to say yes to him as a person . . . which usually meant taking his sense of personhood on *his* terms, hence saying yes to his invitation for dinner.

Then the night the Diamondbacks won the World Series, I went to get a beer (and pretend to study) at an oyster bar sometimes frequented by the O-Zone King—though I told myself I was going there to *avoid* him, in case he was working at Irish Pub that night. He wasn't. Instead he came into the oyster bar with his date for the night—but not until the freckled, heavyset patron at my side had taken my thick sheaf of reading as an opening line instead of a paper bodyguard.

I think we were meant to talk that night; I've never met a man as open to God as him. With most folks, you might get through parts of the Bible's account of life's purpose and how we came to be broken and so hateful of our maker, but generally they object to either God's rather damning assessment of things, or His stringent if gracious terms of repair . . . or something else . . . or everything. These objections usually derail the story midway, leading one down a labyrinthine course of theological rabbit trails.

This time the almost-derailment came from me. Our talk had been going surprisingly well until I looked up to find that my seat at the bar gave me a direct view of the O-Zone King, in line to use the bathroom. At this sudden reminder of him and his date and my obviously lesser appeal as a woman, a pang went through my heart that threatened to wipe out all concentration on the discussion. Before I'd always caved to such internal thunderclouds as if there were no choice involved. But was there? The clamor of baseball and patrons rooting the home team dimmed as I weighed the larger issue. *Was I really committed to serving God or did my "selflessness" exclude guys who offered no balm to my wounded ego? Would I give even when I was getting nothing out of it?*

It took a few exchanges for me to block out my heart's fierce protest, but as I slowly returned to focusing on our talk, I got through the rest of the biblical story, including God's terms for restoring our relationship. My listener still had no objections. Even I couldn't quite believe it, so I recapped.

"Based on everything you've so far said you agree with, you accept the Bible's assessment of things, desire to be made right with God, and recognize Jesus is God's only chosen mediator. What's holding you back from responding to Him?"

It was the only time I'd ever been able to ask that question. I'll probably never know his ultimate answer, at least until heaven, but when I turned to watch the Diamondbacks win the series a few moments later, I savored victory of another sort— in a battle not for that man's soul but for my own. After that I decided it might be time to take a break from bar dates altogether, if not from the bar as my study place. With the exception of my few dates with a blond named Sgt. Ex-cessories, I more or less succeeded in this.

IN A NEW YORK STATE OF MIND

Though still pining over the O-Zone King and flaunting my running-toned curves every chance I got, I found myself hitting a rhythm that year—in everything from running to school to faith—that seemed to precede a major shift. In spring 2002, I was invited to join a symposium for new and experienced scholars in my field taking place in New York City. After five whirlwind days of darting all over two boroughs, I started pondering a move.

There'd never been a question of leaving the desert, just the city where I would settle. Eventually it came down to New York or Berkeley, whose bustling but neighborhood-like streets were the standard by which most other places were judged. But though I had more connections out west, I wasn't convinced I'd left my heart by the Bay, or if so, that I wanted to retrieve it yet. Between my falling out with CS and the eighteen-month crisis with Married Man, I still hadn't really dealt with all that happened three years before. Until I had a better sense why my spiritual life had sustained such damage, how could I avoid repeating those mistakes? Perhaps I'd simply use New York as a launch pad—take a break from school and the suburbs there, then settle down in parts west once life was more sorted out. Besides, I had this vague dream of being a writer someday, and something told me that meant time in New York.

Meanwhile there was my thesis to write and jobs to find. But even though I had an almost-finished master's degree on my résumé, East Coast companies seemed to only see my Arizona address. By late July I started to ponder moving there without a job, based on a potential roommate's promise to hold a room till September. I hardly had any work in Tempe, so, either way, God would have to provide. And though I was barely employed that summer, He'd somehow supplied the means to buy groceries, pay rent, fill my gas tank, even visit Seattle for an impromptu family reunion—all without ever using my credit cards.

For the first time in quite a while, I began taking both God's existence and His *goodness* as facts I could rest my life on. But a jobless move to a pricey city? That seemed the height of reck-lessness. It wasn't exactly a great year for the economy, much less in New York City—not even twelve months into recovery. Still, summer was winding down and I had a small settlement from a car accident (delayed by what might be providence), and weeks left on my lease. If ever there was a time to go, this was it. I decided to pray and fast over it.

To Christians who fast, it's a discipline—like abstinence, tithing, Bible reading, and prayer. But though I'd learned to be faithful in things like running and writing my thesis, I'd never been a very good faster. I couldn't even figure out why you *did* it. All the rest I got: you were either relating to God or funding His work or waiting for His best. But fasting? I no longer had a weight problem, and not eating just made me feel guilty; such days I felt no more spiritual, just hungrier. At least that's how my previous fasts had gone. But this time I resolved to use the fast—and my unemployment—as a chance to take a mini-retreat with God.

There is no magic to fasting; God is no more willing to bargain with us given that chip at play. But this time it was a good fast. It gave me a chance to quiet my heart, reflect on my overall purpose in life and motives for seeking to move, and finally, after some thirty hours, to ask God His thoughts on the crazy scheme. By this point I'd left my house to pace the Tempe Town Lake's south shore, the place I always went to run. A storm was blowing up that night, and the wind whipped my hair in a dance that brought back happy childhood memories of storms and rain in Seattle. But there was no storm inside. As my prayer finally turned to the pressing question, I felt nothing but a peace inside. *Go.* It was not an audible voice, but it was leading as clear as I'd had.

With most of the things I'd ever wanted—especially the men—my heart always felt like the floor of a lazy person's bedroom: mostly swept except for one corner. And though I would try to go to God as if my heart's floor was totally clean and my motives were pure, I always felt that pile of dirt—like grits of sand in a mollusk shell, or corn stuck between your teeth. You always know when it's wrong, and if you pursue it despite the warning, the mess both inside and out gets worse. This time there was no mess. For the first time in a long while—maybe ever—I felt an inexplicable confidence God would bless pursuit of this dream.

The drive home was through a rainstorm not unlike the one Elijah outran from Mount Carmel. As I walked from my car to our second-floor apartment, it was hard to tell the earth's gratitude from my own as the fragrance of ground revived filled my nostrils. And yet, for how clean-swept my heart felt, this new confidence was soon tested.

In case my unreliable heart had been misled yet again, I sought confirmation of God's leading from three parties: my parents, that trusted uncle, and an elder in my church. When I made the first of those phone calls, my uncle advocated caution: "Visit New York to scout for work, but don't move without a job." My parents said the same, expressing concerns about the city and suspicion a cute Catholic thinker I'd met in May had too much to do with my plans to move.

That question was certainly part of why I'd fasted . . . yet God seemed to extend His blessing. Had I misunderstood? Though my feeling of peace did not change, I was committed to moving only with my advisers' blessing. Now there was only one left: the elder from church.

As I drove into Phoenix to meet him over lunch, I had little hope he'd counsel differently. But when I got to the restaurant, my counselor was all for it: "Go! This may be the only time in your life you can take a chance like this."

"But my parents . . ."

"They just want to protect you," he said gently. And then as if to allay their concerns, he promised that if I got stuck in the city, he'd pay for my flight back to Phoenix. Just like that it was settled.

Once the decision was made, everything came together with an ease it seemed God Himself was behind. My folks changed their minds, an Irish Pub pal got me cheap fare on his airline while another one stored boxes for me, I sold my car, packed my things, went through graduation, and boarded a plane for New York all in fifteen head-spinning days.

By the time my flight had departed, I could only imagine clear skies ahead. If I still remembered a strange dream from that summer—in which I rode my mattress through the streets of New York, then entered a bar where patrons got nosy about my sexual experience—I chalked this up to the stress of a major life transition. The symbolism was there, right? Besides, I had chosen New York over Berkeley. How could life in the East ever match the battles I'd come through? Now that God had reset the bone, and I was trying to rein in wayward desires, surely things should return to the rhythm of life before I had to deal with pain.

Rather than trusting God to be good *and* sovereign, you see, I'd clung to a paradigm that took romance out of the picture, and with it His authority over that part of my life. Why would a good God give me desires for marriage that He repeatedly seemed unwilling to fulfill? And why would a good God further show me that what I wanted *did* exist, but in the form of a man who couldn't ever be my husband? As much as I wanted to trust Him, those questions were too hard to answer.

Only once I was in New York and learning from a pastor with a particular gift for connecting sin, God, and grace to the heart did I begin to revisit those issues. Under his teaching, I gradually came to see that what's extraordinary isn't so much the sudden lawnloads of shit, but that God can grow flowers in them. Suffering is a part of life—as much in an emotional sense as otherwise. But as that pastor puts it, the remarkable thing is how God chooses to use the "outer" brokenness of the world to heal the internal brokenness wrought by our sin.

If I had looked more closely at the three years elapsed since Berkeley, I might have gotten a hint of this process. When God allowed me to be tested, it wasn't by taking away my health or means or withholding a good church home, but by letting me struggle through threats to my core desire: community. Life in New York continued this pattern. The second church I visited became my spiritual home, and after a month of looking for work, I found a temp agency that kept me employed full time until I finally got a permanent job in December.

Relationships were a different story.

CHAPTER 11

FIFTY WAYS TO LEAVE
YOUR LONGINGS

Now that I've met you
Would you object to
Never seeing each other again
'Cause I can't afford to
Climb aboard you
No one's got that much ego to spend

So don't work your stuff
Because I've got troubles enough
No, don't pick on me
When one act of kindness could be
Deathly
Deathly
Definitely

You're on your honor
'Cause I'm a goner
And you haven't even begun
So do me a favor
If I should waver
Be my savior
And get out the gun

—AIMEE MANN, *"Deathly"*

n all the excitement of planning the move, I'd barely considered the social cost. Nor did it sink in immediately. The day
after I flew in, a longtime Jesus-freak friend from out west
drove into the city from Philly to run in Central Park. Afterward
I crashed on his couch before we drove down to Virginia for the
housewarming party of our friend from my Posse Pal dream and
tequila drinking with Poster Boy.

But as I settled into my first real week in the city, the novelty
wore off. When the box that should have contained the core of
my library—including all my journals—arrived, just a few
books showed up in an unfamiliar parcel. Slowly it sank in that
I had no church, no bed, and no ready-made communal structure. I was no one's sister or daughter or classmate, had no regular bars or photo labs or coffee shops to idle in, much less the
means to frequent such. I'd moved there with no savings and
just money enough to pay my first month's rent and deposit. All
I had besides the goods I'd packed into four or five overstuffed
suitcases was my laptop, and a dial-up line to the Internet. Perhaps I should check out this "Craigslist" my friend in Virginia
had mentioned . . .

Once I ran out of possible jobs to apply for, it seemed natural to scan the personal ads. With no friends to help me pass the
humid weeknights and weekends, casual dead-end dates
seemed an ideal stopgap. And a couple of them were innocent
enough: no kisses or gropes, just guys eager to exchange coffee
or a Guinness for good conversation.

But that was only one kind of New York man. Two weeks into
my lonely, housebound monotony, I answered some guy's ad for a
Friday-night movie companion. Just to be safe, I warned him that
I first had to visit a Bible study but might have time to meet up
with him afterward. Cue self-deprecating joke about R-ratings.

This tidbit was tossed off in a sufficiently insouciant fashion to give him a good laugh. Or so Ad Weasel said. Because, of course, he called and we talked and then had several flirtatious phone calls and e-mails, over which we built up some chemistry. He had the voice of a middle-aged, portly businessman, but I told myself that hunch was probably off. Besides, this was simply exercise for my brain. So what if "fun banter" might come across as sexually charged flirtation? Ignoring the premonition that I might be headed for trouble, I said yes to a casual date.

When I finally laid eyes on the man, I was relieved to find Ad Weasel a younger, smaller version of James Gandolfini— thirty-one but incredibly middle-aged (as the phone voice hinted). Stout. Two inches under my own five feet, eight inches. I always fall hardest for guys who are tall, blue-eyed, and athletic, fond of thrift stores and acts like the Rolling Stones, Beck, and Ray Charles; Ad Weasel was more like that distant uncle in sales who gets slightly inappropriate when he drinks. After Slobberguy, Sarge, and the others, I figured a man like him should prove no trouble. Surely my own lack of ardor supplied a sufficient barrier . . .

But Ad Weasel was a different sort than previous dates, and I had no game plan preparing me for his brisk fourth-quarter action. I should have known by then that a man doesn't drive you home without the "good-bye" getting messy, but I was still too new to the shocking length of subway rides home—three or four or more times longer than the drive back from Irish Pub used to take—to decline his generous offer. Well, to decline that offer. His second, made after he'd parked across the street from my three-story building, was another matter entirely.

Until that night, I thought sex came with warnings akin to the signs announcing the Bay Bridge. *If you don't want to wind up in Oakland, get off here. Last San Francisco exit.* In sex I figured those signs were things like a spike in desire, removal of clothing, or shutting someone's door. But when I critiqued my date's technique in the midst of our front-seat wrestling match, Ad Weasel offered a compromise that had all the gust of winds on the bridge. In his mind it was probably the most generous offer a man could make to a girl like me while respecting her virginity. But it made me realize I had no interest in ever visiting Oakland—whether by bridge or a north–south interstate—with Ad Weasel by my side.

Without that exchange, I might have realized what was happening too late. But God was neither too prudish nor unmerciful to deny me that gracious wake-up call. If I knew I'd never marry someone like Ad Weasel—would never give him my whole self—I had no business giving him even a part of me physically.

Until that night in his car, my dates with secular men had never forced me to face this stark truth. Ad Weasel did. I might later rue how far I'd let him go, but he did at least help clarify my standards and spare me even greater regrets. I called it a night, went to bed on my floor (I wouldn't get a real one till November), and journaled the hope that God would provide a husband promptly, to get me out of this terrible mess of singleness and libido. How else could I handle the power and danger of desire?

WHEN IN DOUBT, TRY HIM OUT

Roughly one week later, I met the Captain at my new church. A tall, dashing man in natty orange shirt, with an M.A. and job teaching West Point cadets their English, he looked and sounded enough like the Winner to suffice as short-term savior. Since I couldn't actually bring myself to *pray*, "God bring me my husband, if you have one," the Captain's part started out as a guest-star reminder of the sort of man I was waiting for. But since he fit the part so well . . .

Soon I saw potential to extend his run in the anecdotes giggled and gossiped over with girlfriends. *The Captain played volleyball almost as badly as me! He had used the same engagement ring with two different girls but when both fell through he traded it for a camper top for his Land Rover!* Weren't such tales quite endearing? Besides that, we'd become sorta-kinda friends; he read an online paper of mine from grad school days and even praised my use of sources. To cap it all off, he'd bought one of my photography prints—all on his own initiative. It was practically *pursuit!* Considering I stood to see him as often as once a week, this seemed like my healthiest crush since . . . well . . . Poster Boy.

And on some level I was right—frequent contact should have grounded things in reality; the trouble was thinking that sketching the hero's initial bio was tantamount to knowing him. Nothing replaces the intimate knowledge of incidental experience—that growing stockpile of mundane moments from which you slowly discern how a roommate taps her fingertips when she's making a certain point, the look of a sibling's stride seen from a distance, or the way your uncle's laugh tells you if he thought his own joke slightly ribald. I wanted that with the Captain, but I had no way to produce it.

Shortly after I met him, however, two friends of his from college moved to the city—the sort of warm, funny, fascinating married couple one instantly feels a long history with, as if your souls have been laughing and cooking and talking together long before this meeting in the flesh. Soon I was joining the Captain, the Two from Texas, and a few of their other longtime friends on occasional post-church lunches. Their easy banter invited me in, wove a texture of memories and wisecracks so strong even I could attempt a joke or two, like a sixth Beach Boy doubling one part.

But though their community was inviting, at best it was infrequent and it didn't mean they knew *my* songs or the harmonies friends back home used to sing. C. S. Lewis writes in *The Four Loves* that "in each of my friends there is something that only some other friend can fully bring out. By myself I am not large enough to call the whole man into activity; I want other lights than my own to show all his facets." To which he could have added that we're not large enough people *ourselves* to show the whole of our being to others; each holds keys to compartments we cannot unlock on our own.

Not once during all the planning had I reckoned my move could cost me not just friendships but a part of myself as well . . . and yet it started to feel that way. When Hippie the Groper e-mailed to say he was moving to New York, I was delighted. Overnight, life held out hope not just of enjoying a friendship where we shared some history, but maybe finally resolving the summer that still lingered like a long-unhealed wound. Since the Captain had just brought the first of many short-term girlfriends to church, Hippie's timing couldn't have been better.

But though he almost immediately insisted on having dinner with me, my friend had little insight on the spiritual fallout of Berkeley except to tell me its swath cut wider and deeper than just those of us on the project. Turned out most of the Project Pals I remembered no longer called themselves Christians.

Except Poster Boy. Apparently he was off to South America lately, working on some revival there. I'm not even sure why I asked about him, but somehow that news put an end to the way disappointment with other men sometimes brought up fleeting memories of that brief crush, always tinged with sadness and bitterness. Whatever gender fault line once opened between us was a slight thing compared with this unlikely comrade's shared zeal for God in the aftermath of that summer. *The most wounded guy is the one seeking God most passionately? Huh.*

When I spied a likely e-mail address for him in some mass mailing Hippie sent out around October or November, I added Poster Boy to my list for the New York anecdotes I'd begun to e-mail home. Since he never responded to ask I quit spamming him—and I couldn't believe he'd still hold a job he hated three years previously (as the e-mail address suggested)—I decided it must be a dud account that somehow never sent "bounce" announcements.

Not that my updates had high response rates generally. But as I slowly settled in to New York, such brief essays helped me find my voice as a writer—garnering just enough feedback from readers to keep me sending the e-mails. Initially I saw the city through the eyes of a have-not. In an early message, I wrote of it as a "crème brûlée" I hadn't yet managed to eat: "It's both sickening and tantalizing at times, but I can't really get below the surface to enjoy all the exciting contents beneath; seems like I keep scraping flakes off the top."

That started to change on my N train one day, when a man came through asking that we at least give him smiles if not change. I began to see him often and realized my train line must be his equivalent of the corner he would have claimed in Tempe or Berkeley. Though some of his fingers were missing, he had more joy than the scores of others who proved to be part of the subway ritual, whether by begging or singing or preaching or even dancing.

One day I gave him a muffin I had left over from the morning, although it was slightly smashed from my purse. He smiled broadly and said, "I'm gonna enjoy this." If my life in Arizona had been like a houseplant overflowing the pot with tendrils and leaves aplenty, it had been severely pruned for transit and showed no signs of sending out new shoots yet. But when I gave him the muffin that day, it felt like one of those branch stubs bravely crept over the edge of the pot and a new leaf started to unfurl.

Subway Guy was one of my first friends in the city, and nothing made my day quite like seeing him on my train ride home. Whenever a friend or relative came to visit me, I always hoped we would see him so they could meet him. Then late in the year I decided to leave my high-rent flat in Astoria for dodgier digs in Williamsburg. Which meant I'd be riding a different line.

As I lugged my last load of belongings to the N train on a dreary day in January, I realized I hadn't yet seen Subway Guy to announce my move. When the train came, I heaved my bundles into the car and slouched forlornly in an orange plastic seat. But just as I was settling into my sadness, what should I hear from the rear of the train? That gravelly, cheerful-though-weary patter—the most welcome voice I could ask for. When Subway Guy reached my row, I jumped up to hug him, surprised at the tears slipping down my cheeks.

In retrospect, that gracious gift of getting to say good-bye had more in common with my long-ago spring break miracle than I thought to give it credit for. Both fleeting encounters left me temporarily serene, overwhelmed with a sense of gratitude almost too big for one soul to contain. And at the same time, both briefly loosened the grip of panic that God's plan for my life was less than truly good.

Such trust was a radically different posture than most of my encounters with the Captain produced. I made that move to Brooklyn in early 2003, after a Christmas visit from Bro. One day while taking a brewery tour, we bumped into the Captain and a sidekick of his, resulting in several group outings over the holidays. The highlight for me was one slightly muzzy exchange in which the Captain had waxed adorably vexed about the latest Tolkein movie: whereas the first had been guilty of "sins of omission," Part Two he charged with "sins of commission." *A rhymer just like my grandpa, and he was hitting it off with my sibling!*

But though that was probably the best memory of the holiday, the joy it gave was fleeting. Whereas recalling that final meeting with Subway Guy still has a power to calm, thoughts of that bump-in at the brewery were like the well-gnawed bone a miser sucks in hopes there's some trace of marrow he might have missed before. This desperate sense of grasping after a treasure I'd really never had to begin with must have tainted more than my remembering, for I never got that far with the Captain: trying to win over his stomach earned me more disdain than compliments, and when I replaced a much prized if obscure shirt taken when his car was robbed that winter, he said he would have preferred the next smaller size.

You'd think by then a sane woman would have moved on. Especially since, no matter how long I pined and prayed, I couldn't shake a sense that the Captain wasn't God's will for me—at least not now, at least not romantically. The room that held my desire for him had a sizable pile of dust in the corner that nothing could sweep away. And yet in a weird way, that wrongness made him an ideal distraction for my heart. Although we weren't even close to dating, I'd done with the Captain exactly what some do with a string of girlfriends or boyfriends: used him like beer for a thirst you want to silence instead of slake.

It's hardly a novel strategy; I can't count how many friends I've seen get burned by caring deeply for someone, then move on with a safely less emotional thing—whether that be dating a married man or a girl who'd never once make you want to grow old with her. It's shitty and self-protective, but let's face it—giving your whole self to another, risking exposure (and further disappointment) of your deepest longings, seems a price too high to pay once you've been cut down at the knees by one who only wants you defenseless so they can gash up your unguarded heart. Instead we seek to self-tranquilize, to subdue the thrashing and throbbing.

At least that's how people cope with the pain of old wounds; when it's the pain of loneliness, we masturbate. Both lead one to relate to people as objects meant to serve you instead of those you're called to love. (What sort of things do you imagine, after all?) The Bible says the Christian ought to put others' interests before his own—which can't be any less true in romance and sex. But I doubt that most who lament their single and celibate state are missing that chance to serve (except as kindness meets some self-centered need like mine did).

No, what we're missing is *being* served, the pleasure a partner would bring. The truth is, if we wanted to serve, there is no lack of nonsexual opportunities. But when you obsess on your singleness, it's hard not to wind up mourning a void it seems only sex would fill. Unfortunately, that doesn't move you toward satisfaction; it makes it even less likely. In order to be satisfied, you have to actually be hungry—you have to accept being empty. I'd gradually learned that lesson in terms of food, but letting my hunger for relationship go unstaunched by either a crush, a few dates, or even masturbation was much harder.

Once you've become used to grasping, it's hard to accept that the answer might lie in letting go completely. It's like we've all been sent forth into life unclothed except for a sheet we can either attempt to cover ourselves with or wrap around someone more needy than us. It seems that if we extend that aid, it means leaving ourselves exposed to the harsh winds of life. And yet, as far as I can tell, that's exactly what we Christians are called to do—become a radically generous community in which we use what we've been given not for the sake of meeting our own needs, but each others'.

I *did* want to show that kind of love to the Captain in some sense, but most of my seemingly generous gestures were canny attempts to draw him closer to me. This led to sufficient unease and disappointment when he didn't respond as hoped for such that by spring I started to sense I might need outside help addressing my crush. Once I left my first job, for an employer that offered health insurance, I started seeing a counselor.

She gave me a couple books to read, and sometimes I managed to cry in sessions, but nothing produced a major "aha" that cured my soul right then. Finding more first dates on Craigslist didn't help either. Though I didn't realize it at the time, this slowly fueled a growing anger beneath the surface.

Looking back now, it's remarkable both how generous God was in that season, and how patiently He let my sin grow till it was ripe for weeding. By September 2003, I'd come through New York's blackout with more memories than sweat, was settling into a swank job editing music education textbooks, had a fab new roommate with whom I sublet a spacious pad in Park Slope, and a wing woman for my adventures who soon dubbed me her best friend. When Sis came to visit for ten days, it was the perfect chance to parade my posse before the Captain. *These people think I'm cool! Couldn't you find a way to agree?*

SHOCK-N-AWE, OR THE WEST POINT TRIP FROM HELL

Sis had flown out from Seattle to recover and have some fun after a long, intensive summer at what was essentially boot camp for marine officers. Being the typically ignorant civilian, I assumed she'd like to catch an *army* football game. Though Sis made early noises of reluctance (she thought I mostly wanted to scope the Captain's turf), we planned it as a foursome with Best Friend and Guy Friend #1.

Sis had instantly declared the Captain an asshole and was turned off by how much time he appeared to spend readying his appearance each day. But I found hope in an e-mail he'd sent months ago that had eleven gyrating cows GIFs in it, all lined up in a row—eleven cows, inserted after which he had written, "The best effect is achieved by lining up lots of them, but that's too time consuming to bother with." Isn't there some story about the man who gets a "ten-cow wife" when he deliberately overpays the dowry price set by her father? Perhaps this was a sign he deemed me an eleven-cow girl.

Notwithstanding my high hopes that eleven cows = strong interest on his part, the Captain and I maintained a dubious "friendship" outside church, peppered with occasional, goal- or question-focused e-mails on my part, prompt but terse replies on his. (I later learned he liked an empty inbox.) In the football game exchange, the Captain told me how to reach the game but said he didn't think he'd have time to "hang out" with us during, should he happen to see us there. Some matter of long-standing plans with friends.

Sis and I thought this was lame but certainly didn't need him to have fun. We'd have Guy Friend #1 in tow! He would help us split the cab fare from the train station to the game, where Best Friend was meeting us. The Captain assured me the cab number was well marked on signs at the station, and said fare should run fifteen dollars.

We reached the Garrison station fine and sure enough, there's a big yellow sign. Someone calls the number from a cell phone that still has service, and shortly thereafter a van pulls up. We establish a nice rapport with the driver, with whom Sis starts talking military stuff. Everything seems great. Then we pull up to the stadium, and he tells us, "Fifteen dollars . . . each." We just about died. Forty-five for a cab ride!!! A ten- to fifteen-minute cab ride! Coming from New York, it never occurred to us to establish the cab's rate before getting in. Plus, the Captain's e-mail never suggested I might need to do that. Later it turned out he'd never actually taken one of those cabs before.

At least tickets to the game were cheaper than we had expected—somewhat offsetting the forty-five dollars. Still, we three kept telling each other, like thirsty people trying to talk the rain into falling, "Best Friend had better show up, because we need her to drive us to the train afterward." Only problem: terrible phone reception throughout the game, which basically sucked. The reception and the game, that is. Neither Army's offense—or was it defense?—or Best Friend ever showed up. No sign of the Captain either.

By game's end, we were none of us super-chipper. First thing, we start trying to pin down cheap transit back—determined not to get soaked for another half-Benjamin. In this collective mood, the Captain became an easy scapegoat for our troubles. As we were leaving the game, Sis and Guy Friend took to calling him "the asshole" because he was "too busy" to even talk to us.

Desperation hadn't quite caught up with us yet, but as we wandered down the darkening street away from the stadium, hope grew faint. Rather than face the prospect of getting stuck or overcharged again, we focused on finding food, ending up at this little Italian restaurant that probably had a line only given the town's few other eateries. We order the worst excuse for drinks I've ever had, while Guy Friend keeps stressing that phone reception is still as bad as ever, if not worse. (He keeps going outside to confirm this, currying wrath from the restaurant management, who keep shouting at the crowd we barely beat to keep the front door closed while they wait.)

Midway into our second round, the waitress informs us the place has a three-drink per-person limit. Limit—not minimum, *limit*. In a military town. Either we looked like alkies or they hoped to free up our table shortly.

Instead we ordered food. But though we asked that our chili-topped nachos come without any onions (which she'd duly scribbled down), they arrived with the garnish not just chopped but *minced*. Finely.

By then all we wanted was to pay the bill and leave. But this resurrected the old problem. Despite the many failings so far experienced with her employer, we ask the waitress how one finds a taxi. No luck. No one we ask has any ideas, except a cop who suggests we might want to try the police station. That was about as helpful as anyone in that damn town got. Pass the buck.

Past a crowd of kids smoking pot in front of a church (stoned but helpful enough to offer to help us find a phone book—oh but wait! We're not getting service anyway) we end up at the West Point police station. We squeeze into the cramped lobby, peering through a small window to explain our minor predicament to the cop on duty.

"Did you try 866–TAXI?"

We frantically dig out the business cards from our forty-five-dollar driver to make sure that isn't his number.

"Nope."

She calls the number she has, but gets a machine. "Well, just keep trying." She scribbles the number on some paper she pushes through the slotted window, effectively closing our little interview.

Back outside on the curb, we try our nonworking phones again. Eventually I get through to 866–TAXI, but the guy tells me they're "occupied."

With all resources exhausted, Guy Friend and Sis prevail on me to call the Captain for help, insisting he owes us a ride to the station. I call, and get his voice mail. Leave a message.

Guy Friend then pulls out the taxi man's yellow business card, in utter desperation. Decides to pretend we haven't used the service, and to inquire about the price. I suggest he also try the Captain, from *his* phone—in case the Captain is screening his calls or something equally lame. (As far as I know, he's probably getting sloshed with his better-than-us friends in some hip, dive-y West Point bar we'd never have the luck to stumble into.)

Although he'd met the Captain once, and said all of maybe five words to him, Guy Friend makes the call with some reluctance . . . and actually gets through. Sis cannot believe it.

"Captain? This is Guy Friend #1. I met you Sunday. We're in kind of a predicament . . . "

Ah, but desperation makes him brilliant. The Captain is, after all, a literary man. Strategic use of words like "predicament" as opposed to "fix," "situation," or "problem" is bound to be more effectively guilt-inducing.

Between combinations of groveling and mild exaggeration designed to provoke sympathy and obligation, Guy Friend persuades the Captain to come pick us up and drive us to the train station. Apparently he grumbled about losing a prime parking spot, but he agreed to come.

Twenty minutes later, a little white station wagon zips up in front of the Dunkin' Donuts. The Captain waves us over, hurries us in, and takes off at ferocious speed. The man's in this little family car, but he's driving like a *maniac*. Not that aggression is unattractive, of course, but in this case it was hard to tell if the speed was mustered on our behalf or in a desperate effort to regain that golden parking spot. (It later turned out he'd been home when we called, and didn't want to get stuck entertaining us if we missed the ten o'clock train.)

We didn't, but it was a wild ride. Tires are squealing on the turns, but the Captain's all bravado: "Yeah, my tires squeal. It's not like I'm peeling out or anything."

I, meanwhile, after the most crap-ass blue "mojito" I've ever had the misfortune to drink, a whiskey shot on ice . . . and the adrenaline of all this craziness . . . am in rare form indeed. For once, I've overcome my normal fear of talking to the Captain, to the point of interrupting answers to his questions. He's playing the affable rescuer, and making polite inquiries.

"So, Guy Friend #1, what do you do?"

Guy Friend explains the software gig with an Internet start-up he helped to launch, and I interject: "Yeah, he's the originator of this software program that lets people keep a daily journal of things like how often they jack off." Of course, they journal other things too, but I knew the Captain would like this example.

"See! You couldn't get through a conversation without mentioning it."

"Well, I haven't talked about it in a while," I say, all inno-cence. "I usually save all that stuff for when I first meet people. I wouldn't want to end up with some conservative Christian guy . . . "

"Shock and awe," my sister deadpans from the backseat.

As the car erupted in uproarious laughter, I felt both satis-faction at their mirth and an unpleasant sense that Sis had just hit on an unflattering but important truth, the likes of which not even counseling had yielded. Such shtick was more self-protective than flirtatious (except with secular men), but possi-bly I sensed the imminent downturn in our "friendship." If things had to end as I feared they would, at least shock and awe gave me some way to control the grounds on which rejection happened.

CHAPTER 12

KILLING ME SOFTLY THAT HE'S WRONG

There is no worse pain for fallen people than facing an emptiness we cannot fill. To enter into pain seems rather foolish when we can run from it through denial. We simply cannot get it through our head that, with a nature twisted by sin, the route to joy always involves the very worst sort of internal suffering we can imagine.

—LARRY CRABB, *Inside Out*

There were days that fall when I finally cracked through the top of the crème brûlée and scooped up giant, wondrous spoonfuls: one night I got word of a hush-hush concert Norah Jones gave in an act billed as a Willie Nelson cover band. A month or so later, I got to discuss a lesson plan with no less than Les Paul (though I had no clue why this was the big deal I sensed it was; that took research the next day). Those were the almost-free things you could never create or plan on. But when it came to scoring seats for that year's New York Film Festival, I lucked out simply because I made more money now. Well, that, and I was hoping to catch the same show that the Captain went to. I *thought* he'd sort of invited me, but it turned out I was wrong.

Technically he was responding to my attempts to gather a crowd—but who says, "Yes, I'm going to that thing you wanted to see and hoped to attend with others" just for your information? Apparently, the Captain. And since he was the only respondent to my group e-mail about taking in the festival, I had no alternate seatmates when he announced his plans to see that year's headline flick.

I reply via e-mail, asking about the particulars. No response. Attempts to reach him by telephone also fail. He is unreachable. Forced to research things, I learn there are *two* showings—neither of which he's specified. Debate ensues: the Captain has responded to my e-mail, seemingly taking up my invitation to make plans, yet he has proven both unavailable and unforthcoming as to details of said meet-up. Tickets are likely sold out, but the festival website mentions possible standby admission.

Since I'd had such good luck seeing *Letterman* that way, why not give it a shot? I decide to try for the earlier showing, and leave the Captain one last message with my viewing particulars. That, and a casual invite to call if he should be going out afterward—so we can, you know, discuss.

I go, I get a ticket, I get a decent seat with a nice view of all the celebrities there.

I don't get a call from the Captain. In fact I get no word at all until I see him in church Sunday morning, resulting in the muted showdown that was as close as we ever came to actually fighting. In my mind, his actions put him beyond the pale for even friendship, though he claimed neither slight nor invite was intended.

After that, he was the Asshole to me too. How had I let myself get this hurt by a Jesus freak *again?!!* I thought I had fairly carefully held to the line between friendly and more-than-friendly contacts. We were both new in the city, we had many common interests . . . why wouldn't I reach out to another transplant New Yorker? He had seemed to reach back. But when things reached a point he didn't like, did he actually say something?

Confrontation I could have handled, and probably would have respected him for. After all, what I wanted most from him was not necessarily interest but the chance to exchange that conversation I'd so rarely found since grad school. I'd even read books by the author he wrote his thesis on, in hopes of finding a neutral topic to talk about. But when I told the Captain I'd like to hear his thoughts on *Wise Blood,* he asked why I wanted to discuss Flannery O'Connor with *him.*

In retrospect, it's not all that surprising that around the same time as our falling out I made a half-drunken offer one night—when secular guy friend 5 Percent Man had walked me and Best Friend home from a party—to let him come up and "go 95 percent of the way" with me (we'd had one date and several flirtatious IM sessions). Though I'd dated plenty of guys who would have jumped at the chance, 5 Percent Man refused with a chuckle, and left me with just a hug good-bye. He later told me he knew I couldn't have handled something so casual.

At the time, however, I saw this not as God's kindness but as a pattern of Him letting me get hurt. First there was all that went down with the Captain, then just shy of two weeks later I had Ad Weasel treating me as if I were a prostitute. And as if that weren't quite enough, by Halloween I was well on my way to having myself a stalker. Not in the creepy, waiting-outside-your-house kind of way, but in the desperate "You told me emphatically not to call you, so I'm ringing you up to try to resolve this" kind of way. And this was a guy from my Bible study!

Little wonder that by November I thought about actually going back to the Winner. It happened on my bus to the airport, en route to a Thanksgiving trip with my parents. Because they were leaving Singapore at year's end, I'd planned a final trip abroad which, since they wanted to take a holiday, meant meeting up in New Zealand. But while I was still in the States, still riding my bus to JFK, I spy some single guy who reminds me of the Winner, whom I start thinking about: how he's the *last good Christian guy* I liked, the only one who was ever kind to me, and how—*in fact*—the reason I liked the Captain was that he *reminded* me of the Winner.

I am so overcome by this vision, I practically weep. During the five-hour flight to L.A., I fill a sheaf of pages in my journal. All about him.

Because, clearly, a man you've not seen in four years, much less talked to in eighteen months, is quite a prospect indeed. And it's very productive—in general—when current prospects dry up, to simply flip back through the pages of old journals in search of a man you left behind. When true love fails, consult your past. You probably just whizzed by Mr. Right.

Which is precisely what happened on that trip! In a plane, high above, I whizzed right by the Winner's Albuquerque home. It was a most auspicious sign. Once in New Zealand, I dig up a moldy address in my Yahoo! contact archives and send a postcard to his mother. After all, there's nothing like a good connection with his mom to turn a feller's heart to yours! And the Winner's mom and I, though we had never met face to face . . . we had this special bond. I mean, there'd been *phone* calls—more-than-two-minute phone calls! We even had this thing once, when she helped me construct a twenty-second-birthday care package. (Okay, so that was our only "thing"—but still!)

Apparently she got the postcard, but the contact info kindly scribbled in the margin must have been covered with a sticker or something; she never wrote back. Like mother, like son—except he'd had way more chances, thanks to all those update e-mails. And maybe that was a sign too, whether I was willing to admit it or not.

Once back in the States—and sort of back in reality—I resolved to call him up and ask if I should just remove him from my e-mail list. He clearly wasn't into me—was probably by now married to that girlfriend he'd had! If I could just get word of that . . . *Voilà!* All thoughts of crush rekindling safely quashed.

But when I called—and reached him, chatting roughly half an hour—all seemed friendly, even open. Then came the shocker: that girlfriend of three years was, as of recently, the Winner's girlfriend no more. *Oh.* It wasn't exactly an open door, but it left me with enough hope God might yet provide good things in love that I was forced to face the larger issue: *He wouldn't do so on my time.*

This happened to be a major theme in the book my counselor loaned me, Larry Crabb's classic, *Inside Out.* In it Crabb says we must learn to live with both desire and pain—desire because God made us to long for Him and the perfection He first created, pain since those longings cannot be fully met until everything is restored when Jesus returns. To fail to grapple with both is to "maintain the fiction that life is tolerable at worst and quite satisfying at best . . . [In which view] the Cross becomes the means by which God delivers us from something not really too terrible, and the Coming is reduced to an opportunity for a merely improved quality of life."

The hardest implication of this was what it meant for relationships. Crabb says flinching from both desire and pain subtly warps the way we relate to others so that our self-protective motives almost always trump the attempt to love sacrificially. To really love others the way God calls His people to, Crabb said I had to get past my fear of being hurt and disappointed. Not that this was about some sort of Christian masochism where boundaries don't exist, but what did we think Jesus meant when He said that we "take up a cross" in following Him? The kind of love He calls us to is not exactly easy, but that makes it no less worth giving.

That winter, God started to show me how to love both Him and others better, which meant letting go of the focus on *my* "needs" and letting God have His way with my life. I'd wanted the end result, but largely in ignorance of the process it might take to get there. So as God let me stew in loneliness, while Bro proposed to his girlfriend, I got angrier and more depressed. Then New Year's Eve launched another painful round with the Captain and testing began in earnest.

A DAY OF PAIN AND THEN SOME

Last year it had been Bro with me; this time it was Sis, whose ticket Best Friend and Guy Friend #1 pitched in to buy. Between hosting not just Sis but sometimes Best Friend (who still lived a ways out in Jersey) and for a couple nights even one of Roommate's friends from the South, we had ourselves quite a houseful that holiday. For the most part, I loved this. But when said posse met up with the Captain and all his friends in Astoria—plus that sidekick of his, who was visiting from Colorado again—it led to more tears than joy.

The New Year's party went well enough. In fact, on the drive home, to my surprise, Best Friend announced that Sidekick and the Captain wanted to hang with us all the next night to go dancing. Considering the Captain had never been keen on shaking a leg before (except in his impressions of Mick Jagger), I was surprised. Apparently his recent trip to Europe with Sidekick showed him that white men could make peace with their hips.

Sis and I wanted to make peace with our wilder side, so the next day we trekked to the East Village to launch 2004 with our long-awaited "day of pain" (in which she got inked, I pierced). After recovering over burritos and beer, we met the others for drinks and dancing. What they had in mind, however, was neither disco nor swing dance (forms I would have enjoyed), but that strange American pastime of grinding with strangers in dim-lit clubs. Except that this time it didn't mean strangers for the Captain, it meant Best Friend.

All of which was fairly platonic and understandable—caught between chatting up some stranger and dancing with the girls he came with, he chose the latter. And given his awkward history with me, there was no chance he'd single me out on the dance floor. But to be there, in a loud, sweaty club playing music I barely endured, dancing "with" some guy I had no interest in (except that he left some space between us)—while watching Sis grin at me from the arms of *her* stranger and glimpsing Best Friend chatting and dancing with the Captain—was too much.

Though I adored her for many reasons—and most of all as the first friend who'd ever verbalized a commitment to me by calling me her *best* friend—she was the sort of dominant, talented, striking blonde an insecure girl would be terrified to introduce to her crush. I'd always tried not to let Best Friend's strengths intimidate, but it's hard when your friend lives on the same thing you do—male attention—and when she's getting it from the guy whose esteem you've futilely sought for months.

By the time we left that night, I was furious. At and about what, I didn't even know, so when I heard the words of cold rage spilling off my lips, I was just as shocked as anyone. Something in me had broken beneath the strain of misery masquerading as pleasure thanks to the velvet curtain across the door. Never, I vowed, would I endure another evening in a place like that.

Of course it wasn't really the club that had roused such anger, but I wasn't ready to access those wounds yet. Although I'd patched things up with the Captain, we'd never addressed the *real* issue. We never discussed how we should interact as fellow Christians, given that I had obviously liked him and he had no like interest. Instead he gradually backed away, which I took as him dismissing me both sexually and otherwise. I was, as feared, worthless, while, judging from tonight, Best Friend was quite worthy.

I don't remember much of our ride back to Brooklyn, but once we got home to make room for Best Friend on the floor, we found out Sidekick had somehow wound up crashing at our place! (Don't ask me why; I only know it wasn't sexual.) That night we slept six people in our snug two-bedroom apartment.

While Best Friend and Sis arranged things in the living room, I sat at the kitchen table and cried quietly till they found me, which of course led to dismay I was so grieved, and heartfelt assurances Best Friend never meant to hurt me. Which of course I had to accept. The ultimate issue—the way she sought validation from men—was too sensitive and mutual. How could I fault Best Friend for seeking and getting something I pursued just as avidly? Wasn't the main thing that she'd never hook up with the Captain? Though my heart said no, I pledged to forgive her.

By the time I got up on Saturday, Best Friend had driven Sidekick into the city for his brunch plans with the Captain and another guy, which she wound up getting to join. I went and brunched with Sis, while Roommate dined separately with her friend, but food did little for the wounds festering within. It still felt like a wrong had been done, but the only standard to which I could appeal was one I had dismissed as readily as she. Was I ready to deal with how much *I* had fallen short of it?

When Best Friend finally joined us all, for an afternoon tour of the brewery where Bro and I had bumped into the Captain, she brought an invite to see him elsewhere: he and Sidekick and some of their friends were checking out this Lower East Side burlesque bar tonight. Did we want to join? I actually considered staying home, but the fellowship of the group we'd have ultimately trumped my fear of another miserable evening.

As I went into the bathroom to get ready beforehand—a rare, if humid chance to escape the bustle of so many guests—I begged God for strength to make it through the night. And for once I was pleading not for things to work out well (whatever that might look like) but for Him to grant guidance and wisdom and grace and, most of all, His *presence*.

This soon produced a practical quandary, since choosing to go it on God's strength also meant doing things His way: what could I wear that wasn't the fashion equivalent of pulling more shock-n-awe? After some debate, I went with low-key threads: new kick-ass green boots I'd gotten cheap at a sample sale, red plaid pants from a vintage store in Seattle, and a nondescript, long-sleeve black T-shirt purchased in Paris. They were small but critical choices to go with no plan for control or revenge, to let God be my only defender.

SALVATION FROM THE SOUTH

For all that Etta had steered me wrong by promising a man would ease my heartache, I'm always amazed when God allows or chooses just such an instrument for His work in my life. Why

He saw fit that I should catch the eye of the hottest and probably most eligible guy there that night is baffling, but I was more than happy to comply with that plan.

When we reached Burlesque Bar, our advance party had scored seats for us all at two tables near the stage. This was no mean feat as said group included Sidekick, the Captain, a visiting friend of theirs from college, the Two from Texas, plus one other longtime friend of the Captain's who'd recently relocated here with his girlfriend (the pair henceforth dubbed SuperCouple). And that was just their group. Our posse consisted of me, Best Friend, Sis, Roommate, and her guest (whom we'd dubbed George since she hailed from Georgia).

We settle into our early-bird seats, drink up, and admire the premises. From the low tin ceiling to the gilt proscenium flanked by two Victorian cherubs, a DJ stand on the left, and vaguely Art Deco ironwork on a staircase extending beneath the stage on the right, the general effect is much more hip than tawdry—this in keeping with all the Very Cool restaurants and bars outside, chock-a-block on the one-way streets. In fact, it was rather like that neighborhood where I first drank tequila.

Unlike that night, this crush is on surprisingly good behavior (though he buys no drinks): the Captain asks how our day's been, chats with Sis, even winds up talking with me of obedience and Christianity. Somehow we managed to skirt the ethics of seeing burlesque although, while we were chatting, some bored-looking woman in a circa-fifties bathing suit got up and started dancing in front of the velvet curtain strung across the stage.

She carries on for an hour with this strange go-go dance, but watching her pulls me into her boredom. *Maybe this was a good time for a bathroom break.* Shortly before the show starts, I go downstairs to join the coed queue for the toilets.

In front of me is a woman who must be cute but looks impatient because the man in front of her strikes up a conversation that he attempts to extend to everyone else in line. Though I don't really participate, I learn from their exchange that Chatty Gray-Haired Man, who looks late thirties, is here with a posse to see their friend, some comedian.

At that I interject: "Men do burlesque?"

Brief banter ensues until the line moves ahead again and I go back upstairs for the show.

By this time a woman straight from an old-time vaudeville poster has chased away the go-go dancer and started her own, much more impressive show. She is the epitome of what one expects from burlesque, for which the patrons reward her with singles they stuff in her plus-size fishnets—men and *Bust*-reading women alike. It's bawdy, sure, but campy enough we all feel more inclined to wink than leer. *It's a joke, see?*

The club is slowly filling up, and once the show starts, most leave the tables to stand up and push toward the stage for a better view. Our host is a man in a bunny costume, who wears tall clear stilettos like a pro. This portly, blue-suited Cinderella introduces a series of performers, the most entertaining and least naked of whom is a guy known as the Comedian, who comes out to do a high-energy dance as Wonder Woman—small yellow costume and all.

It's his routine that clinches our relief: we're not watching women get naked for our *titillation* but in a sly, ironic sendup of beauty that spurns the oppressive perfection of our fantasy culture in favor (and praise) of normal human curves. It's all so countercultural! And all too soon, it's over, at least for a bit.

During the intermission, Bored-Looking Go-Go Girl returns, and much of our party reconvenes outside for a first- or secondhand smoke break. I come along to chat with Best Friend and a couple of the guys, who are all there to partake of the Captain's fine cigarette-rolling skills (perhaps it had been ash in my heart's corner). Inexplicably, Roommate's friend comes too, although George doesn't smoke and barely knows anyone. She proves a new fan of the Captain, but I am less concerned by their talk than what George says to Best Friend shortly after.

Because of our close contact that weekend, she'd learned a few of our secrets—one of which, in Best Friend's case, George felt free to say she disapproved of. Though she was quick to assure Best Friend she still liked her, I knew George had crossed a line with my friend. Before I could tell if I'd have to smooth things over, however, we heard the Blue Bunny returning for Act II.

I trailed the others inside the bar, but hung back to stand on a bench beside our table, rather than peer through the crowd of shoulders (flat boots gave me less of my normal height advantage, or maybe it was a tall crowd). This new view made me privy to the Captain's ongoing chat with George, but also revealed a strikingly handsome man in the audience—whom I pointed out to whichever girl was at my side. We both agreed he clearly must be gay, if not an underwear model, then turned back to the stage for the Comedian's reprise—this time an all-out version of "Flashdance."

As I'm bouncing around to the song—won over more by the Comedian than the song—it occurs to me this might be the friend of the man in line downstairs. Which might explain why, during that dance, Chatty Gray-Haired Man and the beautiful gay underwear model have moved close to our table and are standing on empty seats to see the performance.

Just then, however, I catch part of an exchange between Best Friend and Roommate, who's being told she should inform George about how I used to like the Captain—if she doesn't already know this. He certainly wasn't my "territory" to claim like that, but as Roommate dutifully dragged George off, I was distracted from saying so by some vague sense the underwear model had noticed me. *Had he just checked me out?* I ponder a pretext for talking to Chatty Gray-Haired Man and as soon as the Comedian finishes his "Flashdance," casually join the cluster of men.

I've barely asked Chatty which performer he knows when I find myself talking to his friend . . . who doesn't seem very gay at all. In fact, I'm getting a kind-of-interested vibe. We start discussing where we're from, and I learn that he's Peruvian. I say I'm from Seattle, and he tells a story of living there briefly and jogging with his girlfriend.

His girlfriend . . . So he's not gay!!! We keep talking, and it just keeps getting better: the Peruvian runs his own nonprofit, and his father used to be high up in the government of his homeland. When a coup ran them out in the seventies, the family moved to New Jersey (hence his friendship with the Comedian), where the Peruvian's dad became a professor at Princeton!!

As I'm attempting to find my jaw among all the feet on the floor, we're sort of, but not really, watching the rest of Act II unfold. Since I'm no longer up on a bench, I can't really see what's on stage, which means standing up on tiptoes whenever there's a big reaction. Then the Peruvian hands me his beer.

"Here, take this," he says, and the next thing I know, he's picked me up so I can see over the crowd and report back on the stripper's routine. That might have been the point when he told me he used to play pro soccer.

Somehow I manage not to swoon or drool, and we keep talking (while mentally I make note that should things ever work out between us, I can say he "swept me off my feet" the very first night we met). When I ask why he lives in New York—as business clearly takes him south, several weeks if not months a year—the Peruvian says he loves the city. Lived in Hong Kong briefly, but loves New York. Oh, and he's looking for a wife. Apparently they're hard to find back home.

If my eyes weren't as big by then as those of the first-timers watching the stage, it was a miracle equaling God's provision that I *meet* this man. Somehow I dodge this obvious chance to mention how many babies I once dreamed of bearing, and instead presume he's found this commitment-eager paragon: "Oh, but I thought you had a girlfriend."

He clarifies my tenses. And thus we establish that he is not only a straight man, but a single one. In search of a wife.

Once Act II concludes, we find a table and move beyond his tantalizing bio. As time goes by and especially after I've reapplied my lip gloss—cheap, but loaded with lots of sparkles—I start seeing something in his eyes I've rarely, maybe never, felt from a man before: a powerful interest reined in by deliberate restraint. (Most guys I'd dated had treated sex like a sprinter's race that went to the guy who got closest before ejection from your embrace.)

The Peruvian was a patient man—at least, he said, with me—and that self-control, combined with his interest, got me all jumpy and giddy inside. What I didn't know until much later, however, was how much my lack of striving had to do with that. When we later had a chance to discuss that night, he said he was quite attracted but knew I was the sort of girl you only got serious with.

Had I been more intent on attention, or dressed a bit more provocatively, things might have gone quite differently. But God had answered my prayer that night, and was quietly showing me how much better His way was than mine. *Trust me. I know the plans I have for you, plans to prosper you and not to harm you, plans to give you hope and a future.* Deep inside, that small big-eyed girl I'd had to build walls of shock-n-awe around to protect began to rouse herself from retreat.

I'd barely begun to relax when we were joined by a string of our friends: first the Comedian and his current girlfriend, then Sis and eventually Best Friend. For some reason she was quite off her game and halfway through introduction to the Peruvian made a horrible joke of his name.

What could have spoiled my golden evening was mercifully deflected as the Comedian willfully misunderstood her, dragging us out of this awkward moment and back to a bantering conversation. Best Friend hung out a few minutes more, then went back to the bar, where I glimpsed another tense exchange between her and Roommate.

"Somehow I feel like there's all this drama I missed tonight," I say to the Peruvian.

"Your blonde friend looks like she attracts drama."

"There's always drama where men and women are concerned." We smile, and go back to exploring the space our conversation has built.

Eventually those seated around us start to trickle away. First Roommate and her friend leave—Roommate probably looking strained and weary—but I barely notice anything until the Captain himself heads off and makes a point of saying good-bye, even giving me a *hug.* I could barely contain my glee that he practically had to drag me away from the Peruvian for that good-bye, but I doubt he noticed. Long after I'd recovered from him, and we'd progressed to some degree of candor, the Captain confessed he and George had gotten sufficiently cozy that night to justify all Best Friend's suspicions and protective interference. But for whatever reason, God's way of getting me through that evening was not interfering with that other attraction, but challenging my notion of what was possible with a man. It wouldn't be the last time.

Once it approaches 3 a.m., the few of us still remaining decide to get pizza across the street. But although the Peruvian buys my slice, I start fighting fear that maybe he doesn't like me that much. He certainly had seemed interested, but since he wasn't all grabby or touchy, paranoia set in. *The only guys who really pursue are the ones who get pretty physical.*

Our party at last gets up to leave, and a sudden dread chokes me that this just might be it: good-bye in a crowd, good-bye under bright lights, and no exchange of phone numbers.

Fortunately it's chivalrous for him to walk me to the car, trailing Best Friend and Sis. In desperation, I switch over to Big Anecdote mode, though sticking with safe stuff like the work I once did on my car, the Eunuch. He still makes no attempt to get more than friendly. *Nothing.*

Once we reach the car, the Peruvian says good-bye to my sister first. They hug, then she gets into the Benz, leaving us the space of silence, if no shield from her and Best Friend's riveted eyes. By now I'm in full-on panic: *He's not going to ask for my number!!*

I step into his brief hug good-bye, and finally he kisses me. Perhaps since my piece of pizza (which we'd shared) was heavy on garlic, it's just a peck . . . but *still.* Beside me I can almost feel the muffled reverberations from the car.

"I hope we see some more of you at Burlesque Bar," he says.

"Definitely!" *Is that it?*

He started to walk away, then slowly pivoted. "Well, maybe we can exchange numbers." We're lucky there was no live feed from my head or the interior of the sedan; he might have had his eardrums blown.

CHAPTER 13

A GAFFE MADE GOOD

I have drifted down a ways along the shoreline,
I just watched these ropes give way where they were tied.
I could have reached out quick when the ropes first slipped, if
I had tried
But I was wondering
where the wind was trying to take me
overnight, if I never did resist, and
what strange breezes make a sailor want to
let it come to this,
with lines untied, slipping through my fist.

—DAVID WILCOX, *"Slipping Through My Fist"*

I f I could go back and counsel the girl who floated into Best Friend's black Mercedes that night, I'd join her in a squeal or two, then remind her how God's purpose for the Winner had apparently been more general than specific. "Maybe He wants to build your hope in His goodness. Besides, is it likely a man you've just met at burlesque night really loves Jesus?" To which Anna Then would have doubtless objected that since the Captain and Roommate and Sis and the Two from Texas were also there, what did that really mean?

Such an answer would show, however, that I was making choices based not on my conscience or seeking to please God, but rather how they compared to hijinks like my errand at the sex shop or the college speech when I did my best impression of an Herbal Essences ad (the point was to argue commercials ought to be rated the same as TV shows, but I wasn't too swift at using the VCR's tape mode). By such standards, burlesque wasn't all that bad. And when compared to most of the men I'd liked or dated, this new guy looked pretty good.

This was more than could be said for my odds of a date with him, as days passed with no phone call. After his silence had stretched into a week, I grasped a flimsy excuse to rectify that. Perhaps a recent text-message issue had somehow erased his call and whatever voice mail he would have left! Despite the customer service assurance that probably wasn't the case, I reasoned the only honorable thing was to call him up and explain my hypothetical woes, reassuring him I did not at all intend rudeness, *had* he called.

Which he hadn't . . . but that didn't matter, for he rectified this by leaving a long rambling message (when my phone had died from a rare case of low battery), while he was at the airport waiting to catch a flight to Peru. For six weeks. In case I wanted to keep in touch, he carefully spelled out his e-mail address.

Although I sent a nice rambling reply, there was no response to my e-mail or its follow-up, sent from an alternate address in case my risqué username (referencing my swing-dance passion) had doomed me to his spam box.

Well, surely he was busy. And what better way to use this wait than doing a little research? When I wasn't reading a five-hundred-page "introduction" to Peru, I began dragging Best Friend to burlesque night, ostensibly as the Comedian's fan club. I'd tried to take a posse there, but both the Two from Texas and Roommate had said they felt uncomfortable returning.

The girl who'd quit reading a library book because two teens went skinny-dipping would probably have shared their unease, but she was buried far away, like a childhood doll discarded somewhere. All things considered, it's hard to say whose soul the battle raged fiercest for that winter: mine or Best Friend's.

When her father's cancer took a very grave turn toward the end of January, she started asking me to pray—and not just when we'd hung up or she'd gone home, but with her there listening. There was a stretch where Best Friend spent almost every Saturday night at our place, crashing there after the show at Burlesque Bar, and often coming to church with me the next morning. She started becoming a part of a circle of Christians including the Captain, the Two from Texas, Guy Friend #1, Roommate, and Sis (albeit the latter by long distance). Never had such a close friend seemed so open to being reconciled with Jesus.

And yet despite my ardent prayers—both for her father's life and Best Friend's soul—I was struggling profoundly to trust God was good at all. One Sunday after a brunch with Best Friend and the female half of the recently disbanded SuperCouple, I went home and almost had a total breakdown. It's right there on the journal page: you can see the sanity breaking apart as the letters grow larger and more erratic, then God slowly pulling me back together with each line that cries out to Him instead of focusing on the pain.

Somehow I pulled through, clinging wanly to an image God gave me that winter of 2004: that this was a kind of surgery, and the pain was a sign of life. If it had been up to me, I would have chosen numbness and death over life, but thankfully God is determined the good work He begins in His children should make it to completion.

It proved to be a season of grace for Best Friend's dad as well. By mid-March, he had improved enough that she took a trip down to Florida for a break. While she was away, I went to the birthday shindig of a near stranger I knew from a random Mediabistro event. Since he'd attended *my* birthday party, I felt I ought to reciprocate, though it meant braving a scene where I knew virtually no one.

I was making my final pass through the room when a blond with twinkling blue eyes above his turtleneck plucked me out of the crowd and drew me into his witty conversation with two others. Though he was full of cultural references I couldn't always match, my tongue proved beguiling enough that roughly a half hour later the Harvard Lickwit had grabbed my hand on the sly for an evening of banter and wordplay that ended in necking against a springy chain-link fence by the West 4th Street F-train entrance.

Although we shared more intellectual chemistry than I'd possibly yet found, his ardor was not that of a man who shared my faith. Not that Jesus freaks are passionless, but you tend to know when you've met one and when you haven't. As this sank in over the weekend, I wept several times amid jumbled thoughts of both the Peruvian and the Winner, and a conviction I should probably quit Burlesque Bar.

When Lickwit e-mailed Monday, however, I couldn't resist the bantering string of messages that ensued. Since Sis was making a spring-break visit and he had travels as well, we agreed to postpone our first date till the end of the month. Which left me free the following weekend to hang out with Hippie the Groper, some of his friends, Best Friend, and the on-again SuperCouple.

Conviction notwithstanding, I wound up suggesting Burlesque Bar, where we managed to catch the second act. It seemed to be our destiny: as we were crossing the street to the bar, I finally saw the Peruvian for the first time since our meeting, though he appeared to be departing.

Once we made it inside, it turned out SuperCouple had

scored seats near the stage—a perfect position from which to volunteer me when the Comedian said he needed help reprising a *Grease* skit we'd missed during Act I. He drags me backstage, squeezing into the closet-sized dressing room filled with the ladies who aren't performing, and tugs on a leather jacket while briefly sketching the skit. I'd barely read through my vulgar lines, scribbled on a half sheet of lined notebook paper, before the current routine was done and we were back onstage.

Lights! Dialogue! Big stage kiss (except, of course, quite real)!

And quietly, on the inside, death of the hope I'd ever go on a date with the Peruvian . . . who had of course returned by then. Once he'd seen this loud shock-n-awe persona vanquish the girl he'd been attracted to, why would he value me again?

TWO STOPS PAST DISCRETION

Perhaps that sense of worthlessness and despair explains how I wound up spending a tense night in the arms of Hippie the Groper one week later. Or maybe it was my increasing anger that Bro was getting married in less than two months.

However it happened, it started when Hippie and I made plans for a casual movie hangout the Friday after my Burlesque Bar debut, which made for a conflict with my Bible study. Since I didn't want to miss that, we agreed to meet up later. But then we couldn't decide what to see, and he was still in Williamsburg, so why not come see his new pad and watch a video there? It was only two stops on the L train . . .

Because he was not just a guy friend, but a connection I had to *Berkeley*, it never crossed my mind to say no. I catch the train, I find his place, and from there we walk to a Mexican restaurant for dinner. Since it's a bit of a walk back to his place, Hippie gives me a "buck" on the bike ride home (i.e., gave me the seat and his middle to hold while he stood on the pedals and steered us back). Although it had the thrill of slight peril, that breezy glide through the night felt like a childhood pleasure I'd somehow always missed out on till now.

Well, that, or the sort of low-key date I'd never managed to have before. But why would I think romantic thoughts when he was just a good friend of mine, and I'd had dinner and drinks that Tuesday with Lickwit?

We get back without a scrape, and settle onto a couch in the big drafty living room of the converted warehouse space, which is bisected by a second half floor of bedrooms. Since it's a little bit chilly, he grabs a blanket beneath which we settle to watch the small, faintly flickering images from the projector he's set up to play *This Is Spinal Tap*. Hippie later claimed we were cuddling by then, but I didn't think it counted since we were only sitting quite close. And hadn't I spent nights like this, watching TV with Guy Friend #1, even leaning against his shoulder sometimes? Nothing ever came of *that*—not even when I had once or twice crashed at his place.

But that had been in a normal apartment, where one of us could sleep on the couch in the living room while the other slept in the bedroom with the door closed. Which probably hadn't been all that wise, but since I'd sometimes crashed there with Sis or Best Friend—and once with all three of us girls sharing his bed together, Guy Friend on the couch—I never gave it much thought.

Hippie's place was different. And by the time the movie finished, the hour was pretty late. I started getting ready to leave, but secretly hoped he'd offer to put me up since the trip from his part of Brooklyn to mine is among the most inconvenient journeys within the subway system, especially late at night.

Sensing, perhaps, my reluctance to leave, Hippie offers to let me crash there. But as I'm eyeing my choice of couches, I can't overlook all the light streaming in through the windows from the street outside. Light I normally would have blocked out with my sleep mask—which is, of course, at home. Hippie's *bedroom*, by contrast, is closed off more like a normal room, and nice and dark besides. Once I've gone up there to get the change of clothes he offers as PJs, it's hard to forsake this obvious comfort. And he's so damn eager to serve!

Well . . . maybe if I just sleep right next to the wall.

Ignoring how strangely thin his borrowed T-shirt is, and the full alarm my conscience is now clanging, I bed down.

Because it was Hippie and we were "friends," there was no sex or kissing. But neither was there peace or sleep. Nothing he did felt completely bad, but what kept me there, and kept me from calling it quits midway—come cab fare, shame, or a long commute—was less enjoyment than tortured curiosity. Two opposing instincts within me were both screaming so loudly, I couldn't tell which one I wanted to follow. Hippie tried to relax things by teasing about my almost prudish passivity, but I spent most of the night more strung out than a cat toward the end of her ninth life.

When I got up on Saturday—rather early, since he had a morning art class—I faced my first real sense of sexual sin and shame. Even though, by some measures, things had technically been less intimate than some of my previous dates, I knew differently. And this had happened with someone I called a *friend*.

As caffeine from the latte Hippie had bought me slowly banished the stupor induced by my sleepless night, a mix of fear and confusion set in, eventually overcoming a vague desire for further exploration. *What had I just done? How had things come to this?* And most importantly, *What was God going to do to me?* Would I get put on intimacy restriction?

The strange thing about adulthood, when you're single, is that it's possible to go for fairly extended periods without facing blatant sin against another. When I still lived at home, disagreements were almost as frequent as meals—and so too apologies. But since I'd been living on my own, it was rare to wrong others in ways that held up such a mirror to my sinfulness. Sure, there was plenty of sin against *God,* but with such infrequent consequence—at least in the form of having to make peace—it was easy to self-congratulate on how much our relationship owed to my "righteousness," generosity, and enlightened theological views. Though for the past twenty months or so I'd been hearing a pastor whose constant theme was grace, it didn't hit home till I faced this proof of what the Bible says God considers depravity.

But in those early days of April, God swiftly assured me that no, He would not put me through some sort of fellowship quarantine till I'd completed proper penance. While this sin might carry consequences more serious than other things I'd done, it was only—as always—through Jesus's death that I could come to Him. It wasn't that I'd been "better" before, but that I'd been more deceived. My fundamental Sin before God had always been much worse than I perceived, but the grace He'd always shown was a much greater gift than I'd ever realized.

Although this sense of forgiveness gave me peace, that "sleepover" launched a difficult month. For the fourth time in less than two years, I had to pack up and move—and that was just the first of several daunting changes to come. Though Roommate moved with me to the cozy new place we'd leased ourselves, I was within a month of concluding my one-year contract job, within six weeks of my younger brother's wedding, and roughly three months from facing my twenty-sixth birthday, still quite single. It was too much change in less than two years; I was ready to be settled. And so, for the first time, I actually said in *prayer* to God, "Please bring me a husband." Whatever had kept me from asking before, I now felt at peace with that request.

Inevitably, this threatened further outings with the Lickwit. The Wednesday after my mid-April move, when I was puzzling over his silence since Saturday, Best Friend confessed she'd actually had an e-mail from Lickwit (they'd met when she wound up chaperoning several of our outings). According to what she forwarded me, he thought I was quite "darling," but not up to their "libertinism." Savvy leaking for a man who'd written speeches for the one-time head of the Stock Exchange.

Although Lickwit's e-mail also said he didn't want to break my heart by helping me break my standards, I'd grown so used to dating outside the church that realizing it could never work was a blow. After work, I wandered west on 32nd Street, then down along Hudson River Park for a long and tearful walk toward lower Manhattan, where I wound up weeping for what I'd "lost" with the Winner. Could there be a man out there as good as *he'd* been?

If I had expected miraculous contact with that man himself, God had a different plan. When I checked my e-mail the next day, during some routine break from work, there was a message telling me Posse Pal wanted to be my Friendster. *Posse Pal?* A shameful tremor went through me. *Maybe Hippie had told him about our . . . hangout.*

Why I should be so alarmed if word had reached that particular circle of people is hard to say, unless you reckon my heart still remembered things my head had long since forgotten. But once I'd clicked the acceptance button—and found out it was not Hippie but our other, Virginia connection that inspired Posse Pal's overture—I found myself wondering whether I might find Poster Boy among his Friendsters.

Well, well. Sure enough.

On a whim, I sent a brief, jaunty message through the site, glossing where these five years had taken me—especially my job in music. Though nothing in Poster Boy's rather dated profile pictures recalled that old attraction, there was still a lingering longing to impress.

Which, apparently, I'd had many chances to do. When Poster Boy *wrote back*—asking if I ever traveled his way and mentioning he had an unexplained interest in seeing New York—he said he'd been following my e-mail updates. *No wonder I got no bounce announcements.* But when I responded by asking about those mission trips I'd heard about—and mentioning my own excursion to India—Poster Boy fell silent, though he added me to his Friendsters. Since this exchange was on par with briefly catching up with some high school chum, I shrugged and returned to IM-ing my sister, Best Friend, or whatever long-distance girlfriend I was whiling the workday away with.

THE WEB SITE THAT CHANGED EVERYTHING

In theory I could have been using the time to scan job ads since I had two weeks left as a working girl, but I had decided to go on unemployment. Though it meant almost a 50-percent cut in income (at a time when I still struggled not to overspend my comfortable salary), I was ready for a break from the frantic blur life had become.

What had happened to New York merely being a "stopover" point? What about the novel I'd told my first boss I hoped would be published in five years? Somehow in the last several months of almost constant socializing and stimulus, I'd lost both the ability to focus and the ear for what my heart was saying—much less the Spirit of God. Not even my languishing, half-finished novel could help: when I finally sat down to resume work on it, I realized I couldn't go further. I didn't know how the characters should resolve their conflict because it was mine too.

When one of that summer's e-mail updates about life on fifty dollars a week provoked a bizarre correspondence with Ad Weasel (whom I'd somehow never taken off my list), I started to think the key to sorting things out was not so much a novel as a *blog*. I'd already launched one under my own name, mostly to post old update e-mails, but what about something exploring the life of one sexless in the city? By the end of my ninth week on unemployment, I had chosen names for several men and myself and the blog, which was launched with a pink template my new guy friend Blogfather gave several crucial tips on customizing.

But though I soon found a purpose and rhythm in posting my near-daily entries, the blog further strained things with Best Friend. Although she'd moved into the city that May, there'd been an increasing distance between us since my return from Bro's wedding later that month. By early July, that distance had turned into tension and an outright ultimatum about my "fail-ure" to be the friend she thought I should be, carried out in a way that made her betrayal especially painful. It felt as if the one person who'd voiced more commitment than any other unrelated individual in my life had just dissolved our friendship like it was a tablet of Alka-Seltzer and she had indigestion.

In retrospect, though, the differences between us were bound to change the friendship eventually. If I came from a tradition whose adage is "do unto others as you would have them do unto you," Best Friend's was "do unto me as I have done unto you." This really wasn't so different from the attitude often in *my* heart, but something she could be quite honest about. I, on the other hand, wasn't supposed to be acting that way—at least if I claimed to be following God. Either I had to ask His help in changing my attitude, or disguise from myself and others this blatant inversion of Jesus's self-sacrificial standard.

But though I'd heard Best Friend insist that others deal with her as she'd treated them, I somehow never thought she'd make that demand of me. And if my defining narrative was that miracle with the Winner—from which I'd gleaned that a loss of control can bring things from God that vastly exceed your expectations (as much as I still feared such total trust)—hers was quite different. Whereas I had suffered relatively little, Best Friend had endured a number of major betrayals and losses from which she learned that when things are outside your control, you're vulnerable to being totally devastated.

Put those two beliefs together, and you have Best Friend attempting to guard my interests—even when I didn't ask her to do it, or always like the way she did so—and expecting that I would do the same for her. The way we thought friends loved each other could not have been more different. Each time she tried to force my hand, demanding I intervene where she thought I could and should help her cause, I dug in my heels. In my mind, acquiescing like that would only reinforce her belief that no one would ever love her "just because," or without her working to somehow earn it. But since she never gave me the chance to love her without prompting, help her out without her asking, I guess my stubbornness seemed like hate. Before I knew it, our difference in values had festered into the rift that made her dump me, the night before I turned twenty-six.

Around that part of 2004, life started to seem pretty grim— in some ways a more realistic view than I had ever had before. Aside from all my personal drama, recent interest in jobs related to public health had forced me to face the suffering caused by AIDS, especially in Africa, in ways I'd never had to do before. Such research was a reminder of the lessons I'd started to learn three years before: life is really broken. Seriously. In fact, when you move beyond the relative comfort of American life, it starts to seem that suffering, not happiness, is the rule, that beauty is the real miracle.

Then while I was making a latte the next week, some line from a Stevie Wonder song I'd recently downloaded into iTunes—about how "true love asks for nothing"—suddenly had me weeping against the cupboard door. Although it is a love song, "As" restored to me a greater vision—not of the love between two friends, or even a man and woman, but one the Bible says Jesus will someday exchange freely with His "bride," the people of God. Finally Crabb's message started to sink in.

It always comes down to heaven, you see: what you think is the ultimate thing, what your soul really longs for. Is it something you want before Jesus comes back, or is it in fact that return? My heart was so good at worshipping God's gifts instead of the Giver himself that it took this second round of tumult for me to finally remember that my *real* hope had been secure and untouched all along. If I had let God have His way for just a few hours or days before, this time the chiropractic adjustments started to last a bit longer.

There were, of course, further relapses, but these mostly involved the Winner, who was proving to be my favorite and most frequent comfort, although this was plainly ludicrous. First there'd been what I told myself was sent as a "letter of closure" (in which I thanked him for being such a man of character). But when in mid-July I figured out how to send an update e-mail with a fairly attractive recent picture, I couldn't resist adding him to the mailing list, one last time. *No harm showing him I'd finally found style and a skinnier self, right?* Although he made no response to either this message or the card, and I swore to exclude him from all future updates, my old obsession showed no signs of fading.

Then one night early in August, on my first date with the Funny Man (on which we went to a rooftop party not far from Burlesque Bar), we met this late-thirties guy I'll call the Talker. Subtle date vibe notwithstanding, Talker later rings me up for an afternoon coffee (I think he hoped to challenge my political views, in advance of a certain unpopular convention that summer).

Although he paid for my latte, the "date" was otherwise very relaxed. Mostly the Talker played shrink for me in the five-hour chitchat that followed. Then, just as I thought things were winding down, the topic of the Winner came up.

I launch into full retelling of the saga, but the Talker is not impressed.

"Can I shake you?!! You need to get over this! . . . You never even told him you liked him?!!"

Finally I agree to consider help, and make my escape.

On the train home, I finished the book a girlfriend had lent me: Paolo Coelho's *The Alchemist*. As therapy goes, I doubtless could have done better than reading a book all about the courage of seizing your dreams, but then again maybe that's what I needed to hear. Once I got home, I called up the Winner, resolved to finally disclose the crush and get a desperately needed dose of reality. Instead, I got his machine, on which I left a short, vague message.

A girlfriend's call briefly upped my pulse, but after discussing my crisis, she recommended I seek parental closure since Mom once said of the Winner, "I don't think you've seen the last of him"—a view I took as prophetic. Once we hung up, I rang the folks.

We talked a while, then finally I fessed up. This time, however, I got both parents' perspectives—a departure from the consults we'd had while they were still in Singapore. Now that there was only a three-hour time difference between us, and they lived in an apartment with two handsets, it was easier to get both parents in on conversations. At the end of the talk, we asked God to help me finally move on from the Winner.

How God would answer, I didn't know, but I was ready—no, desperate—for change. Perhaps He'd have the Winner call back and crush my hope with news of a recent elopement? At this point, even pain would be a good thing. Shaking my head at this splendid way to start my *fourteenth week* on unemployment, I went to bed. *What a Monday.*

The next day passed uneventfully till late evening, when I sent out an e-mail update to the three to four hundred people on my recipient list (without, of course, the Winner). By then it was Wednesday's wee hours, and getting wearisome. Because of anti-spam restrictions, e-mailing so many people had gotten quite cumbersome: recipients must be e-mailed in increasingly constrained batches, each message an hour apart! To get the update out in less time, that night I also used my Anna Broadway account—changing the outgoing name to send as myself.

Unfortunately, the first one hundred folks got an e-mail with the *Sexless* link still at the bottom, though I thought I'd turned the signature off. Not that I was really ashamed of the blog, but news of it was still being disclosed selectively. *Rats*. After scanning through the recipient list, I determined there were no relatives so, since sending a corrected version would mean staying up even later, I decided to let the leak slide. Besides, how many readers did more than briefly skim my e-mails? It wasn't like they all breathlessly followed my life!

This thought a comfort, I finished sending, and toddled off to bed, the gaffe forgotten.

The next day, unusually, I was in Manhattan on a series of vaguely work-lead-related errands, which meant no access to the Internet or the blog traffic stats I'd swiftly grown addicted to. No, not until early evening, when I ventured to Best Friend's apartment for some cautious fence mending, did I eventually get my Internet fix.

Midway through checking e-mail—and of course all stats on the blogs—I checked for new comments. For convenience, I was running them through one account shared by both blogs. This made it less clear whether readers were commenting on *Sexless* or my update blog, but generally I could tell from who the person was, or what they'd said in the comment . . . unless the snippet quoted on the front page was too general.

When such a remark showed up that evening, from some guy with Poster Boy's first name, I figured he'd read the update blog. Especially since it *was* Poster Boy—as I learned from the links he'd left to his e-mail and his *blog*.

His blog!

I click through and scan until I get to an entry with a photograph. *It's almost like he knew I would be curious!* And damn, if it weren't for that Asian girl beside him, I'd be curious *indeed*. I skim long enough to learn that she's just a coworker who had recently moved to Hawaii, then return to sorting out which post he'd responded to. What on earth had prompted him to finally break his silence?

Since last night's update summarized two years' adventures, the online version had several hyperlinks to anecdotes of crazy art parties, crashing a Nike fun run, and the free haircut some weirdo gave me at the Waldorf. This entry—and the older stories it referenced—was "good stuff," in my humble assessment. Funny stuff.

So when I see his comment, knowing Poster Boy reads my updates, I assume he's been amused by one of those old adventures I linked to. I'd completely forgotten the gaffe, you see. In fact it takes some further digging—and rereading of said comment—before I realize that Poster Boy's joking about gold diggers. He had discovered *Sexless*.

Whatever God was up to this time, He had my full attention.

ACT III

THE PILGRIM

We walk along the path, slow, my steps lagging more and more behind. Suddenly we stop and I slump down on a rock.

"You've been questioning My leadership a lot lately. Are you going to follow or not? If not, there's another path over there."

I pause a long time, begin to cry.

At last: "Yes, Lord, I'll follow," through my tears.

"Good. Come on now." He takes my elbow.

"How much must I give up?" I envision parting with a few of the treasures in my backpack.

"Everything." He looks surprised.

Everything. It sinks in as I slowly, numbly slip off my backpack and leave it on the rock.

And so it will begin: every morning—"Lord, how can I glorify you today?" A lump fills my throat. Can't I please feel some of that infamous love now?

He takes my hand to help me along. I feel that wound I am still too numb and stupid to properly appreciate.

"Brother—Elder Brother—I am so very weak for this journey."

"Patience, child. We will make it."

—JOURNAL ENTRY, MAY 27, 2004

CHAPTER 14

WHAT MR. SANDMAN BROUGHT

I'm warning you, don't ever do
those crazy, messed-up things that you do
If you ever do,
I promise you, I'll be the first to crucify you
Now it's time to prove that you've come back
here to rebuild

—STEPHEN DUFFY AND STEVEN PAGE, *"Call and Answer"*

f Married Man had made a shit castle of my dreams, from that
very first comment Poster Boy seemed like the thing itself—
no wife, no girlfriend, and no lackluster faith. In fact, as two
nights' breathless reading of his voluminous blog confirmed, he
had a more serious walk with God than I had yet found in a man
so well dressed, so blue-eyed, and so homeschooled.

This was not, however, what started the biggest and longest
and most bruise-inducing swoon of my lengthy pining career.
Even I could see the tremendous folly of rebounding from a
man in New Mexico for one in California—and rebounding not
just with any ole Jesus freak, but one who'd spurned my interest in him before. Hadn't my prayers for help come from a heart
that was seeking the courage to live in *reality,* be that solitary or
not? Poster Boy finding a place in my life, much less finding me
attractive, did not seem very realistic at all.

Then we started e-mailing. And in one of his earliest

messages—sent in the first couple days of contact—he mentioned he might be coming to New York that fall and if so, would I be around? Luckily I was home at the time, and Roommate was in the kitchen cooking her dinner.

"ROOMMATE! HE MIGHT COME TO NEW YORK THIS FALL!!!!!!"

Could my wildest imaginings have a shred of reality after all? Two vodka-and-OJs later (this was all my pantry could muster), and my freak-out somewhat contained, I hit on an instantly brilliant response plan. If I was blogging about my love life—and writing heavily on the "loves" involved—was it not remiss to exclude the Captain's son-of-a-preacher-man predecessor? It might even be some sort of blogger malfeasance. So on the Thursday after his comment, I gave Poster Boy his debut—very carefully walking the line between laughable past attraction (in which the joke was all on me) and hints of *possible* present intrigue.

He didn't seem to mind the flirtation; in fact he seemed to like it. By mid-October, he'd taken to signing comments not by his own name but as Poster Boy.

FLIRTING MY WAY TO SPINSTERHOOD

By his account, he was as lovelorn as I—which, one day in mid-September, he set out to break down in detail. In that blog entry, Poster Boy sketched the dilemma each time he was out and about and caught sight of some cute girl. Apparently much eavesdropping followed, in which he took note of such things as what she talked about, and how often she chose to swear.

If he was left with *some* hope that she might actually serve

Jesus, he'd consider making a move. But as a rule, most girls had one of four faults: either they were great but "pagan"; great, not pagan, but had a brain "the size of a grape"; great, not pagan, not stupid, but only superficially spiritual; or great, not pagan, not stupid, not even superficially spiritual . . . but taken.

After rereading this once or twice—to confirm I didn't fit *any* of those descriptors—I called Roommate for a consult. She listened to me read through it aloud, then drew the obvious conclusion: "He sure seems to care an awful lot about swearing."

"Aw, shit, you're—AUGH!!!"

That night I had a serious think. This clearly called for response of some sort—but what? I contemplated a witty retort—perhaps suggesting we set each other up with possible dates (by which I could safely introduce the notion we might just hold the key to each other's problem)—then realized both commenting and e-mailing were too direct. Wasn't this after all the man who'd recently lamented, "When do I get to like the girl before she likes me?"

Perhaps I should just *blog* about it, and see how he responds. Besides, he certainly wasn't the only one who had high standards! In fact, mine were so complicated, they couldn't be simply catalogued with four bullet points like he used; no, mine required a Venn diagram.

I spent the evening attempting to draw one that graphed my love life woes, then posted a link to Poster Boy's entry in the morning, noting, "evidently I need to be expanding my vocab beyond good-ole-fashioned cuss words if I want to find a Christian husband."

After some seventy click-throughs from readers referred by my link, Poster Boy conceded, "I think I'M the one who should be taking the vocab lessons . . . I decided I need to add another category to my list of situations in meeting females—the one where the girl is smarter, faster, stronger and cuter than me and I get rejected like junior high jump shot." *Was that girl supposed to be me?!!* If so, he had no clue how bad my basketball was.

In fact as I wrestled with how to sum up my diagram (which sadly there was no way to upload as a visual), I started to realize the quality of my "game" might be more my fault than I had admitted before. For one thing, I tended to go after men I liked with all the enthusiasm of a hungry horse at a carrot stand. This could be blamed on high testosterone (so said the author of *Taking Sex Differences Seriously,* which was my new favorite book that fall) or that more common female fault, impatience. Either way my eagerness didn't work too well—and that was just the attitude. More problematic was how I comported myself, especially my speech. Was it any wonder things went so badly with the Captain, or that I'd attracted men like Ad Weasel and Lickwit (for whom my bawdy banter was a major selling point)?

You might say I'd developed a kind of a comedy act that worked for the folks at the bar I was playing presently, but which I hoped to leave once my big break came along. The longer that didn't happen, though, the more I focused on pleasing the nightly audience, no matter how this might strike any possible agents in the room. I'd kept on pretty long at this, but Poster Boy's appearance in my blog readership was a startling reminder the real deal might yet come around.

That my sometimes-salty tongue and too-often bawdy blog hadn't scared Poster Boy off yet was probably no small miracle. The profile for men like him was eventual rejection, no matter what hints they gave of initial interest.

Surprisingly, though, his attention produced a curious calm—as if I could depend on it, as if it were based on something besides my efforts to attract it. And oh, how I wanted to hope he might stick around—that this time my hope came not from sinful desires, but something the Lord Himself had put in my heart.

Yet precisely because this gift seemed so good, it posed a tremendous challenge. If loving God most had been difficult when He seemed to disregard my desires, what about when He seemed ready to fulfill them? Could I still love God *more* than the sort of gift I'd always idolized in absentia?

As soon as it had become clear that first comment would not be a one-time fluke contact with Poster Boy, I started asking God to guard my heart. The Saturday after the drama began, I even attempted my first fast in ages, to try to keep my priorities straight. "May Your will be done, Lord," I prayed in a journal entry the following week. "Help me seek You first. May I hold and regard this with an open hand."

And then, since I was so committed to not sabotaging my crush this time, why not take to heart his main frustrations with women? I'd started out writing the blog with an eye to holding the interest of readers like those who found me through ads on Craigslist. But why was their attention important to me, if Poster Boy was still reading and slowly becoming a more-or-less weekly correspondent? It wasn't exactly behavior change rooted in what it really should be, since I'd merely switched my search for approval from secular men to Poster Boy, but it was at least a start toward living a life bent on giving glory to God.

That this should be a new direction didn't say much about where my life had been of late, but since the end of spring, I'd been slowly drawn back to a place of greater obedience. One major part of this process was a new Bible study in Brooklyn I'd started attending around the time my job concluded. Perhaps because it was slightly smaller, I found much more accountability than with the group I'd been a part of since my move to New York.

One Tuesday night toward the end of May, the Brooklyn group gathered in a spacious apartment whose decor gave it that rare-in-New-York sense of actually settling in. As I settled into a comfortably worn leather couch, and listened to what the others were saying, I chimed in now and then with the sort of thoughts people often took as insightful. But after I'd made one such remark, our host for the night calmly countered with a statement that registered like a knockout punch: "But the point is *His glory.*"

It was not so much the idea itself that staggered me (though this is something I struggle to submit to every day), but that I'd *forgotten* this. *How had I forgotten this?* I knew it, once. And yet that truth had slipped from me in a gradual downward spiral of small decisions, each less wise than the last, which took their cue not from that crucial, if difficult, axis—God's glory—but what I deemed true yesterday.

Since moving to New York, I've built a few bookshelves—mostly with scrap wood from a futon frame left by a previous tenant, or boards I found on the street near someone's trash pile. One thing I've learned in the process is forming right angles without a level doesn't work so well. You can try to square shelves based on the board they're attached to, but if you keep positioning each piece so contingently, you wind up with a rather rickety structure. Faith is much the same. Not only must you *start* with Jesus as the foundation, you must key every board of the house off that, or you'll wind up with something unstable.

That man's words exposed the structural weakness in my building, and over the course of the summer that followed, it was as if God began tearing things down to the foundation so we could build anew with His glory as the level. In retrospect, it doesn't seem a coincidence that once this work began in me, I started having more of the sort of opportunities for which I'd initially come to New York.

In August I attended the Comedian's end-of-summer party, where I chatted up a mid-thirties writer who described himself as a "very liberal," if previously nonvoting, Democrat—a triumph for bipartisan dialogue even without its significance in spiritual terms. Roughly an hour into the conversation, he asked what books were influential to me as a writer. To both our surprise, I confessed that probably the Bible narrative (which I'd read at least three times completely) topped the list. That, and all the music I listen to.

While I was still absorbing the shock of both my candor and this realization, he probed for more on what must have sounded like some default pious answer. He said he thought Jesus's teachings—especially things like "love your enemy"—had "taken us to another level," but that the Resurrection was an unnecessarily mythic detail detracting from this otherwise salutary story. What did I think mattered more, the Resurrection or the teachings?

Since proofs for the Resurrection seemed more relevant to a modernist defense of the faith, I hadn't thought through such a question before. But maybe this was as good a time as any to reflect on it.

"Well," I said slowly, "when you think about what 'loving your enemies' really entails, it proves pretty radical. In fact, I don't think any of us are ultimately able to do it. If you look only at what Jesus said, the unreachably high standard becomes pretty depressing. You realize you can never attain it. But if Jesus was really man *and* God, which His resurrection would prove, that means He has the power to overcome death, and therefore the power to help us actually approach that standard which we could not reach on our own."

Perhaps sensing I was drawing a bit on the teachings of my pastor, the writer pressed further. What about my *life?* What was more important to *me*—the teachings or the Resurrection?

I paused.

For most of my life the Resurrection has been more of an abstract detail in a story I accept than a life-changing reality—and I admitted as much to the man. However, there was a moment the summer before, when the reality of it broke through in a powerful way. I started to describe to my listener the World Trade Center memorial site design proposal two friends and I developed as part of an open competition in 2003.

One thing we really wrestled with was the geometry of the site. For a while it all seemed completely arbitrary—until we "figured out" a key axis obviously used by the original architects to organize the space. From then on our task became much easier. The next problem we faced, however, was where to put the remains, for which we had to allow so many square feet. At first we were tempted to designate a plot in one of the corners. But as we mulled this over, it became clear that actually the remains were the most important part of the memorial; we had to tackle that "problem" head on.

With this in mind, my friends and I pondered burying the remains in one long line, rather than a square—which fit nicely with the central axis we had "discovered." We began calling this proposed grave site the "line of death." But this created a problem, since a gravestone that long—if continuous—would impede circulation through the site. Should the line of death really be unbroken?

And then, in that curious shift when words sufficiently general glimmer with two sublime simultaneous meanings, the concept suddenly took on a cosmic ramification.

"No. The line of death is not continuous." *Not on that day, and not for mankind.* My voice broke as the realization hit me and brainstorming suddenly became a tearful act of worship. "The line of death was broken . . . because some gave their lives so that others could live." And so, I explained to my friend, the Resurrection suddenly broke into that planning session the previous summer as a reality far more vivid, poignant, and relevant than I had ever experienced. Jesus's death and resurrection backed up His claim that we should fear His Father more than the death our sin introduced to the world. Here was the proof He had the power to fix our biggest problem.

"Ultimately," I told my listener, "life is about hope. You don't get up in the morning because of a set of good principles. You get up because of hope. Death is the one reality of which we are *all* certain. But the Resurrection offers the hope that even *that* can someday be overcome. And so the Resurrection, ultimately, informs all those good statements. Without it, all of that means nothing."

Whatever our conversation meant for that writer, it was one of the most exciting I'd had since the night the Diamondbacks won the World Series. And in the weeks that followed, I felt God drawing me onward to a deeper walk with Him and the courage to let Him use more of my life however he saw fit. This didn't make it easier to voluntarily choose chastity, but if I didn't trust God when it was hardest, how was I trusting Him at all? Besides, through examples like Poster Boy and others, I was beginning to see that maybe God's hard-core servants weren't as rare—or as lame and boring—as I would've thought.

Before, submitting to just how strong the hand of God was in my life had seemed a romantic liability with Jesus freaks and the freaked-by-Jesus alike. In my habit of dealing with God mercenarily, I'd hedged my bets as long as it seemed He was asking more of me than He was giving, at least in the love life realm. But once Poster Boy had "happened" upon my blog, it only increased my newfound willingness to obey. Here at last was the sort of man who ought to be attracted by zeal, and certainly seemed to share it; here seeking God seemed like a win–win situation, no matter my ultimate fate with the boy.

And yet, since that fate was still so uncertain, I couldn't resist installing a few barometers . . .

HOPE ALSO RISES

Toward the end of September, I decided to launch an extended series of contests on the blog. It started because I wanted a chance to report a quote from my final date of the summer—"I haven't made out with a virgin before." Since I was keeping coy about the cause of my ongoing chastity, September's contest was guessing the right missing word in the sentence, and which of the three men I'd dated in August had said it.

Those who got both answers right won their choice of a Gmail account invitation (which still had a certain cachet in those days) or one of my homemade cinnamon rolls. Whoever got *one* answer right won his choice of second prize: a tasteful JPEG of me (since I had kept my face off the blog) or some leftover schlock I'd scored one night at my party's recent political convention.

Despite these fine incentives, not until the month was nearly over did entries show up in my in-box for this first round of the Blog Reader World Series. While Poster Boy's was the first submitted, it was a clearly halfhearted attempt—he said he figured all three of the men had said that phrase at least once in their life.

Then I got even worse attempts—things like "I haven't made out with a Siamese twin before," and what else I don't remember. Had this first challenge set the bar too high? I started to despair of things until a very perceptive Australian, who signed all his comments as Frasier (the one on TV, that is), got both parts of the answer right. If he had been on this side of the globe, I probably would have kissed him.

With answers like that, I had to give Poster Boy one prize, but it wasn't going to be first. And maybe for the guy so keen on poker he even kept a second blog on his games, second place wasn't such a bad thing. I was fortunate he couldn't see the smirk as I gleefully dashed off two personalized announcement e-mails the Friday the contest closed, asking each man for his choice of prize.

Such reader correspondence probably wasn't what the New York unemployment board wanted noted on the record I was supposed to be keeping of job search efforts, but by then I'd grown too comfortable with the routine of daily blogging and all related activities to be that concerned with finding work. As long as I could still pay rent and make do with a mostly meatless diet, it was worth such modest privation to have time for serious thinking.

At times it almost felt as if I were actually relearning this once-familiar mental habit. *I knew this once—how had I forgotten it?*

That conversation in August had rekindled my previous passion for evangelism, and suddenly I was starting to miss that fire in those around me. If we all thought Jesus so great, why weren't we more excited to share the hope of His life, death, and resurrection with others? Something felt like it was missing in my experience of faith. Although I often struggled with a fear that returning to disciplines like Bible reading would bore me, I knew God was supposed to be the defining passion that consumed life, giving it structure, meaning, and purpose. So why was that passion so hard to find in the community of other Christians?

As rays from my south-facing bedroom window sank toward Staten Island that Friday, these questions inspired another round of e-mails. Though not all the update readers shared my faith, I decided to let them eavesdrop on my current reflections, including the thought I wanted to marry a "lifestyle evangelist" like my folks were. The fact that my new crush just happened to *read* these updates didn't escape my notice, of course, but I was curious whether he would respond to anything other than my less godly adventures.

Monday I got a most hopeful indication, when Poster Boy wrote his most flirtatious e-mail yet, regarding the prize of his choice. Apparently he was quite inspired by my interest in evangelists. Well, that and my promised cinnamon rolls:

> So about this prize thing. See, there's a catch. I LOVE cinnamon rolls, but I'm deathly allergic to anything with dairy in it (milk, butter, cheese, cream, cream cheese, cottage cheese, sour cream . . .) so life is rather miserable. This being the case, if you happen to be the Betty Crocker to end all Betty Crockers and can figure out how to bake a cinnamon roll without any of these Poster Boy-killing ingredients, I'll pay the postage to have this kick ass roll sent all the way out here to CA. =) As you said before, the way to a man's heart is through his stomach? (or wait . . . was it his liver??)

First he was riffing on the post about him (in which I described attempting to woo his stomach with apple crisp), then also *chal-*

lenging my baking skills? And actually *encouraging* me to make a play for his heart?!!!

This called for a major consultation with a quorum of friends including Blogfather, Guy Friend #1, and of course Best Friend (with whom I was speaking again). He *was* flirting, right?

Once said tone had been confirmed, I then faced the task of giving the boy some resistance. No sense disrupting the chase he claimed he longed for an opportunity to initiate. Besides that, there was a catch, all right: he hadn't even *won* the chance to choose between Gmail and cinnamon rolls! My e-mail to him had not even hinted at such. But since he was proving a rather loyal reader, I decided a prize *upgrade* could be secured if he sent a copy of a recent CD he'd played on, which record I was too poor to afford. He promptly agreed, and I got down to baking.

Unfortunately, it wasn't so simple a matter to replace all lactose in Great Grandma Broadway's famed cinnamon rolls and still get them to rise properly. In fact, it took not one batch, not even two batches, but *three* to get a dairy-free roll I was finally satisfied could contend for the heart of the first man who'd ever begged for my baking. Once the acceptable sweet had been produced, I packaged four up in a box covered with my brightest red paper, and scribbled a second-prize winner "congrats" card sealed with a shiny, well-lip-glossed kiss.

To send such a wildly audacious note was utterly out of the question if I were writing him *as myself,* but since this was Anna Broadway mailing, and I'd become known for trilling out excess "dahlings" in blog posts and e-mails, why not maximize all efforts to make his heart thrill? Hadn't he himself made that the point?

And strangely enough, in due time he found a way to do likewise for *my* heart, thanks to a couple noteworthy blog posts.

The first announced he'd decided to quit poker completely, after feeling a major sense of conviction. While that in itself was good news—maybe even an answer to prayer (this habit had been his equivalent of the Captain's fondness for smokes)—what really got my attention was how he explained his rationale for quitting. As he went through how he'd thought about the issue, Poster Boy noted that poker was drawing on gifts of discernment he felt God wanted him to use for the blessing of others, except that during games he was doing just the opposite—using that insight against other players.

In the end, he concluded, "Poker . . . is not building up the character of Christ in me but instead is teaching me to be a better liar, to take advantage of people's weaknesses for my own gain, and at its worst may be a form of false worship" (the last part based on his study of one passage from Isaiah). If King of Pseudo Dates ever had explained one of his positions like that, we might have had a whole lot more than pseudo dates.

But the blogging didn't stop there. A couple days later, Poster Boy wrote another post, describing a recent encounter in an affluent suburb near his job. Apparently he'd been walking down the street when he heard shouting from a homeless guy he recognized as a regular on that corner. Since everyone else was ignoring him, and the man seemed somewhat distressed, Poster Boy stopped to ask him what was wrong. The man, who was in a wheelchair, said he needed the blanket beneath him adjusted. This didn't seem much to ask, so Poster Boy readily agreed.

Only when he'd started the requisite tugging did it become clear the blanket in question was saturated . . . with the man's own urine. Poster Boy stuck with the job, then gave the man whatever change he had before sprinting off to the nearest Starbucks bathroom.

Whether because of that image of urine-damp hands or Poster Boy's subsequent dash to clean up, this anecdote left an indelible mark. If the poker post had left me any chance of not falling even harder the second time, it was gone.

And yet, despite such promising measures of character, it's hard to say how long I could have endured this strictly Internet-based friendship. Then October 15 rolled around, the day my rent was due. Normally we paid on time, but this month I'd gotten some freelance work, for which the client still hadn't sent my check, leaving me short a few hundred.

For some reason I mentioned this on my blogs that day—and next thing I knew, here was Poster Boy responding to a previous e-mail, in which I'd tried to broach a conversation about evangelism, with a terse reply: "Call me."

I'm not quite sure what the neighbors thought had happened to me, but they must have heard my shouts throughout the adjoining backyards my bedroom windows looked out on. Although there was no running involved, it might have been a bigger reaction than even my first kiss achieved. We hadn't yet progressed to *instant messaging* and he wanted to answer my questions by way of the *telephone?!!*

After I'd gotten my palpitations somewhat under control, however, I realized the peril of being the one to *initiate* the call. Far better for him to call *me*—especially since he had the much more restricted schedule, and who knew how long our talk would go?! I let a suitable interval pass, then dashed off a quick reply to that effect.

"Oh, I just wanted to talk about your rent," he wrote back. *My rent!* Not even my own family had been that generous! (Mom and Dad believe strongly in supporting their children's financial independence.) Although I knew there was no way I would ever let him loan me the money, we worked out that he'd try to call me later on that day.

When I described this brainstorm to Guy Friend #1—complete with reenactment of my initial shouts—he noted one major flaw in my plan: "Now you're going to hyperventilate every time the phone rings!"

"Aw, crap. You're *right*."

I paced and fretted till close to 5 p.m. West Coast time, then finally decided I could call Poster Boy on the grounds that I wouldn't know how to answer the telephone otherwise.

This pretext determined, I slowly picked up the phone. But as I began punching in the numbers, my heart seized with a phone anxiety far worse than I'd ever felt before. This time my chest was actually, literally *burning!* Everything seemed to hinge on the fragile fiber-optic fulcrum between my fingers.

It was something like a moment described in *The Alchemist:* "I'm afraid that if my dream is realized, I'll have no reason to go on living . . . I'm afraid that it would all be a disappointment, so I prefer just to dream about it." Did I? No. It was time to take this fearful step toward actualizing whatever was really *there* between us, even if that were less than I was hoping for.

Ignoring the fact that phone nerves like this almost always preceded contact with the guy's voice-mail service, I dialed his number a third time and pressed the "Talk" button, praying God put my heart's thudding on mute for the call.

One or two rings later, a warm male baritone I hadn't heard in five years announced his name.

"Hey. I decided I should call *you* so I wouldn't have to worry which name to give when I answered."

Pause. He realizes who he's talking to and chuckles with relief I'm not the work-related caller he said he'd feared.

"Hey, Anna."

Was that the sound of a smile in his voice?

I slowly remembered to breathe again, no paper bag required, and felt my way through the strange reality of this first-ever phone call with the only man who'd ever prompted the prayer "Please guard my heart." Twice.

CHAPTER 15

LESSONS IN HEART SECURITY

The tumult in the heart
keeps asking questions.
And then it stops and undertakes to answer
in the same tone of voice.
No one could tell the difference.

Uninnocent, these conversations start,
and then engage the senses,
only half-meaning to.
And then there is no choice,
and then there is no sense;
until a name
and all its connotation are the same.

—ELIZABETH BISHOP, *"Conversation"*

While that mid-October call didn't lead to the lengthy discussion of ministry I at first envisioned, it wasn't long before we'd progressed to chatting online. It started out as tech support for my sometime-ailing iBook (whose platform turned out to be Poster Boy's day-job specialty), but by the third day of chatting that week, he gave me not just the bad news on my laptop but a glimpse inside his life not divulged on the blog—which was soon taken off-line anyway, when an ex-girlfriend stumbled across it.

Poster Boy worked for a large university in those days, and after a recent gig, he'd come back to work for some reason, only to encounter a bunch of freshmen involved in an annual school ritual he compared to a low-grade orgy. The anecdote and the dismay with which he shared it of course reinforced my view of him as a virtual saint, but also ushered me into a place I hadn't expected him to invite me, where we could somewhat vulnerably commiserate over the loneliness and struggles of balancing life in both the Christian and secular worlds.

Although I might have hoped things would take a clearly romantic turn soon after, I had to admit that building a friendship first was certainly wise. Better to start things platonically, with someone where there's ample room to pursue eventual attraction, than start romantically without determining whether you even can be *friends*. Life has plenty of moments where roses and ambiance get you nowhere, but knowing the sort of joke that will make the other person relax a bit makes all the difference. And if there was one thing Poster Boy and I seemed to do well, it was to make each other laugh . . . or at least type "lol"— which, when rendered in all caps, I assumed meant literal laughing out loud and not just that you'd typed something funny. That was how I distinguished the two forms in my use, anyhow.

But all our banter notwithstanding, I had no interest in friendship unless it was going somewhere. It was proving far too easy to build the sort of rapport that would surely terminate once either of us started dating, because we would then find such intimacy with that new partner.

So, by late October, I started looking seriously for jobs outside New York. After all, if I had high rent, no family, and no job on the East Coast, why restrict my search to a cold-winter state when I could pay equal or less rent for a pad near two of my relatives and a much more temperate latitude? When you added to these inducements the number of community colleges on the West Coast that actually offered religious-studies classes (which called for teachers with M.A.s like mine), it was almost entirely irrelevant that California was also the home of the old crush recently so attuned to my dating, financial, and computing woes.

But however much our newfound friendship seemed to enjoy God's blessing, that didn't include me getting the first West Coast job I applied for. Shortly before Thanksgiving, I came home from my first day on the job at a temp assignment to news that I'd been passed over for a community college teaching assignment whose detailed application packet had taken much of October to get in order.

It wasn't so much the time investment that made me burst into tears, of course, but the fear this blow somehow meant I'd never find a way to move west and therefore into Poster Boy's affections. *How could he ever think highly enough of me to pursue a relationship across three thousand miles?* Still reeling from the rejection letter (though at least they'd had the decency to notify those passed over for interviews), I opened up my laptop and went online. I'd barely completed dial-up (since my budget was too tight for cable) and opened my instant-messenger program when who should IM but Poster Boy!

On other occasions, I might have stayed in my funk a while longer, but somehow he sensed the best response to my discouragement was helping me joke my way back to a calmer, more hopeful place. Besides which, our conversation reminded me that though he hadn't yet stated his reasons for following my life so closely, the distance had proven no hindrance to him pursuing a friendship. *Maybe God wasn't limited to working through open jobs around the Bay Area.*

Maybe, in fact, the best thing was to make a weekend

stopover there! I'd have to venture westward anyhow for an annual visit with the family—and since said relatives also included
an aunt and her brother living near San Jose, why not take this
chance to explore the region that just might become my new
home?

INTO A SOVEREIGN WAITING ROOM

Once tickets were booked for a glorious twelve-dollar fare
(thanks to another chunk of frequent-flyer miles), I sent out a
casual e-mail to all conceivable friends and relatives in a swath
from San Francisco to Vancouver, announcing the trip strategi-
cally billed not as a tour of California but the West Coast. No
chance was I going to initiate a hangout with Poster Boy, other
than in the sense of a group FYI.

While I don't remember feeling all that guilty about proceed-
ing with the trip, it must be admitted that I hadn't exactly fasted
over it either. Not that this was a totally invalid form of decision
making; in his mammoth tome *Decision Making and the Will of
God,* Garry Friesen says reason and our desires can be perfectly
valid factors in making decisions—in fact that they're often part
of the means God provides us to make choices pleasing to Him.
During earlier seasons of deliberating, this notion had been a
great comfort.

My college years had presented a different challenge, however. In those days one of the biggest struggles was learning to
think through a decision instead of asking God to just tell me
what to do. I was learning how to apply His principles to things
like my finances and commitments. But by 2002, when I had to
decide if I should leave Arizona, thinking through what choice
would most honor God had gotten a lot more complicated.

I no longer had to fight the fear that what I desired must by default be bad, but what about when your desires verge on what one former pastor has called an "over-desire"? That was the reason I not only tried to think through my possible East Coast move and seek advice from wise counselors (both practices Friesen advises), but embarked on a two-day fast. Somehow I knew *that* decision came down to what my motives were, and whether the reason for making that move was based on an interest in the cute Catholic I'd met on my first trip to New York. Only when I had laid my heart bare before God as best I knew how, and still felt a peace from Him, did I commit to the move.

Catholic Boy was a minor threat next to Poster Boy, though—and probably that's why both the times I've liked him began by asking God to guard my heart. If you'd asked me at the time why I felt the need to pray a request like that, I probably would have speculated that it was to protect against getting hurt, or else some version of trying to follow that verse from Song of Solomon about "not awakening love" until it pleases. I don't know whether or not such a reading of that line is accurate, but where the Bible discusses "guarding your heart," the context is neither emotional caution nor learning to love a man only once he's first shown love to you.

Guarding your heart is most specifically mentioned in a verse in one of the Proverbs, which says our heart is the source or "wellspring" of life. In order to make sense of this, though, you have to look at what else the Bible says about the heart. It isn't just the source of emotions (though God's followers are called to love Him with our whole heart) but also the basis of our actions and decisions. Jesus says our speech is part of the overflow of the heart—implying it's also the seat of character. To guard your heart then has something to do with protecting the very core of who you are.

So why would I sense that Poster Boy somehow entailed a threat—that I might not guard my heart so well around him? Most likely because what you pursue at any cost, the thing you spend your life in search of, has a great effect on your actions. When I finally consulted that favorite uncle about what the Bible says on guarding your heart, he mentioned Jesus's Sermon on the Mount. Sandwiched in between the Lord's prayer, and Jesus's advice on worry, He talks about where we ought to really invest; what we ought to make our "treasure" in life. In contrast to all earthly and material things—which death will take from us or us from them, if something else doesn't get them first—He says we ought to make treasure of *heavenly* things, "for where your treasure is, there your heart will be also."

Just a few verses later, in His vivid remarks about worry, Jesus concludes with the note that "pagans run after" things like food and clothes, but since our Father knows we need all that, we should seek first His kingdom and His righteousness, and trust God to provide everything we require. In other words, we should not assume our security comes from a winter coat or food in the fridge—or friends and a spouse and a 401(k), or whatever else we think we will die without—but the God who gave us life in the first place. Seek *Him,* and He will sustain our lives as long as He has appointed we should breathe to praise and serve Him.

I think the reason God prompted me to pray, "Please guard my heart" was that He knew how great the risk was that I'd find my treasure in Poster Boy's interest—value the man more than his Maker. And yet, perhaps the really astonishing thing about how God deals with His people is the giving of gifts He knows we won't give Him His due for. Even though we value physical comfort far more than restoration of the relationship lost at Eden, God doesn't consign us to a life of unrelieved misery. I'm not sure I could trust someone I loved that much, but He does—over, and over, and over again.

This is not to say God isn't jealous, though. While He gives with unfailing generosity, we may at any time have to reopen our clenching fists around the gifts He's given. Abraham had just begun to enjoy the long-awaited son God promised (through whom it was said he would father many nations) when he faced a soul-shattering command: take this very son and kill him, as a sacrifice to the Lord. He was ultimately spared that loss by a ram that God provided, but not until both the man and his Master had seen what was really in his heart. God makes no apology for His jealousy about that which is His.

The first time He began testing what I loved most was the Monday following Thanksgiving, shortly after I'd booked my holiday travel and sent the group e-mail announcing my grand tour of the West Coast. Although we were both online that day, there was no instant message or return e-mail from Poster Boy. This silence was so crushing that it sent me into a tailspin once I got home from work to the privacy of the apartment. Since Roommate wasn't home yet, I sat down on the couch and slowly started to process what was really going on behind this despair. It proved, of course, to be a felt threat to what I'd made my trea-sure, as I confessed to my journal:

> *I want to rant of God's unfairness. Blame Him for tricking me into facing my deepest desires. Cry out in anger now my vine wilts.*
>
> *"But I admired the vine! The branch of the Vine! Which is admiring the Vine!"*
>
> *. . . Somehow I must reach through this pain to the God who will surely go with me into death.*

Not until I have forsaken all others but Him can I even truly love the others beside Him.

It was a strange process of writing out things I knew to be true in a "head" sense but was still struggling to live out. Maybe the reason that Jesus analogized faith to a tiny mustard seed is that God will work with even our faintest effort to turn toward Him and obey.

Although my motives for yielding to His gentle but firm conviction were far from pure (I hoped such obedience would eventually bring me closer to Poster Boy), it was clear that "I must let something die to be satisfied" in God. "The very desire which brings me here must in some sense be burned away in this death," I realized. It was the first of several such major battles of the heart—even though I still didn't fully grasp why this had to happen or how it might be an answer to prayer.

When at last God had brought me from struggle to submission to peace, I finally went online to check e-mail.

Poster Boy had written. And not only was he adamant we should meet up, he extended a chance to hear a sample track from the still-overdue CD (apparently mailing it was right up there with digesting foods with lactose). An Internet station was featuring one song for free download, giving listeners a chance to comment on whether it should join their airplay lineup. As small a thing as it was, that e-mail so vastly exceeded what I had been hoping for that I wept at God's extravagant kindness. It wasn't exactly a ram, but it was a resurrection of hope much sweeter than I had dreamt was possible.

And that was just His goodness at the top of the week. Thursday night when I copied Poster Boy on an e-mail tipping a number of West Coast friends off to Starbucks' annual holiday party (going on that day, with free drinks for all), he e-mailed back letting me know that he and a friend were in L.A. for the day, in some very important meetings about their music! As thrilled for him as if it were my own success, I dashed off a quick note about how much Frasier, Best Friend, and my No-Cali uncle had liked the sample track—writing not as a groupie, of course, but someone helping promote her friends' keen licks. (Or so I told myself, anyway; maintaining a peer-to-peer rapport was crucial, no matter how low key it forced my praise of their music to be.)

But that didn't mean I couldn't rejoice in his progress . . . Once I left my temp job for the night, I called up every friend I could get on the phone, to share Poster Boy's good news. This happy buzz carried into the next night's ninety-minute online chat with Poster Boy, who seemed as tickled as I by our conversation. "Great chatting with you," he said as we finally signed off. I sank back into the futon with a happy sigh of agreement and shook my head at the marvelous things God seemed to be doing. It was about as good a Friday—much less a week—as I could have asked for.

Or so I thought.

About the time I closed my laptop, Roommate came home for the evening. We traded greetings and small talk while she slowly took off her coat, scarf, and hat, showing no signs either of us had exciting news to share.

Only when she was taking belongings into her bedroom did she remember. "Oh, by the way, you have a message," she said with the slightest hint of a secretive smile.

"I do?" I thought I'd been checking the voice mail online from work each day—though none of the West Coast companies I was applying to had called yet.

"Yeah."

"Who's it from?"

"Oh . . . I think you should just listen."

"*What?!!*"

Heart pounding madly, I dashed to the wall phone. Sure enough, once I pushed the right sequence of buttons, there was that familiar baritone, no question about the smile this time. And oh my God, he was *rambling,* he was *up!* Their meetings had gone really well, and when they got stuck in traffic during the six-hour drive from L.A., he thought to call me to *talk.* He called! For no reason but to *talk!!* To *ME!!!*

I think that message about made up for all those days of silence from the Peruvian, and the months waiting for an e-mail from the Winner . . . and quite a lot of other letdowns besides.

FALLING WHERE WISE MEN FEAR TO TREAD

By then I was roughly two weeks from the visit . . . and what would be the biggest first date of my life. It didn't start out looking as if it would be any more than a coffee hang with Poster Boy, but once we'd established the best day to meet—the Saturday after my Friday-night flight—it turned out he wanted to meet up in the evening. Since he wasn't free till on the late side, owing to double or triple booking that day, I figured our meeting would just be for drinks.

Around this time, a random Tom Jones fan in the San Francisco area wrote back to one of the Jones-themed blog promotion posts I'd put on their Craigslist, offering me a spare ticket (I guess he didn't realize I lived in New York). Although it was fairly unlikely the show the ticket was for fell during the few days I'd be out there, and even unlikelier still that show was the one night I was supposed to be seeing Poster Boy, I decided the lad might need one more chance to feel like he was fighting for my time. (Not that his threats to cancel our meet-up on account of a cold had any bearing on this.)

Hence a blog entry only five days before our date, in which I pondered the merits of possibly standing up Poster Boy for an unknown fan of Tom Jones. After all, while it was not unusual for men from San Francisco to be on the odd side (witness the financier who gave me that free haircut at the Waldorf), surely I was not responsible for the timing of a once-in-a-lifetime chance to get caught in a storm of middle-aged ladies' underwear, which I'd heard Tom Jones attracted.

Poster Boy quite agreed, although that wasn't exactly the plan: "If you don't go to Tom Jones with a middle-age Craigslist troller instead of going to dinner with me, ya'll should take down this here blog," he commented. "You'll have stories for a WEEK out of that."

Only one word of that registered. *Dinner?!!* If not for the stately confines of the Park Avenue real estate office where I was on assignment, there would have been no rein on my decorum and my vocal chords. Forget wondering if it was too much to infer from a boy buying cocoa that it was a real date (on that long-ago night with the Winner), if it was *dinner* Poster Boy had in mind, this was most certainly a date.

By the time the big day arrived, it was all I could do not to have a total meltdown. I knew, somehow, that if the fragile connection between us wasn't strengthened by this trip it wouldn't survive beyond my West Coast visit. And this wasn't just any crush!

In an effort to tranquilize wayward nerves, I took an afternoon run through my uncle's neighborhood, and changed my outfit at least three times upon returning. If Poster Boy hadn't found a way to pick me up one hour earlier than planned, I might have had to start a second jog by the time he finally arrived.

At last when I was upstairs putting on lip gloss, I heard a shout from my uncle's girlfriend, who'd heard the doorbell: "He's here!"

Unbelievable, but at twenty-six, I was finally having the closest thing to an almost-textbook first date, complete with the boy driving to pick me up, and a male relative on hand. Sure, the uncle in question was my dad's youngest brother and more laid back than protective than other forty-year-olds might be—but still.

While I came downstairs and dragged out the process of buckling the straps on my three-inch heels, my uncle and his girlfriend carried on avid small talk with Poster Boy, whose music I'd successfully turned them into fans of. After I finished donning my footwear and jacket (a silk piece I'd designed and knitted myself), I quietly stepped into their talk for a few more minutes.

Once alone in the car, however, we had to fend for ourselves. It was by no means terrible, but it certainly was surreal. And since we were dining on his turf, a twenty-minute drive from my uncle's, we had plenty of silence to fill. As easy as it was to talk online, once side by side in the new-to-him Subaru Poster Boy picked up that very morning, there was only so much material I could get out of the virtues of manual transmissions (which his sporty silver station wagon came with). In fact, had I not actually met a friend of his the month before, when Poster Boy set me up with him on a very platonic wedding date near D.C., we might have struggled a bit for topics.

We were much more used to talking about each other than things liked in common or people we both knew (who were few anyway). But arguing whether or not Poster Boy was a closet romantic was one thing when we were safely secluded behind our respective laptops; in person it was quite another to ask bold questions like how far I'd gone with 5 Percent Man—which he had queried at random not long before. (Since the story was fairly innocent, and the question seemed that of a boyfriend hopeful, I didn't refuse to answer, though I probably should have rebuffed him.)

Finally Poster Boy pulled off the freeway and into a more dynamic environment than the grim industrial section we'd driven through. Since he still owed me the now nearly two-months-overdue CD, we first made a stop by where he lived to scrounge in the pickup replaced by the Subaru, then took a tour of the house he shared with several other guys.

Although Poster Boy had a ground-floor bedroom, the bulk of the rooms were upstairs, including a funny one at the top of the flight leading down to the kitchen. This last space had a pitched roof and walls adorned with a number of rather unusual bumper stickers. For some reason this inspired me to launch into an ill-considered anecdote describing a slightly risqué bumper sticker purchased for Best Friend at a New Zealand thrift store.

It wouldn't have been like Poster Boy to frown at the punch line, but only as it passed my lips did I remember my pledge to cut back on the bawd. *Oh crap! I'm not supposed to be so naughty anymore . . .*

While this horror wasn't audible, it somehow transpired at the top of the staircase, at the very moment when I should have been thinking about my footing. Next thing I know, it's down on both knees in a tumble of red pants and multicolored sweater. *So much for the "She's a lady" campaign . . .*

Remarkably, I managed to fling an arm on the right-side railing and stop a couple steps short of the landing. And then, as if it were standard course to begin first dates with a headfirst crash down stairs, I wobble back up on my heels for a careful trip down the second flight.

Somehow this leaves enough brain cells unused to actually carry on banter about the follies of female fashion. Frankly, I'm not sure which was more shocking: the tumble itself (which left bruises for several weeks) or my swift recovery. Well, I should say, my *mostly* swift recovery. When Poster Boy pressed for why women still wear heels—despite the evident risks—the strain took a toll on my wits.

"Sometimes we're a bit misogynistic," I tossed off, without really noting which M-word I'd used. By then we'd made it to the door of his bedroom, where Poster Boy thought he'd put a book he owed me.

"Misogynistic?" It was perhaps my first real eye contact with that electric blue gaze. He furrowed his brow in a puzzled face not unlike the one my brothers make. "Misogyny is the hatred of women."

I'd just fallen almost a full flight of stairs on the biggest date of my life, then proceeded to make a subtle misstep in word choice, which Poster Boy then *caught*—and he had done so without arrogance! After all the Captain's blunt grammatical checks, such gentleness was unprecedented. Forget not spraining or breaking anything, it's a miracle I didn't swoon right onto Poster Boy's bed.

"*Oh!* I . . . I meant we're *masochistic.*"

The bright side of two colossal gaffes was that one couldn't do much worse after that. We made our way to dinner without event, and carried on conversation mostly without pause, though it was also mostly without flirting.

As we found ways to talk about each other's lives that neither covered old ground nor pushed too deep, I kept wondering how I measured up to his expectations. At least I was much skinnier and had better taste in clothes! But was it true what Dad had always implied about solid Christian men? I'd never had a real date with one—at least in such a formal sense—so I didn't know how to read things.

Secular guys would probably be playing footsie by now, or would at least have made *some* point of contact. I was too nervous to even maintain *eye* contact long. Though in the event he *didn't* like me, this probably was a good thing—forget about wearing your heart on your sleeve; mine was probably glowing right there in my eyes, not even dimmed by the lens of glasses for once.

But other than one point when Poster Boy seemed determined to bait the saucy girl of the blog, there was little hint of the flirt he'd sometimes been online. And without assurance where I really stood with him, I hadn't the courage to snap back with my usual moxie.

By then we were almost done with the meal, which probably meant the evening—and therefore our contact for the trip . . . until I remembered the next day was Sunday. Normally that meant church in the morning. But since I was the guest of a secular relative . . .

Scarcely had I started to sketch this dilemma when Poster Boy hit on the obvious solution: I could come to church with *him*. He warned me that they weren't having a typical worship service—some outreach in the community would take up much of the day—but said I was welcome to join if I wanted.

"I don't need to be just a consumer about things," I shrugged. And since my flight didn't leave till Monday, there was no reason I couldn't spend Sunday on the peninsula, helping him and his church. As long as Poster Boy didn't mind hauling my luggage and me to the BART station afterward, so I could ride to Berkeley to meet up with friends, it should be no problem.

Nope, no trouble from his end. As long as his parents okayed me coming, it should be fine for me to visit.

His parents? Oh sure, of course. I'd had many first dates of this magnitude, which preceded meeting *the family.* Somehow I managed to keep breathing normally while he called his folks, who apparently pastored the small congregation. Once the Poster Parentals had approved my visit, we sorted out what time he should pick me up in the morning.

That did it for the evening. Next thing I knew, Poster Boy pulled up in front of my uncle's two-story condo. He made no move for a parting hug, but as I reached for the door handle, Poster Boy flashed one of those cocky, flirtatious grins I remembered. "So are you going to blog about this?"

"Oh, I don't know . . . " I waved a hand vaguely, attempting to play it cool. "Sometimes a small thing becomes a whole entry, and sometimes a big thing barely gets mentioned at all." *CRAP! Had I just let on . . . ?*

"Well, see you tomorrow, then. Eight-thirty sharp."

"Right."

I made it inside without further spills—even seeming to make contact with the ground—and presented my uncle and his girlfriend with the CD Poster Boy had given me for them. If you had asked me what I thought of God that night, I doubt I could have found words.

CHAPTER 16

IS YOU IS, OR IS YOU AIN'T— NO MAYBES

There is the old joke made by the Marx who laughed about not deigning to belong to a club that would accept someone like him as a member—a truth as appropriate in love as it is in club membership.

. . . Marxists feel their core self to be so deeply unacceptable that intimacy will necessarily reveal them to be charlatans. Therefore why accept the gift of love, when it is sure to be taken away imminently? If you love me now, this is only because you are not seeing the whole of me, *thinks the Marxist,* and if you're not yet seeing the whole of me, it would be crazy to grow used to your love until such time as you do.

—ALAIN DE BOTTON, *On Love*

God, of course, was supposed to be the point of things—but with a church visit that would entail meeting *the family,* it was hard to remember that. Especially since each comment and glance gave me further data to contrast with the strangely persistent peace in my heart. Were these last few months the start of the story I hoped they'd tell, or would this be one more thing written off as another catastrophic judgment call on my heart's part? So far things looked quite hopeful . . . but still.

When I got up the next morning, I couldn't deny the sense

of excitement in my stomach as I dragged my luggage down-stairs to the Subaru, where we found room for my two suit-cases. Once on the road, I rambled along, making conversation about things like music and parent relationships, uncertain of Poster Boy's mood. He sure seemed awful quiet. *Was he regret-ting my company, or was this just his pre-morning-coffee de-meanor?*

Maybe it was merely concentration. After we left the 101, the road became more windy. When Poster Boy changed the ra-dio to a station playing classic jazz, I scrunched down happily in my seat, enjoying the tune and the boy and his car, and his competent handling of the frequent curves. There's nothing quite like the acoustics inside an automobile, and I have always loved a good snaky highway. Put these together with Poster Boy's company, and you had yourself one fine Sunday morning. I started to relax about his silences more.

Once we dropped closer to ocean level, the road wound through a flat section lined by pumpkin fields, where Poster Boy told me the rotten ones sometimes exploded from all the gases inside. Shortly after we'd turned onto the northbound coastal highway, he stopped at a coffee shop with a small deck over-looking the Pacific. He paid for our lattes and breakfast pastries, then led the way to a table outside, where we browsed parts of someone's discarded newspaper.

From time to time we glanced up to take in the view, which included a small family at an adjoining table. One of their two young children was a boy whose glasses made him imme-diately darling. Apparently Poster Boy noticed. After we were midway into breakfast, he announced apropos of nothing in his sports page that he was ready to have children. No mention of the wife involved, but children, yes, he'd like 'em. Soon, if possible.

Honestly, there are moments where I can't fathom what men are thinking when they say the things they do to women—since we, of course, presume they're thinking five or more things at once (as we are), all cagily bent on some grand master strategy to bedevil and attract us. How else could you explain how well they do so?

In an effort to look blasé and unfazed by Poster Boy's evident need for a Basics of Biology review course—or a wife—I took a huge gulp of latte, surely worthy of Lucille Ball herself, and pondered the best course through this conversational minefield. Later I thought of a thousand witty replies, all safely disinterested and casual, but at the time I was left speechless. From the few details Poster Boy had divulged about his friendships with other women (all of which had proved similarly ill fated), it seemed any sign of interest would be deadly.

So how on earth could I reply without sounding like I was volunteering to help? Silence seemed the safest response.

After a moment, Poster Boy clarified: not more than one kid at once, of course. *Was this supposed to sweeten the deal?*

"Oh yes," I rushed in. "But it's not good to grow up without siblings. I've known some only children . . . "

Which response, as safe as it seemed, somehow led, mysteriously, to a neutral discussion of how many children we each envisioned—he wanted three, I was hoping for three or four. *How nice. We wanted about the same.*

This agreement established on one of the three major issues couples fight about (at least according to my prof in an undergrad sociology course—the others are money and sex), we polished off breakfast and returned to the car.

FAMILY REDEFINED

After pulling back onto the highway and driving a few miles north along the ocean, Poster Boy turned in to another small town, drove up the hill, and parked on a sleepy street not far from a post office building. This proved to be the center of town, although the handful of retail buildings wasn't much of a shopping district. He led the way to one such structure and opened the glass door to a small space that could have easily functioned as a coffee shop or boutique. Inside there were two or three families spread out on couches and chairs, in the midst of what turned out to be a sharing time.

An animated, gray-haired woman, whose gaze shared with her son's the glint of the salt water out the window, seemed to be halfway through a story, so Poster Boy made the briefest of introductions as we scurried for seats. I squatted down beside the woman who would become Girlfriend #6, while he found a square of carpet near a blond guy who was surely one of his three younger brothers.

Slowly I gathered that Poster Mom was reporting on their outreach the day before. But since her son hadn't given me much background on the church, her story said more about its teller than the events. Whenever she paused to laugh about something, it seemed to pull more sunlight into the room, yet there was also something in that low voice that evoked the strength of a delicate ironwork gate. *So far, so good.*

About the time I was starting to pick out who the rest of Poster Boy's kin were, they broke for lunch, and the man who proved to be Poster Dad came to greet me. I started to rise from my seat on the floor, but he warmly deterred me. "You don't have to get up, you're family."

In a spiritual sense, of course, I quelled my galloping heart. He didn't seem to notice my widening eyes.

Poster Mom was busy directing the setup for lunch, but Poster Boy's two middle brothers and his sister-in-law also hastened to make me welcome, though it seemed he had never mentioned me before.

After a brief meal eaten in the sunny backyard of the building, everyone gathered around some photocopied maps of the town and assigned the remaining streets not covered the day before. Apparently they were canvassing all one thousand homes with gold-mesh-wrapped narcissus bulbs—a Christmas gift from the church to all their neighbors, except those who wanted no part of such kindness.

Poster Mom prayed over each of us and asked God to bless our time in their community, then we all split up into various smaller groups. There were some instructions about a verse to pray over each of the doorways—which I forgot all but the gist of—but I cheerfully set out with Poster Boy and his married brother, walking up and down quiet streets and leaving behind narcissus and prayers except for the houses marked "do not deliver" on our list.

I hadn't done anything close to such an outreach since my summer project in Berkeley, but this proved a radically different experience. It was no burden to show a small kindness in the name of Jesus, and to connect such generosity to faith gave the deed more solidity somehow. Maybe not since India had I felt the peace of actions so logically wedded to belief.

Sadly, such experiences are all too often limited to "special project" status—at least in most of the churches I've attended. We may have great theology and a powerful preacher, but few hands-on settings in which we're actually working out what it means to see God *first,* both in relationships with each other and those outside the church. Something in me had deeply desired that growth—longed for a context in which you're constantly putting sweat, tears, and prayers into learning just how hard, yet how holy and good, is the life Jesus calls us to—but not until that Sunday had I found a context so American and mundane for that sort of faith in application.

When I wound up delivering bulbs to houses whose owners were home, I faked my way through the conversations with a surprisingly genuine sense of goodwill though I scarcely knew whom or what I was representing. Not until one of the final houses did I get asked who the bulb was from.

"I don't really know," I admitted sheepishly, "but my friend might." I gestured toward Poster Boy's lanky silhouette, waiting for me at the base of the stairs. He must have been too far away to discern this gesture as a call for backup, so I fumbled through the rest of the interaction on what little I knew of the church. Finally I was able to break away and rejoin Poster Boy.

"What were you two talking about?" he asked when I'd made it safely down to the street.

"Oh, he asked who the bulb was from. I said I didn't know."

"What?!" Poster Boy's yelp wasn't that far off one of my own.

"Well, I wasn't given talking points."

Realizing this was true, he then explained that their church ran a small but thriving community center. While much of their outreach was to youth, their aim to love and serve by no means stopped there. That was only one part of an effort to bless and engage the community in a holistic sense. In fact, as I would learn, the winter calendar of events included a number of lectures and classes similar to what a YMCA might offer. Though the church made no secret of their faith, they certainly didn't restrict their programs to the overtly "spiritual."

Much of this I gathered later, once we reconvened at the

Poster Family home—this time in a living room I'd never entered during that long-ago visit on the Fourth of July. After Poster Boy briefly took on Poster Bro #3 in a voluble video game, he turned to discussing some PowerPoint presentation with his dad and Poster Bro #2, an expert in graphic design.

Since this involved some text about the community center, which I'd skimmed during the video game, it finally gave me a chance to make a more confident contribution. Even from my quick read, it was clear the copy could use some tightening up in places. Poster Boy and his dad both seemed wiped out by then (it was already late afternoon), so they gamely let me carry on with Poster Bro #2.

Midway into this powwow, we were joined by Poster Mom. As the conversation slowly shifted from one between the men and me to one between us two women, the guys all slipped away. We went back and forth a few rounds between Poster Mom's vision of what the text should say and what I thought would be most effective from an editorial standpoint, until she suddenly stopped the conversation.

"Who *are* you?"

Poster Mom is one of those people whose focus can be so intense you almost feel ignored when she's concerned with something else, but when her attention shifts to you it's like time in a spotlight. Up until then, I think she'd been so consumed with all the other tasks at hand that she hadn't noticed this strange interloper tagging along with her oldest son.

I had no idea how unusual or routine it was for Poster Boy to bring home female guests—how typical or special was the family's instant warmth toward me—so I steered clear of all but the vaguest terms describing my connection to him. Far better to sketch character indices, like how I'd been homeschooled and came from a solid Christian family, than spend too much time defining my unlikely acquaintance with her son.

Once we finally concluded our interview, Poster Boy was ready to drive me to BART. Though I was flying back in less than a week to try to chase down a permanent job, these precious few moments alone seemed a crucial juncture to figure out whether our friendship would survive the trip. Had Poster Boy seen enough to finally make a more than friendly move, or was he disappointed by the reality?

Our conversation during the twenty-minute trip to the station gave me no clue where I stood with him, but when he finally pulled into the drop-off zone, his farewell was warmer than the night before. As Poster Boy dragged my two suitcases out of the car, he teased me for having so much luggage, then reached for a comfortable hug good-bye. At least we were progressing! And wasn't a good guy likely to take things slow? Secure in the thought that clearly I wasn't *losing* ground, I headed up to the platform for the trip to Berkeley, my first return in five years.

After a brief visit with Girlfriend #1 and Family Friend—now married and working in Berkeley as staff with College Students—I flew the final leg up to Seattle. Mom and Dad picked me up at the airport with Sis, then we drove two hours down to my grandparents' place.

With the weekend stopover still so fresh in my mind, conversation naturally gravitated toward Poster Boy and the visit to his church. Mom and Dad had been apprised of developments since fairly early on, but this time I even dared filling in my grandparents, though I'd not confided a crush to them since the Winner.

Family was always the litmus test of interest: was this someone I could tell them about, much less imagine bringing to meet them and the rest of my more religiously conservative kin? Most of the time it wasn't, and such silence exposed how far from the mark was the guy I liked. Poster Boy, finally, was someone I'd be proud to bring, even eager to introduce and see what conversations transpired. And since I'd already met *his* kin, why not give my grandparents some hope that the ninth of their seventeen living grandchildren might not wind up a spinster after all?

More than describing the whirlwind five months of going from no contact to a friendship where I'd even met his family, however, I found myself marveling over the time at church. As I told Dad on a walk one day, worshipping and serving with them had been like putting my hands inside an electrical socket. Not that it had felt like this at the time, but there was no other way to describe these powerful aftershocks. Maybe because their notion of church hewed more closely to those described in the book of Acts, the Spirit of God seemed present among them in a way I'd never encountered before. It wasn't so much a sense of people defined by radical piety, though, as it was their love for God. I imagine the early church was much the same.

The first Christians certainly were no less sinful than us (just read some of Paul's epistles!), but somehow there's a definite all-or-nothing-ness to their faith. While every other religion of the day was accepted as part of Rome's pluralistic mandate, the Christians refused to treat Rome as their ultimate authority. This same church would later take care of other people's sick when the plagues hit Europe, but their unique approach to "religion" was controversial enough that it led to the deaths of numerous martyrs at state hands.

While there might be some in America's churches today who seem like they'd die as readily for their version of the truth, consider how Jesus went to His death. Instead of defending His in-

nocence, He was silent. When Peter cut off the ear of one soldier, Jesus immediately healed him. Or look at Paul and Silas:
when an earthquake shook the prison holding them and everyone's chains were released, the men stayed and kept their jailer
from taking his life, instead of running to safety.

These were churches where people risked beatings, imprison-
onment, and stoning—but they stuck with it. These were
churches that faced internal challenges like overcoming genera-
tions of racism as they slowly became multiethnic, and other issues of class and gender—but they stuck with it. These were
churches that struggled with how to resolve their conflicts outside of court and had to face sin from legalism to sexual
immorality—*but they stuck with it*. At the same time, the author
of Acts reports that God's Spirit moved among them with great
power, even miracles. Is it any wonder? When we're willing to
decrease so God can increase in us, His people can become
something quite remarkable. That, I think, is what I saw unfold-
ing in the midst of Poster Boy's church. One Sunday wasn't
enough.

PLANTED BY THE PRAYERS OF ANOTHER

After four days catching up with family, I flew back to San Jose
for Christmas day and a frantic two-week search for work.
When I managed to land two interviews during my final week,
I started sketching a madcap move plan, whereby I'd fly home
for maybe a week, pack up everything, and fly back to stay with
my aunt until I found permanent housing. Never mind I had almost no money to do this, it would entail breaking my lease,
and the jobs I was looking at were a good hour's drive from my
aunt's house—surely God could do miracles!

My final Sunday at Poster Boy's church (it was the only place I'd gone to worship that trip, though after the first time I always drove myself), I must have mentioned this harebrained scheme to his mom. Before I left for the day, she made sure everyone gathered to pray over me. Although I'd spent a couple days thinking and praying and even discussing these plans with Roommate and was "75 percent sure" I'd follow through on the move, Poster Mom saw things as being much more uncertain. She asked God to plant my feet wherever He wanted me to stay.

The drive away from church that day was difficult—and not just because of this gentle reminder God might not be as committed to my move campaign as I hoped He was. Somehow there'd been a curious retreat by Poster Boy, so subtle I could barely discern what was wrong, and yet he hadn't pursued my company since that first weekend. I tried to give him space at church, though he was the one I knew best, but something had changed. Although he kept reading the blog and leaving occasional comments, Poster Boy made no further efforts to see me while I was in town, and spoke only briefly after the services.

Both Family Friend and my aunt said things didn't look hopeful, but I found his actions confusing. If Poster Boy had lost interest, wouldn't he simply do as the Captain had? Why was he still reading the blog at all?

When I attempted to suss things out in the great debate over a suitable prize for the soon-to-be-crowned Blog Reader World Series champ—polling readers on the choice of either a date with me or beer as possible trophies—my crush claimed it hinged on the beer. "Well, no disrespect to our lovely blog-mistress, I do have to say that a choice between ANY date and six pints of Guinness is barely a choice at all!" Only if the beer were Pabst Blue Ribbon did Poster Boy say I might have a slight advantage. *Hmph!*

At that point I should have probably canceled all Poster Boy Fan Club memberships, but things had gone so astonishingly well on the whole—at least until quite recently—that I still couldn't conceive of all God's evident blessing on this friendship being for a purpose other than romance. It had been one thing to risk my heart on Married Man, despite all monstrous red flags, red lights, red *everything* to the contrary, but I didn't even have *dust* in the corner with Poster Boy! Even Poster Dad agreed that I must have gone to their church by some "divine appointment."

It was, however, Poster Mom's words that lingered longest in my head, as I returned to a frigid New York and eventual rejection from the second company interviewed with (the first had already told me no). *God certainly seemed to be planting my feet in New York.* The news about the second job had come in the midst of washing some dishes or making a latte, so I stood at the counter absorbing the news and wondered how I'd make it through this latest disappointment.

There was a lot of history in that kitchen. Here was the cupboard I'd wept against that day Stevie Wonder reminded me of heaven. Here was the phone from which I'd listened to Poster Boy's voice mail roughly a month before. Here was the sink I'd emptied of dishes so many days this month as one small way to grow in discipline, hence love God and my roommate better. And one other way I wanted to love Him was by rejoicing no matter what happened jobwise. I'd even asked God for the strength to help me do so. Now I had the news, would I rejoice?

It was at least definite closure. And what was a few months' delay? Perhaps spring would be a better time to move, once Roommate was finished with school and we'd fulfilled our one-year lease. It might even give me time to save some money! Deciding a small celebration might help me decisively rejoice, I tugged on boots and went out for cake mix to make a special dessert recipe I learned from my grandma at Christmas.

Though choosing to praise God didn't raise the bitter outside temperature, it did begin to teach me about contentment no matter what my actual circumstances. Staying in New York forced me to depend on God to reveal Himself apart from the community and encouragement I'd found in California. Not that my own church or Bible study were lukewarm or heretical, but God seemed to work through them in less dramatic ways than the house church on the West Coast. And after all, to think that I would grow more in the presence of Poster Boy's church was overlooking the fact it was *God* who'd matured them, God who ultimately supplied the training and knowledge as He saw fit. My job was to seek Him and humbly accept whatever means He chose to use in my life.

Besides, the issues that needed the most work tended to be much more basic than I wanted to admit. It doesn't take some particular spiritual gift to spot idolatry at its ugliest; it takes faithful love like that of several dear women in my Bible study, who prayed with me week in and out, confronted me without rancor or timidity, and backed up their words with consistent demonstration of concern for my well-being. That, plus my own willingness to listen, proved more than adequate for the growth God had in mind.

For the few things I faced that were beyond the experience of those women to help, my needs were met through other means. During the first several months of the year, I stayed in frequent contact with Poster Mom, who had begun to take on an informal sort of mentoring role toward the end of the California stay. Once I returned to the East Coast, it was natural to keep contacting her with questions or updates on ways that she could pray for me and, eventually, for news on ways that I could pray for them. To my surprise, it wasn't long before she took to signing e-mails "Love, Poster Mom." Since I felt a rapidly growing affection for her, I soon responded with like signature.

Such contact was a comfort given the growing infrequency of my chats with Poster Boy. His increased silence was so dramatic that after running it past my parents, I called him up in late January to ask if I'd done something to cause his retreat from friendship—meaning, of course, to press the issue of whether it had been friendly interest at all. If he claimed I'd misread his intent, then why the sudden distance? Only if he'd had and *lost* interest could this silence be explained (though, if I had thought about it, I would have realized he probably wouldn't have owned up to this anyway).

Poster Boy gave none of the answers expected, to my absolute befuddlement. He pled the demands of extreme overtime (claiming work weeks of something like seventy or eighty hours), then temporarily quelled my fears that he was backing off by asking about my search for work and giving advice on a quandary over a recent freelance project.

Despite these signs of concern, however, that phone call was one of the last times we talked until a few days before Valentine's Day, when he IM-ed to thank me for his prize as the Blog Reader World Series champ (I swear he was the unanimous choice of my unbiased, three-person team of judges—and entries had no identifying marks).

Things started off well enough when Poster Boy made a joke referencing previous e-mails about the prize, which was a handheld muscle massager given me by my aunt during New Year's cleaning. But then he swiftly pushed the joke much further with a remark that, after three weeks of silence and his reduced initiative in contact, left me feeling used. Though what he'd said wasn't that much more obnoxious than a few of his more shocking remarks before Christmas, the context was quite different. Then I'd been slightly taken aback but viewed such boldness as flirting, on which grounds I let it pass without comment. What exactly was I supposed to think now?

Fine—he'd lost interest. It was painful, but I could deal. To resume chat with such an immediate reference to the provocative, though, suggested he had little interest in me except as a source of the safe kicks my earliest blogging had provided. But hadn't he noticed how I'd been trying—for months, no less—to minimize such content? Here I was striving to take to heart his inadvertent feedback, even though what motivation his interest once provided was fast declining, and he seemed to care only for my former self. Maybe good guys didn't like character as much as they claimed to.

We traded a few more strange remarks (my half of which probably left Poster Boy more confused than my misuse of "misogynistic"), then he fell into a lengthy, unexplained silence. After a bit, I made some excuse about lunch and ended our chat session, then went off to an angry, multiday mope. Internal peace be damned!

When my snit completely defeated attempts to fast on Valentine's Day (which I spent mostly seething instead of praying), I decided this called for a letter of confrontation. I've always had a peculiar affection for putting literal ink to tactile paper, one advantage of which is thoughtfulness—and in this case, more contrition than I expected.

Thinking about the bottom-line issues, and why I felt I could confront Poster Boy, meant appealing to a higher standard—which, once again, I had to admit I hadn't met either. There was no way to object to his words without admitting the bawdy climate I'd created with *Sexless*. Although I'd very assiduously avoided such talk whenever we were communicating directly—

for fear he'd presume from any apparent flirtation that I actually *liked* him—it wasn't fair to expect him to read my mind or hesitate over private remarks akin to what I boldly said in public.

Given the surprising degree of confession in my three- or four-page letter, I felt at peace about the words slipped into a jaunty turquoise envelope two days later, after Mom and Dad approved an e-mail version. If there was any lingering hesitation as I slipped it into a postal bin, self-protection steadied my hand on this attempt to provoke the conflict that would surely hasten his ultimate rejection of me. Far better that such a parting happen on my terms than he catch me by surprise.

God, however, seemed to have other plans. Poster Boy probably got that letter the same day he flew out of state for a trip through the end of February (which I knew of either through his mom or my growing contact with Girlfriend #6). The month went by, I waited in dread—the trip was apparently more than a week in length—and right about when I expected he might be finally home to read my letter, I returned from a day of temp work to find a fistful of mail in which was a strangely familiar turquoise envelope.

That shocking flash of color was like getting a cosmic version of the shoulder-blade pinch my mom had once perfected for getting our attention. *What?!!* I turned it over to verify the letter was unopened, then peered at the slash marks through his address. Scribbled in what looked like a masculine hand were the words "Not at this address."

Not at this address! But I'd sent so many packages there! And surely he hadn't moved . . .

As I slowly walked from the mailbox, there was a shocking sense of having smacked into God's sovereignty: *Beyond this point, you may not go.*

CHAPTER 17

TEARS, FEARS, ONE MORE YEAR

Prosperity will have its seasons
Even when it's here, it's going by
And when it's gone we pretend we know the reasons
And all the roots grow deeper when it's dry

—DAVID WILCOX, *"All the Roots Grow Deeper When It's Dry"*

There have been crushes where the biggest struggle was simply letting go of hope: when some man has become your treasure, it's hard to walk away from the loss unrequited or failed love feels like. It can even seem farsighted (if not noble—aren't you loyal?) to persist like a losing gambler, who refuses to leave the table because he's sure that a few more hands will recoup and multiply his investment.

That's self-protection of one kind, but it's not the only game our hearts buy into. Other times, the goal is not avoiding the loss itself as much as losing in a certain *way*. Eventually I had to admit this was the ultimate point of the letter: attempting to maintain control over how much Poster Boy could hurt me. I don't know why I thought God would care more about false hope than such manipulation, though, especially since the latter had started coming up a lot not long before the letter was written.

It all began the very first weekend of February, when I became convicted that change was needed not just in the way I spoke around men, but in my actual approach to friendship. I had become a user of men, feeding needs God hadn't yet chosen to meet with a husband through ambiguous, intimate friendships that were almost a kind of emotional dating. However often the guy in question was looking to me as a similar kind of stopgap didn't matter.

I started to realize chastity meant saving more than physical intimacy for marriage. Spouses share more than just sexual closeness, after all. So as a rather belated resolution for 2005, I decided to give up dating (at least in the sense of casual romance), and even most one-on-one hangouts with guys. No matter how deep my desires for relationship, it was God's right to bring blessings into and out of my life as *He* saw fit. If there were needs I thought He should meet, or ways He was "underusing" my talents and youth, this so-called lack and waste were really His problem, not mine.

Flowers don't fall short of their purpose if they bloom and fade unseen by human eyes, after all; it is enough if they delight their Maker. It is in fact in seeking to delight Him that they enthrall us as much as they do. I had spent most of my single life attempting to enthrall every guy who went past, and consequently wound up less healthy and deeply rooted than I might have otherwise. Find sustenance on the surface, though, and you have no root to hold you down, come storm or someone determined to uproot you. Better to let thirst draw your roots down deep.

This was the lesson hammered away that February weekend of decision. As I told my journal:

> *It's like you've got to drill down deep, deep into the core of the earth. For a time as you sink down deep in after your spade, it looks like you're pulling away from all the stuff on earth: friends, sky, rain, trees, flowers, laughter, all of it. But it's really*

just taking you in to the core of it all, to the Life and Love who made it. And you have to sink your roots in Him, after all. You have to find His water underground . . . Only when your roots are drinking from that stream can you grow tall enough and strong enough to reach out into the world and maybe even make a little shade for others. To grow up tall and strong so as to bless the soil of others' plots of ground—that's what we're meant to do. The branch or plant, after all, doesn't worry so much about "growing" hard or stretching up strong, but sinking the roots down deep into the waters of life. And then, because of how God's made us, the life and springing upward is a mostly natural consequence of that drinking, sinking, rooting.

While this vision initially gave me hope and great release from the stress of seeking men's attention, sinking in after my spade soon proved quite difficult—for sinking away from Poster Boy meant trusting God with our friendship to a much greater extent than I wanted.

After the letter came back around the beginning of March, I started to realize this wasn't about trying to prematurely end things before my deepest longings were drawn out then completely disappointed, but about trusting God to know what was best—trusting God even with the thousands of miles between us. So much for the illusion of control!

And yet, even though unemployment had run out, I couldn't quite bring myself to start looking for a *permanent* job—at least in New York City. Hence a series of temp assignments that were, in their way, a vocational kind of cohabiting. In retrospect, this eagerness to beat a path to the West Coast is almost comical. Right around the same time I'd made the pledge to give up dating and be more careful in friendships with guys, I'd started thinking about writing a book based on the blog. Maybe there was a story in my struggle to be chaste—which would, with any luck, wind up looking like some Christian *Bridget Jones,* except with Poster Boy as Colin Firth (at least a girl could hope for that).

Once I managed to score a strictly "informational" interview with an agent I sort of knew, I even threw together a book proposal for his review. That meeting didn't go well. At all. Less than one month later, however, an editor friend of Blogyenta's—whom I'd met at a stitch-n-bitch—e-mailed to ask if I'd thought of turning *Sexless* into a book. By the middle of March, we'd gotten together for drinks to discuss my proposal, which she had several suggestions on how to improve but already hoped she'd be able to buy for the publisher she worked for.

If I'd stopped to think about it, a possible book deal might be good reason to stick around a bit longer. And wasn't my writing partly why I'd come to New York in the first place? Perhaps if I had been driven more by career than the hope of marriage, this would have been reason enough to stay. But not even the prospect of such a major creative coup could combat the fear of sabotaging any chance with Poster Boy by staying put on the East Coast. Wasting that rare confluence of opportunity and aptitude seemed less tragic than potentially wasting the last few years of my youth in a singleness that might be avoided with a canny relocation.

Not that I was totally confident God considered this the best for me—*au contraire.* Hence a gradual distance between us, as I tried to skirt the deeper, more honest prayer times in which I feared God would press the issue.

This lasted until a week before Easter, when I finally realized what I was doing. On Palm Sunday, I walked to the large city park in my neighborhood, dragging my feet in dread at what I suspected lay ahead.

As I entered the west side of the path belting Prospect Park's diamond-shaped perimeter, my prayer turned toward the heart of the issue. After a bit of crying out in my fear and longing to exit Brooklyn, I finally conceded God didn't seem to be blessing such a departure. Though He'd worked plenty of miracles when I left Arizona, present conditions—even for a summer move—suggested God wasn't supporting an exit at this time. What did He want me to do?

Give Me one more year here.

I burst into tears. It certainly wasn't an audible voice, but that thought was quite distinct in my mind—and far enough from what I wanted to hear that I was pretty sure it was God. But that didn't stop this small bit of clay from arguing with her Maker for the rest of the hour-plus walk, on through the night (even after I'd gone to church), and into the wee hours of the morning. Only once I was finally sinking into the wounded sleep of submission did God's peace begin to comfort me, along with what seemed assurances of how He would bless me.

Once I agreed to obey God on moving, all the energy occupied with that dead-end project was transferred into the book proposal. At the same time, all the details came together with the same swiftness and ease my move from Arizona had—as if, once again, God's blessing were upon this. By the end of May I had an agent for the book, and one week later, a last-minute interview for a big piece on chastity in a national magazine, which was on newsstands by the middle of June.

SOMETHING ROTTEN IN THE STATE OF FRIENDSHIP?

Poster Boy, meanwhile, had fallen silent for part of that winter and spring, but eventually we returned to occasional chats online. By May he'd tried to help send some freelance editing my way, and had drawn me into consultation on a project he and a friend were preparing to launch.

As these discussions continued into the summer, I got a firsthand glimpse of how other Christians were working out the implications of faith in their work and art. This wasn't just about what sort of songs they wrote, however, or striving for integrity, but thinking through how their success could prosper others. Poster Boy and Poster Friend, you see, perceived means as a stewardship one was given primarily for the purpose of blessing other people. It wasn't really a new idea—if you read your Bible—but their effort to live this out began to quietly change my thinking in radical ways.

Yet even as my involvement with them began to spur such fruitful reflection, I started to realize the friendship with Poster Boy wasn't all that healthy. Though there'd been no flirtation between us since February, I was still battling not to give him God's place in my heart. And from little things he'd said here and there, it seemed I might be resurrecting a few of Poster Boy's own relational struggles. After my national interview raised fears he would soon reject me over my sinfulness, these issues in our friendship became unavoidable.

Maybe if I'd had more than one night's notice from the reporter, and a tad more than two hours' sleep to prepare, I wouldn't have answered his follow-up queries about one of my more regrettable indiscretions. Instead I gave in to my usual tendency to explain till the questioner was satisfied—forgetting that this time I had no editorial control over how these details were pieced together.

By the Friday before the article photo shoot, I was well on my way to a full-scale, four-alarm freak-out—all over what Poster Boy would make of my ill-considered disclosures. This tension eventually leaked into our chat that night.

The session began as a consult on whether I should hang out with a church guy or not, since my recent ban on even friendly dates was loosely based on a book that Poster Boy had recommended. As I'd only skimmed a few chapters at the bookstore one day, I hoped he could give me some Cliffs Notes on the dilemma. Did he have time to talk, or was he "crazy-mad busy" as usual?

"MAD busy. But I got time for ya."

And as casual as his reply was, therein lies the mystery of how the human heart extends and receives love. What to one person is common courtesy is to another tender words of life—and by the same token, what one person intends to show as great affection may be to his beloved an irrelevant show of frivolousness compared to the kindness of simply doing the laundry sometimes. Poster Boy doubtless had no clue, but from that sentence onward he held my fearful, nearly tearful heart in his hands.

All this stress and fragility had almost nothing to do with the pretext of our talk, of course. So after debating the wisdom of the one-on-one hangout in question, I finally got around to my less-than-stellar interview. Naturally, I couldn't get into what I was *most* afraid of him learning, without it seeming weird, but I tried to give him a pretty good gist of it.

Poster Boy said "hoo boy" a lot, as I sketched the sort of quotes that might make it into the story, but mostly just kept teasing me. Somehow the combination of that almost folksy reply—not far off something my mom's relatives might say—and his gentle ribbing did as much good for my heart as if he'd directly addressed my stated fear that "no Christian guy would want me as a wife" after my portrayal in the article.

It was this sort of offhand kindness, by which he made me feel more loved as a friend than he might have intended, that fed my growing frustration with his remoteness. While Poster Boy had no trouble entering graciously and generously into *my* life, this new phase of friendship was marked by general silence on his own life and struggles; even general questions prompted cursory remarks dashed off before he invariably had another meeting.

Eventually I realized this had to stop. However much I enjoyed Poster Boy's concern for my life, however healing his humor had often been, it wasn't good for either one of us to maintain this fairly one-way flow of intimacy. I clearly couldn't expect him to invite me into his life the way he readily entered mine, so if I wanted a mutual friendship, I'd have to learn to reciprocate his distance.

I started another letter. This time the main thrust was asking we quit communicating by chat. It certainly was a painful stand to take, but seeing whenever he was online and wondering if he would or why he didn't IM me was slowly eating away at my sanity. Besides, since e-mail and phone calls were implicitly more intentional ways of communicating, the shift away from a fairly casual medium might subtly raise the question why we were in touch at all.

I don't remember much else about the second letter, except that it went through *four* drafts at least—reviewed by my parents and Roommate—and struck me as so understatedly eloquent, it was hard not to keep a copy for myself. In keeping with my custom of mailing such missives near important dates, I sent it on Poster Boy's twenty-ninth birthday, while he was down in South America for another trip. This time, however, I took him off my buddy list, and even explained to Poster Mom I thought it best we cease our regular contact. She was quite understanding.

Weeks went by, and no word came from Poster Boy. Although he and Poster Friend were gearing up for the launch of their project, it incensed me to think he'd gotten the letter and just ignored it, as well as the issues raised within. Hadn't our friendship meant more to him?

Five weeks after I'd mailed the letter, and one week after my book proposal sold, their big project launched. When I went on-line the next day, a girlfriend and I embarked a lengthy catch-up session, heavy on talk of Poster Boy and Poster Friend. Forty-five minutes into this, and not long after I'd filled her in on the letter requesting IM silence, a new tab pops up in my chat window. For a conversation with Poster Boy.

Let's just say if I'd been on a radio station just then, I might or might not have met the FCC's standards.

After we traded a few lines of greeting, all fairly clipped on my part (however nice it was to see him working to have a conversation), I asked whether Poster Boy had had any interesting mail lately.

He hadn't, aside from a package sent back with Girlfriend #6 after she flew out for five days in May.

No letters?

No. Was he supposed to get one?

Holy freaking crap. God blocked the second one too! Apparently we needed to talk about all of this more directly.

In many ways we did. Looking back, though, I think we barely began to address the deepest issues—at least at a level acceptable to a female mind. After a couple IM sessions hashing things out, we returned to silence. No talk of what this friendship meant to each of us (which probably wasn't the same), or if we therefore could continue it, and if so what that would look like. Nothing. Had I not wound up back in California that October, in fact, I'm not sure when we would have spoken next.

Once I finished teaching a one-month class in September

(one of the various part-time gigs that paid my bills during book writing), it seemed a good time to take a West Coast vacation, visit with friends, research the book . . . and finally catch Poster Friend and Poster Boy in a live performance. Though I flew out with some hope the trip would help clarify how on earth I ought to end the book I'd just sold, there was a good bit of dread things might be rather awkward between us.

My first weekend of the ten-day trip, I crashed with Girlfriend #6, which meant attending church with Poster Family the next day. Though Poster Boy greeted me warmly enough when I saw him briefly Saturday night, his conversation Sunday consisted of asking about the weather. *Fantastic.* Would my gut sense that more was still in store for the trip be borne out? With only God to trust, I drove to Monterey for a visit with Girlfriend #3.

After a good couple days catching up (she'd recently returned from two years with the Peace Corps), I drove back to the city for the much-anticipated gig. I'd tried to round up a posse of my local friends, but wound up joining only those whom I knew because of Poster Boy, drat the man. When would I get a chance to show I had *friends,* for God's sake?

Dancing around to Led Zeppelin later almost made me some *new* friends among a few of the guys at the bar, but Poster Boy made as few efforts to approach me as I did to approach him. Once I was finally getting ready to leave, though—which would be the last time I saw him on this trip, maybe ever—it seemed rude to not say good-bye.

He was standing near the stage with a small knot of guys, clad in one of the jackets he wears like some sort of hepcat uniform (invariably, it's blue velvet or tan leather). How the man could look unfailingly attractive seemed the height of unfairness, but I didn't have so bad a getup myself—nor should I have, for how many weeks in advance a suitably casual-yet-hot outfit had been planned. And hadn't he even admired my thin khaki jacket Saturday?

Mustering all the height my new three-and-a-half-inch black retro pumps afforded, I strolled near and waited until he caught my eye, attempting some casual writerly diffidence that wouldn't lead to further spills.

Apparently my Jane Dean aloofness relaxed him enough to delve beyond the climatic differences between our two states, but this meant asking how I was doing. *Crap! How was I sposed to answer this now?*

I must have paused too long.

"Not good?"

Still I hesitated. Finally I told him, in a gentle reminder of our previous talk, that if he was going to ask about me, he had to be prepared to tell me how he was doing too. *Reciprocity and all that.* Cue: standard spiel on how extremely busy he was.

Somehow, though, this led us into discussing the "research" component of my trip. Explaining that I'd quizzed Posse Pal on the summer we all met, I heard myself say offhandedly, "In fact, I'd love to talk to you about that summer too." *That wasn't planned!*

"Sure!"

Next thing I knew, we were making tentative plans to meet or talk that weekend, even though he was leaving for a mission trip days later.

There were several times when I thought it wasn't going to work out, but finally we met up Sunday night at a sports bar near his home. I made a couple opening queries about the summer we first met, but to my surprise the conversation gradually took a fairly personal turn. It wasn't what I'd expected of the night, but as if he'd known the questions I longed to but didn't dare ask, Poster Boy wound up sharing as openly as he'd ever done.

At some points, it was all I could do not to spring across the table, and wrap myself around him like a human tourniquet for the pain still there years after some of the incidents he described. Since I feared he would spurn any sign of caring, I let his words pool quietly inside me, until God reclaimed them a few days later in ardent prayers and weeping for him.

Toward the end of our talk, Poster Boy said flat out he wasn't interested in anyone currently, but I left feeling humbled and grateful for how much he'd let me in, and much more at peace about our friendship.

I would have been quite content to end the trip with that conversation, but then he unexpectedly IM-ed the next day—chatting with an unusual ease and expansiveness on his part, as if our conversation had been a great relief to him also.

It felt so good to talk and joke around like that, at first I thought we might pull through with an intact friendship after all. Then I wound up dropping a couple things off that night in the small town where his parents lived and stopping by their house on one of those errands. Once Poster Mom and I settled on their couch, she asked how things were going with her son, which led to a conversation I should have probably foreseen.

Not until my plane took off the next morning, though, did I process things enough to really cry. Then the tears flowed freely throughout much of my flight, as I struggled to draw up the boundaries suggested during my talk with Poster Mom. First I sketched an e-mail saying I couldn't be friends at all. But that didn't seem right. Wouldn't this be an ultimatum presuming that Poster Boy would never draw sufficient boundaries himself? Next I tried backing toward the truth—an e-mail warning that while I'd never *ask* for more than friendship, I couldn't promise I'd never *want* more. Except, of course, the "hypothetical" was already true. *Dammit.*

By the time I reached Brooklyn, there was no "event" too small to merit the weeping due a real tragedy; mercifully it was a rather unremarkable subway ride home. After another cry once I walked in the door, I got ready for my Tuesday night Bible study. When they saw how distraught I was, the women in my prayer circle were unanimous that I cut things off with Poster Boy. As I continued to hesitate, one finally asked if I had ever told him that I liked him. *No* . . . That would be the very worst thing imaginable! No matter how much I might scheme and passively hint at interest, I never, never, *ever* told a guy the state of my heart—at least not until such feelings were past tense. If I crossed that line with Poster Boy, he'd never get the chance to think he liked me first!

Walking home bareheaded through the increasing drizzle later, though, I decided honesty might be the best thing after all. Why drag out this drama any longer? After battling pride through several far-too-naked choices of words, I finally found a phrasing I could live with, then dialed his number.

Voice mail. Seeing this as a blessing, for once, I said my three-sentence speech of interest disclosure and pressed the red "end" button. Strange, it should be so physically easy to tear asunder a friendship like this—shouldn't there be more work involved?

When I got home, I caught up with Roommate briefly, had some wine, turned off my phone, and cried myself to sleep.

LIFE, REPURPOSED

After I awoke the next morning, there was a cryptic, two-word text message: "Roger that." And to think I ever presumed I somewhat understood men! However much confusion this "response" created, though, God's grace was unmistakably upon me during the next few days.

At so many points my way had seemed unclear, but once I'd told Poster Boy, I saw how unavoidable and crucial it was. In light of how much openness and honesty had characterized our talks in California, there was no way to continue our "friendship" with any sort of integrity while carrying on the pretense of disinterest. I had had to let him know. And now that I had, things were completely, finally in God's hands.

When I went to Blogyenta's monthly stitch-n-bitch ten days later, one of the women remarked on my painful disclosure, saying that it could "really release God's power" in my life. I didn't quite understand at the time—how could my simple honesty be so powerful? Perhaps what she perceived, however, was how that phone call put a nail through the heart of my idolatry. While staying in New York had been a sacrifice of the possible, telling Poster Boy I liked him had been a sacrifice of the actual. Once I'd lost that old life, who knew what God would provide?

The late-October ground was still damp from rain that night as I walked home from the subway later on. In keeping with my recent habit, I turned onto the block I'd been praying for weekly since around Easter. That night, however, I passed a soggy mattress sheltering what looked like a person, whose plight became the focus of my prayer for the block. Once I turned the corner onto the avenue down to my street, I started praying about how this person's need touched *my* life.

Certainly I couldn't dream of offering to let him or her crash at my place, with two unprotected women—but what about some day? It struck me then that should I ever marry, I wanted a husband who'd be willing to pray intensely with me about such things—even be open should God lay on our hearts a response of radical hospitality. Though in some ways this thought only expressed more explicitly the things I'd wanted for a while, I went home with a strange feeling it pushed me closer to a great discovery.

When I went to church the next night, the sermon was all about justice and God's profound identification with the poor. I couldn't shake the sense this was connected to my prayers somehow. *What was God trying to show me?* It was like I was holding a box that would open once all the proper pegs were inserted.

Tuesday night at Bible study, discussion about the sermon led to talking about encounters with the homeless. After I realized how little extended contact most of my friends had had with the poor, I challenged the group to think about sharing a meal with a beggar that week—or at least offering food to one. Who knew what blessing the Lord might have in store for their courage?

If I had thought God meant my words for them, though, I spent the rest of the workweek surprised at how much they haunted *me. What was so familiar in the way I'd described my moments with the poor?* I had even choked up in talking about Subway Guy.

Friday I got what proved to be another peg while I was waiting for my train into the city. Almost out of nowhere, a seemingly random question skittered through my head: *Which would bring me greater joy, a husband and child, or seeing someone come to God?* Right about then the train came, but as I stepped inside the car, I realized probably the latter would.

Not until quite a bit later that night did the box get shaken just right and I realized the pegs were finally in place. Then it suddenly dawned on me that helping the homeless and talking to people of Jesus—especially the conversations most centered on why His life was of such consequence for history—had *both* moved me with an intense sense of my humanity and purpose. Suddenly my pastor's recent teaching, all that contact with Poster Boy's church, and what he and Poster Friend were trying to do with their project all fused into a staggering epiphany. *The things that moved me most were instances when I was most involved in bringing God's kingdom to bear on this earth.*

I had spent the last fifteen months attempting to sort out where I could find my purpose in life and suddenly here it was. The ultimate satisfaction and purpose wasn't sex/marriage/family as I had so long believed, it was participating in the restoration of God's kingdom here on earth. But for the first time I saw that this was *not* the rather boring set of discrete goals I'd always taken it for—things like virtuous living, helping the poor, and telling folks about Jesus. Nor was it some sort of individual crusade.

Seeking God's kingdom was everything my pastors had said about church as a "family of families" and a community called to bless both each other and the city they lived in. It was both preaching the gospel *and* helping the poor, both what we'd done in India *and* Poster Boy and his friend's approach to professional and creative success. Most importantly, rather than being a nebulous course of obedience, it was a purpose that could encompass marriage or singleness, writing or motherhood.

No matter what the future held, if I found my purpose in seeking God's kingdom, my identity couldn't be shaken. As I fell asleep that night, the words of Jesus rang in my head like some kind of love letter: "Seek first His kingdom and His righteousness . . . Store up for yourselves treasures in heaven . . . "

CHAPTER 18

THE WORTH OF THE BLUES

What most of us spend the energy of our lives warring against is reality—the fact that life is awful and the truth that this world is not our home . . . [N]o one will choose a path of sacrificial, courageous love if this life is either all there is or is nearly as good as the next. One will choose the better only if the present is faced as it is—not worth living for, but worth dying to change.

—DAN ALLENDER AND TREMPER LONGMAN, *Bold Love*

In that long-ago dream of dying a virgin, two lies were exposed: one regarding the true nature of this earth, and one regarding my identity. Both stemmed from a distorted view of what "good" was. Though I'd been trying to skirt the error often made by the church—demeaning the physical world—I only bought into the lie more common in secular thought: that ultimate good and pleasure are found in *this* life. Not until I started to grasp the significance of the kingdom could I recognize the truth and error in both.

When you read Jesus's parables or stories of the kingdom, you encounter lots of talk about *cultivation*. Whereas most people tend either toward denial of life's pain or minimization of its beauty, Jesus finds *both* lack and worth. Thus He affirms our sense of the goodness in life while firmly asserting the painful result of our sin: how fleeting and imperfect are those joys, how often our wretchedness destroys them.

It is by no means easy to try to reconcile those two; some of the difficult intervals one is forced to play in so doing may not resolve into music until we reach heaven. And yet in heaven alone—in being fully restored to fellowship with God—is there the promise of something wondrous enough to meet and exceed our deepest longings. That is a hope that cannot be shaken by anything. As this realization began to sink in, I felt the chains of an idolatry I had started to think I'd never overcome actually giving way; I was finally slipping free.

But if I'd thought such healing meant the blessing of marriage—or at least a boyfriend—might follow on its heels, I'd misunderstood the reason that God liberates His people. When, for instance, we read about the Israelites, it might be easy to take from the story the notion that God's redemption was to bless them with the Promised Land. And that was certainly part of the plan, no question. But if you read more carefully, the line always taken with Pharaoh is that God wants to bring them out so they can *worship Him*. As it turns out, that isn't a canny lie; it is the truth.

Worshipping God starts right away, and as my heart is only recently starting to learn, He's not the lesser gift but the greatest. Until you see that, no good gift can be properly enjoyed.

AT LEAST

Shortly after my spiritual breakthrough, Poster Boy and I finally worked out the terms of our parting as friends. What proceeded with reasonable humor initially, though, eventually got messy—

so much that by my next trip to California, two months later, I was prepared for the worst, most awkward meeting possible. That proved a slightly pessimistic outlook on the New Year's Eve party we both got invited to, but neither was said shindig a chance to learn if he'd accepted an apology I'd e-mailed earlier.

Then I had to call Poster Boy three days later, with a minor fact check for the book. Though he'd made the briefest attempt at teasing me New Year's Eve, I wasn't sure he'd want to talk any more than absolutely necessary. As far as I knew, even having him review the chapters he figured in was asking quite a lot, since earlier that fall he'd gotten mad enough to de-Friendster me. (Admittedly, our parting hadn't gone down in the most adult fashion.)

When he finally called back, I'd just cleared security at the airport and had plenty time to talk. Though he was watching a football game, to my surprise it turned out that he was in no hurry either. After we'd worked through most of the matters at hand, he asked how I was. Since this showed more openness than I expected, I shared a little bit of my research the last couple days, then asked what he'd thought of the chapter I'd sent. As it was still fairly muddled at that point, any feedback he had would be quite helpful.

Initially Poster Boy focused on more general flaws, like places where the story lacked direction. But as I kept responding calmly, he ventured into the heart of the problems he saw, both in the chapter and my writing on the blog in general. I'd already had several tense confrontations with Dad on this trip—and even an unexpected one with Poster Mom—but as I listened to her son, it seemed the point of those prior discussions was getting my attention for the words that God gave Poster Boy.

As our talk continued for a staggering twenty-five minutes,

he went on to balance some of the harshest words my writing—
and, by extension, my spiritual life—had ever withstood with
frequent affirmation of both my gifts and, at least implicitly, my
worth. In him, I faced my worst fears: observations I'd thought,
if heard from another, would pretty much destroy me. Surprisingly, his didn't. Running through every word he said was a tone
of concern and esteem so strong and so shocking that I sat
speechless for at least two hours after we talked.

Never had my shame been so exposed to another or addressed with such love. He had said all that to me, and yet said
he respected me. Not even love—*respect*. I actually had to consult my laptop's thesaurus to confirm that "respect" meant what
I thought it did.

I guess I've always seen part of love as really a kind of pity
(or at least, that's how it has sometimes come across in others).
Just because you're committed to loving need not mean there's
much *worth* in the loved, only that you, the lover, have much
integrity. Depending on who and how and why you love, that
emotion could be directed up, across, or down. Others who
have confronted me may have *said* they loved me, but in those
moments I felt like they mostly meant they pitied me, this sinful rag of a wretch. It felt as if their "love" was directed down.
How then could Poster Boy see such sin and hypocrisy but still
find something to value in me—something that made him look
not down but maybe even up to me? It was perhaps the first
time I began to really *get* what God's grace means.

Grace not only embraces you at your most shameful, it's the
most effective antidote to sin. As the impact of Poster Boy's
words sank in, I had no choice but to heed the correction it
seemed God had lovingly spoken through him. Every time my
usual self-protectiveness rose to deflect a change implied by his
words, memory beat that back. *But he said that he respected me.*

Instead of consigning me to a heap of ruins because of my sin, he wanted to clear off the filth that was tarnishing what he saw beneath my disgrace. His words were not meant to protect *himself* (from my impurity), but the God-given worth in *me* that I kept dragging in the dust. Therefore I had to listen to him, and take to heart what he'd said.

Some man had finally cared enough to point out my shock-n-awe for what it was, and then to stick around and talk to the terrified woman behind that shield. Over the year since then, it's launched me on an exploration of grace that's changed my life, although it hasn't changed my circumstances in exactly the way I hoped.

Poster Boy ended our talk that day with the comment he "still considered me a friend" but said he thought it best we part ways so we didn't keep on hurting each other. Other than occasional talks about this or that part of the manuscript, we haven't been in touch since then.

In many ways, that loss has been profound. Forget my early, distorted views of Poster Boy as near saint—here was a man with the guts to *confront* me! If I'd been dismayed before at my seeming inability to reciprocate what a blessing he'd been in my relationship with God, it was far worse now. As the months dragged on and contact decreased, however, God began to show me that even this "waste" of love was His business. Was not God the ultimate agent behind all my growth? Weren't Poster Boy's needs *His* job to fill? My place was to offer praise and gratitude to God—and if He someday chose to share that blessing with Poster Boy, so be it. But if He chose to *not* use me for comparable good in Poster Boy's life, that was His prerogative too.

By the beginning of summer, I was starting to find peace with all this, to even find contentment in my singleness and my loss of almost all contact with the friend who was once so dear.

Then toward the end of July, Poster Friend texted me with news on an upcoming gig . . . in New York. They were finally playing my town.

While he never actually said as much, I knew without a doubt this meant Poster Boy was coming too. Never mind how much his long-ago mention of a possible visit had started, this news fulfilled something I thought God had promised more than a year before, the night I finally gave up my move scheme: he'd bring Poster Boy to New York. Now it was finally happening! Would God at last accomplish what I'd been longing for nearly two years now?

Though there was little in Poster Boy's recent actions (and total silence about the visit) to support a positive outlook, I was paralyzed by emotional indecision. On the one hand, I didn't want to hope for too much and face total devastation if I was wrong. But on the other, I didn't want to *self-protectively* hope for the worst and therefore fail to trust God would bring good through this regardless. Somehow I had to put my hope in *God's character,* and not a specific outcome—trust that God alone knew what was best for me, the very thing I'd always been so loath to do.

As if that weren't enough to manage, this drama commencing nearly three weeks prior to the show presented a serious threat to my writing, already several weeks behind schedule. So over the course of the next few weeks, I started taking walks to pray—first just a few nights a week, then almost nightly, then even *twice* a day when the strain was greatest. These forty-minute laps up and down an avenue near my house were not so new, of course—they had their start in my long-ago, long-forgotten loops round a campus track—but I'd never walked and prayed like that so consistently.

Somehow in those stretches of pacing the sidewalks, I found

a focus not usually possible when I tried to pray that long while sitting or kneeling, and an intimacy with God I'd never known before. For the first time, my prayer life became less a means of crisis management (though that was usually a good chunk of the walk), more a ritual of relationship that daily grew in its preciousness. Maybe it had not been so strange after all that early e-mails describing my "seek first His kingdom" epiphany likened the words to a love letter.

Love is, of course, the word used to describe our expected relationship to God—"Love the Lord your God with all your heart and with all your soul and with all your strength" (what Jesus later calls the great commandment). Somehow, though, I had always treated my heart more like my money, whereby God was entitled to maybe a tithe and then some, but certainly not the sort of lavish affection long reserved for a husband. Even though I had long since overcome those childhood days when not even *some* hint of feeling was possible, I still couldn't see how God could ever possibly inspire such depth of devotion and passion . . . until I started walking to pray every night.

By about the third week, I was starting to feel a sense of truly *worshipping* God—in my very posture of being—that had always before been directed toward whatever man I liked at the time. I was so used to feeling slightly guilty at wanting to praise someone so emphatically, it was a shock to realize the truth. *This was the only time I couldn't possibly be guilty of overstating someone's worth, integrity, and character.* This was, in fact, the very Someone I was meant to find such exalted language for! And even at my best, I would still fall utterly, grossly short of giving adequate praise to God. "Were the whole realm of nature mine," as the hymn goes, "that were a present far too small."

How did a simple walk have such an impact on my heart? I

don't know, exactly, but somehow those nightly strolls began to undo a lie believed long ago when Etta James's words crept in with the answer to my loneliness, while writing letters to Musical Man or pining for him on the curb outside my high school job. *Stormy weather? Must be the man.* Now I was taking bigger and bigger chunks of my day to *God,* running His way each time I grew troubled and confused. Prayer became the default response pining once had been, and God the One I knew could get me through things, no matter what.

Well, actually, that's not *quite* right. Not until the weekend of the gig did I find out just how much God could get me through. In the beginning, their only show was on a Sunday, which proved a difficult time slot to sell folks on. Though I promoted the concert to more than a hundred in my address book, my invite yielded only three attendees—not quite the New York welcome I'd hoped to provide.

This turned out all right in the end: Poster Boy didn't prove keen on socializing much with anyone—even, or maybe least of all, with me. Though we chatted briefly after the show, he was almost rude at one point and certainly not that happy. Not until I was taking my subway ride home, though, did I realize what a burden he'd left on my heart.

I was totally wiped at that point, having done a prayer walk just after dawn, slept maybe three hours, then gone to a neighborhood morning church service since I was skipping my usual evening sermon to hear him and Poster Friend. By the time I got home, I pretty much headed straight for bed . . . but I couldn't sleep. Though I was all but one tiny part unconscious, that one holdout staunchly refused to give up beseeching God on Poster Boy's behalf. Finally I turned on the light, prayed through the book of Philippians for him (as I'd sometimes done in the last several months), and when even that didn't totally give me peace, told God I couldn't pray any more that night. Hard to say if it was Poster Boy's drama or mine that was too blame.

When I finally awoke, a restless edginess over the second, last-minute "show" they were playing Monday night followed me through the day. Though what had so far transpired hadn't been anywhere near what I'd thought might happen, I hoped God would bring resolution with tonight's meeting—just as long as I left rejoicing. That was my only request, and something I'd learned in the last several months was often the best thing I could ask for. Whether because of nerves or erratic sleep, though, I didn't do much praying that day, until my train ride into the city. Even then, scattered thoughts conspired to keep me from finding the sense of peace I wanted.

Their second gig was at this strange place co-owned by some Big from a couple of major TV shows, who seemed to favor aging but well-preserved blondes in miniskirts and tube tops— judging from the bulk of the wait staff, anyway. When I got there, shortly before the ten o'clock set, there was almost no one in the sprawling front room of the place. Evidently the small crowd there was cheering on some twelve-year-old and his band, who treated the back room to a series of covers by Living Color, Nirvana, and many others (or so I learned). Though Poster Friend started out shaking his head at the whole thing, the kid's chops wound up impressing him and Poster Boy, who recognized far more of the songs than I did.

Once Boy Wonder wrapped up around eleven, a stream of musicians carrying instruments started filing back for the Monday night "jam," which Poster Boy and Poster Friend had been invited to participate in. *That* was their gig. Maybe half an hour later, the house band went up, led by this aging sax player whom I randomly recognized from some volunteering I'd done for a music nonprofit; he plays with one of the Tri-States' favorite home talents.

House Band played a couple songs, then brought Poster Friend and Poster Boy up to play. For a brief, horrific moment (Poster Friend's wife and I sat there shaking our heads), the house band seemed to think the guys would need some backup. Fortunately this got cleared up swiftly, leaving Poster Friend to belt out two songs like he was making a pitch to a label to sign them. Even his wife looked surprised at the way he took one note, but I guess it was the strange ambiance of the place. (We're probably lucky he didn't try to borrow some guy's gold necklace—though there were options, if he'd wanted to.)

After their set, we lingered for another round and a few of the local talents, including a jazz jam with a lot of the horn players who'd come to play that night (one notably single trombone player launched this spurt of break-dancing, instrument in hand—including one move akin to doing a full-body car wash). Afterward, several female singers sang fairly convincing covers, mostly of songs Etta James made famous.

This became an ironic soundtrack for my uncomfortable interaction with Poster Boy . . . and the unexpected peace that finally came. Though his mood had clearly improved from the night before, there was a peculiar tension between us I couldn't quite understand. When I finally remarked upon his earlier gloom, he told me some of the background—in the process revealing a recent and short-lived relationship. I'd even met the girl—what were the odds of that? Though it was all past tense by this point, somehow his news hit like when I'd learned of Married Man's new relationship with Photogirl.

We talked off and on a bit after that, while watching the

setup for jam night, but the tension was so thick between us, I started to wonder what I was really longing for—*this?* This miserable, unpleasant interchange?

Finally when they'd played their set, and Poster Boy was hanging back along one wall with a beer and Poster Friend, I had a moment to process it all. While some woman sang a credible version of "At Last," I stared at the poster-sized paintings of rock legends on the opposite wall. The pain inside reached such intensity it was like flames licking through my rib cage. *Is this it, Lord? Am I completely over him for good? What have I lost? What is my future now?*

Normally I'd have done anything to stop the hurting—including believe all the reasons I thought God had given me to *maintain* hope were just lies. It would be trying to manage my heart yet again, but when muting all the thwarted longing behind my pain promises relief, it's been a bargain I've often willingly accepted, no matter how much it hardens my heart in the process. This time, though, with Crabb's words in *Inside Out* still fresh in my mind from one of the chapter drafts, I was willing to let the hurt continue unchecked.

All right. Maybe You have a purpose for the pain. I'm going to try not to run this time, but simply let it pass through me, and trust You still have my best interest at heart.

Perhaps it was about then that I remembered our nightly walks—remembered each time I had been on the verge of freaking out or breaking down, or otherwise forced to trust God in a way that seemed really scary, because it meant having to actually *trust* Him, not just fake it. Each of those times, He'd always been there, always come through, always in the end helped me to get a better perspective on things. Always. Every time I sought Him with all my heart, God had revealed Himself and proven to be as faithful as the Bible record claims. And no matter how deep my grief at losing all former closeness with Poster Boy—probably for good—this didn't affect my recent intimacy with God. Not one bit.

The pain began to ease then, as the peace that had eluded me throughout the day began to wrap a tender hand around my heart. *Poster Boy wasn't my treasure anymore—God was!* As this slowly sank in, I didn't even have to wince at hearing a favorite Etta James song from the stage. Maybe it was even more appropriate than I realized.

As Ad Weasel (of all people!) had once remarked, perhaps my ideal man was really God. He probably made that remark thinking I should be a nun (partly why I had always feared being "too" content with God—what if He then decided I didn't need a husband?), but Ad Weasel had grasped the germ of a crucial truth. All the ultimate longings I'd attached to romance were the cry of a heart still mourning Eden's loss. As a result of all of this, I'm finally starting to see that only if I love God with my whole heart, soul, and strength could I actually love a husband in the self-sacrificial way that spouses are called to. To save my life, I must lose it and find it only in God.

I still don't know why everything had to happen this way; sometimes it seems like life sure woulda been easier if Poster Boy and I simply never crossed paths again—online or in the flesh—and all that pain just wouldn't have happened. But if I wish the hurt away, I lose how much I grew to love my God through this, and how could I ever, *ever* want that?

If I were to insist that all of life operate like songbook jazz—that breathy, earnest catalog of odes and paeans to love and the beloved—I could possibly make a case for things gone wrong (at least to myself). But that would be missing a whole other genre of music that seems largely evolved to pick up the pieces of wistful jazz songs after they skitter dangerously and disastrously into something that sounds like either a dissonant modern composer or a toddler at the keys. That genre is the blues, which, at its best, redeems our suffering with a telling so honest yet so beautiful you can't help receiving hope in the hearing.

And if such music is possible, the question then is if you're willing to sing the songs you've been given.

TO SING OR NOT TO SING?

You might say I've lived most of my life as a strangely warped musician—a child reared by an orchestra, who grew up more obsessed with finding a band to play in than with learning to hone her craft. By the time that Poster Boy found me, I'd taken up residence at a bar, where I hoped my cheeky songs of the reluctantly chaste might catch the ear of a bigwig who was seeking a talent like mine to seed his band.

As I walked up to the counter for my postshow drink that night, I saw a man who somehow seemed familiar. I realized he played piano in one of the rooms I'd rarely been into. His shows must have been the same time as mine on most nights, for we never—till then—had crossed paths. But as I squeezed through shoulders and wallets to catch the bartender's eye, I realized I knew this guy from some gig long ago. He turned to greet me and was for once friendly.

We chatted while he finished his one drink, then he left for the night—unheard of for the sorts of musicians who drank there. I watched him go, half curious, and also by then half tipsy. But when the next night came, he stopped by for the end of my show again. We started to talk and eventually to play jazz together—when the crowd had thinned out and there was no one around the stage.

In the beginning we mostly joked around with the music, trading solos and counterpoint as we played through a songbook of easy standards. He was always more serious than I, though, more committed to doing things well, so after a while I started to listen—go home and figure out some new chord he'd played, or even attempt a few scales!

Things went on quite well for a while—especially when he brought some other musician friends to play with us. After that I figured it was only a matter of time before he suggested we become a formal band of some sort. Surely we weren't just playing together because we both needed a practice partner, but as a way of exploring our unique sound. Why else had we drifted so quickly from banging out the melodies to lingering over the solo sections? Once I'd gotten to know his voice, and how he tended to handle certain material, I couldn't wait to try other tempos, keys, and chord progressions.

Then one day I found out he had no long-term plan at all. And since I'd set such store by that hope, we probably shouldn't play together again. Looking back now, I'm honestly surprised I didn't swear off duets for good. When I went home, I looked at all my music books, all the records I'd been listening to, and cried.

While I was running an errand later on, however, I passed a person who looked so sad, I stopped and sang a song to him. I have to admit, I was so down myself, I just picked a simple blues tune I knew—but *singing* my pain cheered me up a lot. It wasn't like life was suddenly sunlight and birthday cake, but not like it was weeping through sleet on the day you forgot to pack your umbrella, either. That got me thinking.

As I passed a coffee shop, God fell in step beside me. He didn't speak, so after a bit I started to answer the question His very presence seemed to raise.

"I know. Was I starting to practice simply so he'd ask me to be his partner or so I could make better music for You? I *thought* I had good motives . . . But why can I only play jazz with other people? On my own I just seem to play the blues."

Not that the form itself was really so bad. Unless you were singing of tying yourself to a railroad track, the songs themselves were beautiful somehow—even when they told a story of sorrow. At least, that's how the better blues were.

So whose ears had I really meant to please? Maybe, regardless of whatever happened with my now-departed friend, it was essential to pursue my music alone for a time. How else would I ever know that it was truly for God's pleasure? Everything might sound good at first listen, but I'd be sliding the notes a bit, and someday when we hit a really unusual or challenging chord, my superficial practice would be unmasked—perhaps with fairly disastrous results. Whether or not I wound up being a solo artist or playing in a band, I had a lot to learn as a musician.

"But I want to be in a *band!*" I cried. "I thought we played so well together. So well." I looked at God to see if this sparked sympathy.

To my surprise, I saw not just the reflection of myself but of my pain—the gaze of one whose beloved is rejecting his love again. *Love* . . .

I looked away quickly and stole a cautious hand to my chest then, feeling the bloodied gouge marks left behind by all the ill-fated auditions and short-lived tryouts over the years. My heart was still trembling and shuddering between the spasms of pain and the siren enticement of numbness.

"I thought . . . I thought if I left the blood flowing there, it might run into the street and bring the death of me," I whispered, not yet daring to look at God again. Yet even as I said it, I felt accused by my own words. To leave those parts of my heart dead meant there was less of me to love God with, and quite honestly, there'd been more of me dead before Poster Boy.

But could I stand to revive the parts that longed to keep making music with him? Those parts that once played jazz?

A bit sooner than I wanted to, I slowly took God's hand and fit His wounds against my own. Tears began rapidly drumming down on His hands, then, as if my heart were slowly beating a strange new song.

God pressed a gentle kiss into my hair. "Come now, and I'll teach you more of the blues."

SONG AND POETRY CREDITS AND ARTIST INFORMATION

All quotes in this book were made possible by the generous permission of the artists and their publishers. To purchase the mp3 soundtrack online or to learn where to buy their albums, go to www.sexlessinthecity .net.

QUOTES IN ORDER OF APPEARANCE

Chapter 1: "Stormy Weather" as performed by Etta James on the CD *At Last* (1961).

Chapter 2: "You're Nobody 'Til Somebody Loves You" as performed by Dean Martin on the *Swingers* sound track (1996).

Chapter 3: "A Kiss to Build a Dream On" as performed by Louis Armstrong on the *Sleepless in Seattle* sound track (1993).

Chapter 4: "Human Cannonball" from the David Wilcox CD *Turning Point* (1997). For more information about David and his music, visit www.davidwilcox.com. For more information about Ric Hordinski (David's cowriter on this song), visit www.richordinksi .com.

Chapter 6: "Looks Like Rain" from the eponymous CD *Tal Bachman* (1999). For more information about Tal and his music, visit www .myspace.com/talbachmanmusic.

Chapter 8: "What a Good Boy" from the Barenaked Ladies CD *Gordon* (1992). For more information about the Barenaked Ladies and their music, visit www.bnlmusic.com.

Chapter 9: "10 Cent Wings" from the Jonatha Brooke CD *10 Cent Wings* (1997). For more information about Jonatha and her music, visit www.jonathabrooke.com.

Chapter 10: "Jackass" from the Beck CD *Odelay* (1996). For more information about Beck and his music, visit www.beck.com.

Chapter 11: "Deathly" as performed by "Aimee Mann on the *Magnolia* soundtrack (1999). For more information about Aimee and her music, visit www.aimeemann.com.

Chapter 13: "Slipping Through My Fist" from the David Wilcox CD *Underneath* (1999).

Chapter 14: "Call and Answer" from the Barenaked Ladies CD *Stunt* (1998). .

Chapter 15: "Conversation" from *The Complete Poems 1927–1979* by Elizabeth Bishop (1999).

Chapter 17: "All the Roots Grow Deeper When It's Dry" from the David Wilcox CD *Big Horizon* (1994).

CREDITS